# CALENDARS OF GWYNEDD.

# Kalendars of Gwynedd;

OR,

CHRONOLOGICAL LISTS OF LORDS-LIEUTENANT, CUSTODES ROTULORUM,

SHERIFFS, AND KNIGHTS OF THE SHIRE, FOR THE

COUNTIES OF ANGLESEY, CAERNARVON,

AND MERIONETH,

AND OF THE MEMBERS FOR THE BOROUGHS OF CAERNARVON AND BEAUMARIS. TO WHICH ARE

ADDED LISTS OF THE LORDS PRESIDENTS OF WALES AND THE CONSTABLES

OF THE CASTLES OF BEAUMARIS, CAERNARVON,

CONWAY, AND HARLECH.

COMPILED BY EDWARD BREESE, F.S.A.,

CLERK OF THE PEACE AND OF LIEUTENANCY FOR MERIONETHSHIRE.

WITH NOTES BY WILLIAM WATKIN EDWARD WYNNE, ESQ., F.S.A.,

OF PENIARTH; SOMETIME KNIGHT OF THE SHIRE AND AFTERWARDS HIGH

SHERIFF FOR MERIONETHSHIRE.

LONDON: JOHN CAMDEN HOTTEN, 74 AND 75, PICCADILLY.

1873.

TO THE

RIGHT HONOURABLE EDWARD MOSTYN, BARON MOSTYN,

LORD-LIEUTENANT OF MERIONETHSHIRE,

THIS LITTLE WORK IS

Inscribed,

AS A SLIGHT THOUGH GRATEFUL ACKNOWLEDGMENT OF

MUCH KINDNESS AND CONSTANT FRIENDSHIP

WHICH HIS LORDSHIP HAS

DISPLAYED TOWARDS

THE COMPILER.

# PREFACE.

SOME years ago it occurred to me that authentic lists of the Lords-Lieutenants, Custodes Rotulorum, Sheriffs, and Members for Merionethshire, might be compiled by me during my frequent visits to London. It was not till I commenced the task that I formed any adequate notion of its difficulty. At that time I had not seen the Lists of Sheriffs and Members published by Mr. Wynne, in the "Archæologia Cambrensis." Neither had I seen those for Anglesey in Rowland's "Mona Antiqua," nor the List of Sheriffs for Caernarvonshire in the "Cambrian Register." I set about my self-imposed labour by going to the Public Record Office and commencing, at first for Merionethshire only, lists extracted wholly from independent and original sources. I considered it right to start from the beginning, and therefore began my Sheriffs' Lists from the date of the first appointment to that Office in Wales, 12 Edwd. I. In the course of my searches I found the names of so many officers connected with the two other old Counties of North Wales, that I allowed my original intention to expand to a compilation which should embrace the three old Counties of Gwynedd or North Wales. But vast as are the sources for such a search in the Record Office and British Museum, I found they would not afford complete information, and that serious gaps would break the long line of names, extending over nearly six hundred years, which I wanted to make as consecutively perfect as possible.

Private and local sources had therefore to be explored, and it was then I was led to consult Mr. Wynne, of Peniarth, whose reputation as an accomplished Antiquary, and as the possessor of the finest MS. collection in Wales, pointed him out as the best authority. Mr. Wynne not only at once approved of the undertaking, but offered to render every assistance in his power. He subsequently went carefully through the draft Lists, comparing them with his own, and at my request, most kindly consented to add notes, which should "illustrate" some of the older names, and identify the later ones. This task he has accomplished in a manner which adds infinite value to such a work as this. His notes ear-mark with the "nôd" of historical truth the names of a great number of the different holders of the offices referred to. Besides Mr. Wynne's valuable personal assistance, his splendid collection(1) has been a source of much help. The great collection at Mostyn Hall(2) was also most kindly thrown open to me at all times by Lord Mostyn, and much valuable information was obtained therefrom, and especially from the "Vaughan" and "Mostyn" volumes of correspondence, &c.

No compilation, such as this, is entitled to public confidence unless every source from which information has been derived is mentioned without reserve. The following is therefore inserted as a list of the original public MSS. and documents consulted :—

### AT THE PUBLIC RECORD OFFICE.

Parliamentary Writs and Returns.
Patent Rolls.
Welsh Rolls.
Chapter House Documents.
Domestic State Papers.
Calendars of State Papers.
Crown Office Docquet Books.
Fines and Amerciaments (Wales).
Repertories.
Sheriffs' Allowances.
Special Commissions.
Tax Accounts (Wales).
Escheators' Accounts (Wales).
Petitions of Allowances on Sheriffs' Accounts,
  alias Sheriffs' Proffers, &c.
Pipe Rolls.
Sheriffs' Books.
Sheriffs' Warrants of Attorney.

States and Views of Accounts.
Land Revenue Records.(3)
Documents relating to the Appointment of
  Sheriffs—Elizabeth and James I.
Sheriffs' Accounts—Cedule Vic.
Welsh Records, viz. :—
  Ministers' Accounts.
  Plea Rolls.
  Docket Rolls.
  Bail Rolls.
  "Papers" (Declarations, Pleas, &c., &c.).
  "Memoranda," Files of,
  Gaol Files.
  Judgments, Docket Books of,
  Cause Books.
  "Continuances" (of Actions).
  Imparlance Books.

### AT THE BRITISH MUSEUM.

Harl. MSS.
London Gazettes.

Pamphlets and Single Sheets.
Journals of the House of Commons.

---

(1) The well-known Hengwrt Library and MSS. were bequeathed to Mr. Wynne by the last Sir Robert Wms. Vaughan, Bart.

(2) This is historically better known as the famous Gloddaeth collection.

(3) Also the Records at the Land Revenue Record Office, Spring Gardens.

In the Anglesey List of Sheriffs, some few names, not obtainable from public sources, have been taken from Rowland's "Mona Antiqua." I do not guarantee the perfect accuracy of these names—especially as I find many errors in Rowland's lists when I compare them with those which I have derived from original sources. Browne Willis' "Not. Parl." has been referred to simply for purposes of comparison, and where the names therein were found to differ from mine, I have retained my own, as being derived from the fountain-head—the Writs, and Returns, and the Journals of the House of Commons. In compiling the lists of Members it was considered expedient to make full extracts from those Journals. They will accordingly be found in the foot-notes, and will furnish some curious information respecting many of the contests for the several seats, and the Petitions presented against some of the Returns. The Lists of Lords-Presidents, and Constables of Castles, have, like the others, been constructed from original sources.

Since the work has gone to press it has occurred to me that misapprehension may arise with regard to some of my observations on the original constitution of the North Wales Counties. I may not have made it appear as clearly as I intended, that although Flintshire was constituted a County by the Statute of Rhuddlan, the greater portion of it was not formerly comprehended within the boundaries of ancient Gwynedd, which consisted of the "three old Counties of North Wales" (as Anglesey, Caernarvon, and Merioneth were always formerly referred to) and the Berveddwlad. This latter District consisted of five Cantreds, of which one only— Tegengl—became part of Flintshire. I have therefore adhered to the old method, and have confined my observations and lists to the three old Counties.

I would also desire to point out in more explicit terms that the division of County, *sub eo nomine*, did not exist in Wales previously to the Statute of Rhuddlan. But that the three old Counties of North Wales had prievously existed as separate Provinces or Districts there is abundant evidence. In Sir John Price's description of Wales, augmented by Humfrey Lhoyd, it is stated that "This land (Gwyneth) was of old time divided to foure parts," which he proceeds to describe as the three Counties and the Berveddwlad. The "Parthau Cymry," in the Llyfyr Coch, has a similar arrangement of the names and districts. Other authorities might also be cited.

It is almost certain that amongst upwards of two thousand names, spread over half-a-dozen centuries, errors have crept in. But I have conscientiously laboured to make accuracy and authenticity the foundation of the work, and I believe that sins of omission may be more easily charged upon me than those of commission.

I am much indebted to the Deputy-Keeper of Her Majesty's Records, Sir Thomas Duffus Hardy, D.C.L., for his courtesy and kindness, by means of which I was enabled to secure the assistance of some of the gentlemen connected with the office. Not that such assistance is ever begrudged to anyone going about a search at this office with an intelligent and intelligible object. On the contrary, the officials here, from the highest to the lowest, are distinguished above all others in our Public offices for their unvarying good temper, (often under circumstances of great provocation) and their prompt attention to all who appeal to them for rational assistance. One of them, Mr. A. T. Watson, has given me much valuable service.

Mr. Wynne's Notes are distinguished by an asterisk at the commencement, and the initial W. at the end of each.

E. B.

*Morva Lodge, Portmadoc, August* 3, 1873.

# CONTENTS.

# VENEDOTIAN NORTH WALES.

## CHAPTER I.

### ANGLESEY.

IN peering through the legendary mists that obscure British History prior to the invasion of the Romans, we vainly endeavour to fix one authentic record which bears directly on our West-Celtic landmarks till the invasion of Anglesey by Suetonius Paulinus, A.D. 61. From thenceforward, to the occupation and distribution of the Province of Gwynedd, or Venedotia, by the sons of Cunedda Wledig, in the sixth century (referred to more fully in the third chapter), we have scarcely any other than meagre legendary accounts of this part of Britain. It is not here intended to give any account of the famous little Island of Anglesey, nor to dwell upon the elaborate historical and archæological particulars relating to it which have been supplied by various authors—and notably by the learned Henry Rowlands in his "Mona Antiqua." It will be sufficient for the purposes of this work to state that Anglesey, since the first formation of Counties, has necessarily, from its geographical position, been a distinct territorial division, and is still bounded by its ancient and natural limits. Its population, according to the Census of 1871, was 50,919, and the numbers at each Census taken during this century were as follows :—

| Year. | | | | Population. | |
|---|---|---|---|---|---|
| 1801 | ... | ... | ... | 33,806 | |
| 1811 | ... | ... | ... | 37,045 | |
| 1821 | ... | ... | ... | 45,063 | |
| 1831 | ... | ... | ... | 48,325 | Increase in 70 years, |
| 1841 | ... | ... | ... | 50,891 | 17,113. |
| 1851([1]) | ... | ... | ... | 57,327 | |
| 1861 | ... | ... | ... | 54,609 | |
| 1871 | ... | ... | ... | 50,919 | |

---

([1]) The large increase in the population at the Census of 1851 is probably to a great extent accounted for by the number of workmen employed on the New Harbour of Holyhead, and the Railway Works in the county. The gradual completion of those works may account for the decrease in the numbers in 1861 and 1871 respectively.— *Vide* following tables.)

The subjoined table gives the acreage, population (in 1861), and annual value of each Parish. It may here be stated that the sums which appear in the column headed "Annual Value" are the amounts upon which each Parish is assessed to the County Rate, and such sums do not indicate even approximately the actual letting annual value or rack-rents of the tenements within such Parishes.

| UNION. | PARISH. | Area in Statute Acres. | Population in 1861. | Anual Value. £ |
|---|---|---|---|---|
| BANGOR AND BEAU- MARIS. | Llanddaniel Fab. . . . . | 1,679 | 442 | 1,959 |
| | Llanddona . . . . . | 2,387 | 567 | 1,461 |
| | Llandegfan . . . . . | 2,760 | 900 | 3,355 |
| | Llandysilio . . . . | 917 | 1,359 | 3,749 |
| | Llanedwen . . . . . | 1,939 | 273 | 2,468 |
| | Llanfaes . . . . . | 2,297 | 243 | 82 |
| | Llanfairpwllgwyngyll . . . | 952 | 695 | 1,636 |
| | Llanffinan . . . . . | 1,267 | 138 | 1,024 |
| | Llanfihangel Esceifiog . . | 2,889 | 1,026 | 3,205 |
| | Llanfihangel Dinsylwy . . | 833 | 54 | 574 |
| | Llangadwaladr, or Eglwysael . . | 4,718 | 526 | 2,071 |
| | Llangoed . . . . . | 1,343 | 618 | 1,777 |
| | Llangristiolus . . . . | 3,936 | 881 | 3,528 |
| | Llaniestyn . . . . | 1,663 | 212 | 627 |
| | Llansadwrn . . . . . | 2,891 | 419 | 2,952 |
| | Penmon . . . . . | 7,180 | 240 | 707 |
| | Penmynydd . . . . | 3,153 | 446 | 3,182 |
| | Pentraeth . . . . | 4,013 | 962 | 3,313 |
| | Trefdraeth . . . . | 3,135 | 921 | 3,349 |
| CAERNARVON. | Llanidan . . . . . | 4,645 | 1,323 | 5,061 |
| | Llangeinwen . . . . | 5,388 | 913 | 4,569 |
| | Llangaffo . . . . | 1,590 | 122 | 1,605 |
| | Llanfair-y-cwmwd, or Llanfair-yn-y- cwmmwd . . . . | 166 | 37 | 214 |
| | St. Peter Newborough . . . | 7,410 | 918 | 2,098 |
| ANGLESEY. | Amlwch . . . . . | 9,221 | 5,949 | 11,826 |
| | Bodewryd . . . . | 526 | 26 | 509 |
| | Coedana . . . . . | 1,627 | 275 | 1,311 |
| | Gwredog . . . . | 936 | 42 | 790 |
| | Llanallgo . . . . | 659 | 430 | 570 |
| | Llanbabo . . . . | 1,743 | 138 | 1,345 |
| | Llanbadrig . . . . | 4,097 | 1,187 | 4,061 |
| | Llanbedrgoch . . . . | 3,193 | 356 | 1,322 |
| | Llandyfrydog . . . . | 3,819 | 706 | 3,116 |
| | Llanddyfnan . . . . | 3,506 | 720 | 2,636 |
| | Llaneilian . . . . | 2,398 | 1,282 | 1,831 |
| | Llanerchymedd . . . . | 15 | 67 | 94 |
| | Llaneugrad . . . . | 2,695 | 276 | 1,106 |
| | Llanfairmathafarneithaf . . . | 1,949 | 757 | 1,321 |
| | Llanfairynghornwy . . . | 2,135 | 293 | 1,664 |
| | Llanfechell . . . . | 3,637 | 958 | 3,129 |
| | Llanfihangeltrerbeirdd . . | 1,570 | 356 | 1,496 |
| | Llanfflewyn . . . . | 1,265 | 128 | 1,080 |
| | Llangefni . . . . . | 2,426 | 1,696 | 4,245 |

| Union. | Parish. | Area in Statute Acres. | Population in 1861. | Annual Value. £ |
|---|---|---|---|---|
| | Llangwyllog . . . . . | 2,301 | 207 | 2,280 |
| | Llanrhwydrys . . . . . | 1,143 | 136 | 1,118 |
| | Llanwenllwyfo . . . . . | 1,756 | 546 | 1,625 |
| | Llechcynfarwydd, or Llechgwenfarwydd . . . . . | 1,964 | 366 | 1,982 |
| | Penrhoslligwy . . . . | 2,894 | 473 | 1,980 |
| | Rhodogeidio . . . . . | 1,003 | 284 | 1,022 |
| | Rhosbeirio . . . . . | 369 | 26 | 414 |
| | Tregaian . . . . . | 2,066 | 160 | 1,442 |
| HOLYHEAD. | Aberffraw . . . . . | 6,252 | 1,238 | 5,509 |
| | Bodedern . . . . . | 4,235 | 1,084 | 3,308 |
| | Bodwrog . . . . . | 1,813 | 319 | 1,435 |
| | Ceirchiog . . . . . | 613 | 174 | 496 |
| | Cerrigceinwen . . . . | 1,582 | 465 | 1,414 |
| | Heneglwys . . . . . | 2,062 | 510 | 1,745 |
| | Holyhead . . . . . | 6,988 | 8,773 | 18,334 |
| | Llanllibio . . . . . | 826 | 59 | 716 |
| | Llanbeulan . . . . . | 2,943 | 315 | 2,600 |
| | Llanddausant, or Llanddausaint . | 2,011 | 565 | 1,833 |
| | Llandrygarn, with Gwyndu . | 2,430 | 359 | 2,036 |
| | Llanfachreth . . . . | 1,887 | 532 | 1,720 |
| | Llanfaelog . . . . . | 2,732 | 763 | 2,027 |
| | Llanfaethly . . . . . | 2,629 | 445 | 2,109 |
| | Llanfairyneubwll . . . | 1,279 | 357 | 1,038 |
| | Llanfigael . . . . . | 484 | 121 | 536 |
| | Llanfihangel-yn-hswyn . . | 1,404 | 222 | 813 |
| | Llanfwrog . . . . . | 2,017 | 246 | 1,550 |
| | Llangwyfan . . . . . | 1,828 | 200 | 1,479 |
| | Llanrhyddlad . . . . | 2,679 | 790 | 2,147 |
| | Llantrisant, or Llantrisaint . | 4,447 | 488 | 3,542 |
| | Llanynghenedl . . . . | 2,965 | 427 | 2,026 |
| | Llechylched . . . . . | 1,783 | 635 | 1,754 |
| | Rhoscolyn . . . . . | 2,580 | 462 | 1,420 |
| | Trewalchmai . . . . | 1,700 | 768 | 1,539 |

# CHAPTER II.

## CAERNARVON.

AS mentioned in the following chapter, there are good reasons for supposing that originally Caernarvonshire proper was comprised within the strong barrier of mountains beginning by the sea at Penmaenmawr, and extending thence, crescent-shaped, in a south-westerly direction beyond Clynnogfawr to the Rivals. Before the conquest of Wales, though how long it is difficult to decide, the county had swollen to nearly its present size, and embraced the whole of the country extending from Conway to Trefriew, Bettws-y-Coed and Penmachno. The Commote of Ardudwy-uwch-artro appears to have been severed from Eifionydd, (with which anciently it formed one Cantred), and added to Merionethshire. By the Statute of Rhuddlan, the Hundred of Creuddyn (¹) was incorporated with Caernarvonshire. Giraldus Cambrensis, in his Itinerarium, speaks of Lleyn as part of the Province of Arvon; so that as early as the year 1188, when this learned Prelate accompanied Arch-bishop Baldwin, who preached the 3rd Crusade throughout Wales, the fertile Promontory and the adjacent Commote of Eifionydd had been recognized as forming part of the same "Province." Giraldus does not speak of Shires in North Wales.

In the Statute of Rhuddlan the divisions of the County are briefly described as follows :—

*Vicecomes de Karenarvan, sub quo Cantreda de Arvan, Cantreda de Arthlencoyth, (Arlechwedd), Commotum de Cruthin (Creuddyn), Cantreda de Thleen (Lleyn), & Commotum de Yvioneth.*

The County was part of Britannia Secunda, and was entirely within the ancient Kingdom of Gwynedd.

It is bounded on the north by the Irish Sea; on the north-west by Anglesey, separated by the Menai Straits; on the west and south-west by Caernarvon and

---

(¹) In the "Parthau Cymru" contained in the Llyfr Coch, the Commote of Creuddyn is placed among those in the Berveddwlad. There is no doubt that prior to the Conquest of Edward I. Creuddyn was an unannexed territory, with the Castle of Deganwy as its principal fortress. This Castle, by old writers is called Gannock.

Cardigan Bays; on the south and south-east by Merionethshire: and on the east by Denbighshire.

It is 51 miles in length, and 22 in breadth, and has a sea-board line of 95 miles. Its towns, all of which are sea-ports, are Conway, Bangor, Caernarvon, Nevin, Pwllheli, Criccieth and Portmadoc. The watering-place of Llandudno has also become a town of some consequence, and is the resort of a very large number of visitors during the summer.

It has an area of 579 square miles, or 370,273 acres.

Like Merionethshire, its geological formation is the Silurian, and its minerals are the same except as regards gold, which has not been found in it. Its blue, red, and green veins of slate are extremely productive. The great quarries at Penrhyn and Llanberis, belonging respectively to Lord Penrhyn and Mr. Assheton Smith, each produce over 60,000 tons of slate a year; and the vale of Nantlle has several quarries, at which a large number of men is employed. Throughout the County it is estimated that there are about 10,000 workmen employed in connection with these quarries.

The principal mountains in the County are Snowdon (Y Wyddfa), 3,571 feet high; Carnedd Llewelyn, 3,469; Carnedd Davydd, 3,427; Moel Siabod, 2,878; Moel Hebog, 2,584. There are several other peaks of considerable height; amongst them being Penmaenmawr, 1,548 feet, at the eastern, and The Rivals (Yr Eifl), 1,868 feet, at the western end of the crescent of hills which bounded the ancient Shire-ground. In both these last-named hills there are quarries of sett-stones worked—in the first on an extensive scale.

The population, according to the Census of 1871, was 106,122, and the returns of each Census during the present century, with the total increase in the seven decades, are as follows:—

| Year. | | | | Population. | |
|---|---|---|---|---|---|
| 1801 | ... | ... | ... | 41,521 | |
| 1811 | ... | ... | ... | 49,655 | |
| 1821 | ... | ... | ... | 58,099 | |
| 1831 | ... | ... | ... | 66,818 | Total increase in 70 years, 64,601. |
| 1841 | ... | ... | ... | 81,093 | |
| 1851 | ... | ... | ... | 87,870 | |
| 1861 | ... | ... | ... | 95,694 | |
| 1871 | ... | ... | ... | 106,122 | |

The following table contains the area, population (in 1861[2]), and the annual value of each Parish in the County:—

[2] The Census tables for 1871 have not been classified.

| HUNDRED. | UNION. | PARISH. | Area in Statute Acres. | Population in 1861. | Annual Value. £ |
|---|---|---|---|---|---|
| UWCHGORFAI . | CAERNARVON . . | Llandwrog . . | 9,516 | 2,825 | 8,437 |
|  |  | Llanwnda . . | 11,459 | 1,660 | 4,359 |
|  |  | Clynnog . . . | 12,060 | 1,671 | 5,510 |
|  | PWLLHELI . . | Llanllyfni . . | 7,521 | 2,362 | 4,396 |
|  |  | Llanaelhaiarn . | 6,698 | 736 | 3,169 |
| ISGORFAI . . | CAERNARVON . . | Llanbeblig . . | 6,792 | 9,937 | 21,492 |
|  |  | Llanfaglen . . | 1,884 | 253 | 1,149 |
|  |  | Llanrug . . | 4,516 | 2,139 | 4,339 |
|  |  | Llanfairisgaer . | 2,474 | 1,060 | 3,084 |
|  |  | Llanberis . | 10,431 | 1,364 | 7,995 |
|  |  | Bettws-garmon . | 2,759 | 94 | 489 |
|  | FESTINIOG. . . | Llanddeiniolen . | 9,024 | 5,747 | 14,253 |
|  | BANGOR & BEAUMARIS . | Beddgelert . | 20,608 | 1,066 | 2,113 |
|  |  | Bangor . . | 7,543 | 10,662 | 25,617 |
| (ARLECHWEDD) UCHAF . | BANGOR & BEAUMARIS . | Aber . . | 8,833 | 582 | 2,585 |
|  |  | Llandegai . | 16,100 | 3,381 | 33,888 |
|  |  | Llanfairfechan . | 6,521 | 1,199 | 2,872 |
|  | CONWAY . . | Llanllechid . | 18,111 | 7,346 | 9,057 |
|  |  | Dwygyfylchi . | 5,794 | 1,386 | 5,709 |
| ISAF . . . | CONWAY . . | Conway . . | 2,437 | 1,855 | 3,708 |
|  |  | Caerhun . . | 13,402 | 1,314 | 4,279 |
|  |  | Gyffin . . | 3,705 | 715 | 2,416 |
|  |  | Llanbedr-cennin } Dolgarrog. (³) } | 4,909 | 355 / 134 | 1,048 / 523 |
|  | LLANRWST . . | Llangelynin . | 2,017 | 234 | 1,318 |
|  |  | Maenan(⁴) . | 2,902 | 373 | 1,637 |
| CREUDDYN . | CONWAY . . | Eglwysrhos . | 3,735 | 832 | 5,562 |
|  |  | Llandudno . | 2,729 | 2,316 | 13,299 |
|  |  | Llangwstenin . | 1,314 | 674 | 1,911 |
|  |  | Llysfaen . | 1,900 | 908 | 2,321 |
|  |  | Eirias . . | 941 | 295 | 1,468 |
| NANT CONWAY . | LLANRWST(⁵). . | Bettws-y-Coed . | 3,537 | 509 | 1,100 |
|  |  | Dolyddelen . | 14,384 | 811 | 1,474 |
|  |  | Eidda(⁶) . . | | 396 | 1,118 |
|  |  | Llanrhochwyn . } Trefriw . . } | 9,576 | 532 / 483 | 1,377 / 945 |
|  |  | Penmachno . | 11,208 | 1,425 | 2,933 |
|  |  | Gwydir or Trewydir(⁷) | 7,621 | 400 | 1,295 |

(³) Dolgarrog is a Township in the Parish of Llandrillo-yn-rhos.

(⁴) Maenan is a Township in Eglwysfach Parish.

(⁵) "The Abbey," formerly extra-parochial, has become a Parish for the purposes of Act 20 Vict. c. 19. Its area, population, and annual value, are included in those of this Union.

(⁶) Eidda is a Township in the Parish of Yspytty.

(⁷) Gwydir is a Township in the Parish of Llanrwst.

| HUNDRED. | UNION. | PARISH. | Area in Statute Acres. | Population in 1861. | Annual Value. £ |
|---|---|---|---|---|---|
| EIFIONYDD . . | FESTINIOG . . . | Dolbenmaen . . | 2,145 | 387 | 874 |
| | | Llanfihangelypennant | 8,844 | 753 | 2,729 |
| | | Penmorfa . . | 10,157 | 1,104 | 2,975 |
| | | Treflys . . . | 999 | 91 | 391 |
| | | Ynyscynhaiarn . | 6,546 | 3,138 | 6,365 |
| | PWLLHELI . . . | Criccieth . . | 1,678 | 769 | 1,625 |
| | | Llanarmon . . | 3,753 | 556 | 2,487 |
| | | Llangybi . . | 4,519 | 622 | 2,412 |
| | | Llanystumdwy . . | 6,780 | 1,126 | 4,468 |
| COMMITMAEN . | PWLLHELI . . . | Aberdaron (including Bardsey Isle) | 7,508 | 1,266 | 3,978 |
| | | Bodverin . . | 511 | 50 | 266 |
| GAFFLOGION . | | Bottwnog . . | 487 | 138 | 421 |
| COMMITMAEN . | | Bryncroes . . | 3,646 | 889 | 1,822 |
| | | Llanfaelrhys . . | 1,679 | 208 | 832 |
| | | Llangwnadl . . | 1,243 | 272 | 766 |
| GAFFLOGION . | | Melltyrne . . | 1,519 | 265 | 1,112 |
| COMMITMAEN . | | Penllech . . | 2,187 | 261 | 1,251 |
| | | Rhiw . . . | 1,653 | 370 | 759 |
| GAFFLOGION . | | Denio . . | 1,278 | 2,420 | 4,011 |
| | | Llanbedrog . . | 2,548 | 469 | 1,604 |
| COMMITMAEN . | | Llandegwning . . | 1,488 | 142 | 1,054 |
| | | Llanengan . . | 4,354 | 1,021 | 2,575 |
| GAFFLOGION . | | Llanfihangel-bachell-aeth . . | 2,915 | 312 | 1,441 |
| | | Llangian . . | 4,835 | 1,088 | 3,085 |
| | | Penrhos . . | 555 | 104 | 343 |
| | | Carngiwch . . | 1,344 | 130 | 415 |
| DINLLAEN . . | PWLLHELI . . . | Bodvean . . | 2,572 | 382 | 1,323 |
| | | Ceidio . . | 1,081 | 153 | 915 |
| | | Edeyrn . . | 1,380 | 613 | 1,392 |
| | | Llandudwen . . | 1,331 | 94 | 1,050 |
| GAFFLOGION . | PWLLHELI . . . | Llaniestyn . . | 4,256 | 1,012 | 2,942 |
| | | Nevin . . | 1,816 | 1,818 | 2,370 |
| | | Pistill . . | 3,949 | 495 | 1,302 |
| | | Tudweiliog . . | 2,241 | 371 | 1,480 |
| | | Llannor . . | 5,553 | 1,023 | 3,978 |
| | | Abereirch . . | 5,962 | 1,652 | 5,227 |

# CHAPTER III.

## MERIONETHSHIRE.

**I**T is impossible to determine, with any degree of certainty the date of the first constitution of Merioneth into Shire-ground. English Counties were formed by, or about the time of, King Alfred. Camden accepts this on the authority of Ingulphus of Croyland, who wrote, as he states, in the 10th century. Hallam, however, in his "History of the Middle Ages," says :—

"It has been usual to ascribe the establishment of this system among our Saxon ancestors to Alfred, upon the authority of Ingulphus, a writer contemporary with the Conquest. But neither the biographer of Alfred, Asserius, nor the existing laws of that Prince, bear testimony to the fact. With respect, indeed, to the division of Counties, and their government by Aldermen and Sheriffs, it is certain that both existed before his time ; and the utmost that can be supposed is that he might in some instances have ascertained an unsettled boundary. There does not seem to be equal evidence as to the antiquity of the minor Divisions. Hundreds, I think, are first mentioned in a Law of Edgar. But as Alfred, it must be remembered, was never master of more than half the kingdom, the complete distribution of England into these districts cannot upon any supposition be ascribed to him." (¹)

It is very uncertain when the three old Shires of Gwynedd, or North Wales—viz., Anglesey, Caernarvon, and Merioneth—were constituted into similar Divisions. Howel Dda, who governed Wales about the middle of the 10th century—a Prince of remarkable intelligence, and the founder of the great Venedotian Code of Laws named after him—does not refer in his laws to any such Divisions. That Code, as it has descended to us, was compiled by Iorwerth ap Madog, at the end of the 11th century, and we may therefore assume that Counties in Wales were not then formed. Anglesey, from its insular position, was always a distinct territorial division. Caernarvon, as we have seen, at first comprised only the tract of land known as Arvon, extending from Clynnog-fawr to Aber. Merioneth was in Britannia Prima, and was

<hr />

(¹) Middle Ages, A. Murray & Son's Edit., 1870, p. 506. The great historian ignored the mention of Hundreds in the laws of Moelmutius, translated for Alfred by Asserius (*see* post).

divided between the two Kingdoms of Gwynedd and Powys, the greater part being in Gwynedd.(2) According to Welsh legendary history, it was so called after Meirion, son of Tibiawn, son of Cunedda Wledig a Northern British Prince, who lived in Cumberland in the 6th century. About the year 550, A.D., he is said to have sent his eight sons against the Gwyddelian Picts, who then occupied North Wales. The Cuneddian heroes are represented as having utterly overthrown and expelled the Irish, and occupied the country. The eldest, Eneon Urdd appears to have appropriated Caereinion (in Montgomeryshire), and his eldest son, Caswallon llaw-hir, was sent against the Picts to Anglesey, which he subdued and occupied, having slain Serigi Wyddel, their prince there, with his own hand. Meirion settled in Meirionydd, and his uncle Edeyrn in Edeyrnion, afterwards and now part of Merionethshire. Another son, Dunawd, is said to have delivered the Commot of Ardudwy, " in Eifionydd," and called it Dinodyn, or Dunodig. (3) It is open to much doubt whether this nomenclature, founded on the legend of Cunedda, can be accepted as literally accurate. It is more probable, as has been conjectured by a modern Welsh scholar, that in this we have the names not of individuals, but of various petty tribes of common origin, which moved down gradually from North Britain, and expelled the Gael from their seats in Gwynedd.(4) Some writers say that the province was called Mervinia, from Mervyn Frych, the father of Roderic the Great ; and under this title Leland mentions it—

" Porrigitur vasto fluvii trans ostia Devi
Tractu terra potens hastis Mervinia longis." (5)

In the 12th century it consisted of little more than the Cantref of Merionydd (comprising the modern hundreds of Talybont and Estimaner), Penllyn, and probably that sea-board portion of Ardudwy which lies between Traethmawr and Barmouth. In Sir John Wynn's " History of the Gwydyr Family," it is stated that Conan ap Owen Gwynedd had for his part the County of Merioneth, and in a note it is added that it

---

(2) Camden says that five counties of North Wales—viz., Montgomery, Merioneth, Caernarvon, Denbigh, and Flint—belonged to the Ordevices, and he traces the etymology of the latter word to the position of those counties with reference to the River Dovey. " That as they" (the inhabitants) " settled above the two Rivers Devi—which rise from contiguous springs, and run different ways—and *Oar Devi* (Ar Ddevi), signifies in British *upon the Rivers Devi*, they might thence be called Ordevices. Nor, indeed, is the name of Ordevices totally extinct in this tract, great part of it which lies on the sea, being still called by the inhabitants ' Ardudwy,' which the Romans seem to have softened into Ardovie and Ordevices."— Camden's Britt. (1789), Vol. II. p. 530. Camden's theory as to the name of Ardudwy is, however, too far-fetched. Ardudwy is as soft as Ardovie. It is more probable that as the tract of country which bears that name lies between the two estuaries of Traethmawr and Abermaw, it was therefore called " Ar-dy-dwy"—that is, " Upon the two Rivers or Estuaries."

(3) Nennius. Hist. Brit. Achau Saint. Iolo MSS., p. 521. Camden's Britannia—Title Merioneth. Lloyd's (Powel's) Wales, p. 14. Rowland's Mona Antiqua (1766), p. 146, *et seq.* Henry Rowlands is not very accurate. He states that Meirion lived in the seventh or eighth century, and was the son of Owen Danwyn, and the brother of Seiriol, Patron Saint of Penmon, in Anglesea, and of Eneon Frenhin, whose cloister was at Llanengan, in Llyn, Caernarvonshire. The latter was son of Eneon Urdd ap Cunedda, and cousin of Meirion.

(4) Vestiges of the Gael in Gwynedd. By the Rev. W. Basil Jones, M.A.

(5) See also Colt Hoare's Giraldus, Vol. 2, p. 79.

2

was therefore always styled by Giraldus Cambrensis "Terra filiorum Conani" (6). A portion, if not the whole, of the Commote of Ardudwy formed at that time, and afterwards, but one Cantred with Eifionydd, under the name of Dinodyn, and was allotted to and held by some other child or children of Owen Gwynedd, probably by Roderic. (7) It is mentioned as one of the 38 Commotes of the 15 Cantreds of Gwynedd in the Parthau Cymru contained in the Llyvyr Coch o Hergest,(8) and with the Commote of Eivonydd, is assigned to the Cantred of Dinodyn, in the county of Caernarvon. It would also appear by the same topographical list, that Edeyrnion and Glyndyfrdwy were not, prior to the Conquest of Wales, part of Merioneth or of Gwynedd, but formed part of the Principality of Powys Vadawc. Up to the same time, and possibly much later, the Cantred of Arwystli, or Arustley,(9) which now forms part of Montgomeryshire, belonged to Merioneth. It is not mentioned as included in it by the Statute of Rhuddlan, but in all the old records of the period (10) this Cantred, with its three Commotes, is assigned to Merioneth, and undoubtedly formed part of it prior to the year 1284.(11) It has been assumed that the fact of its forming part of the Archdeaconry of Merioneth at the present day, is evidence that at one time it was also part of the county. The addition of it to the Archdeaconry is, however, of modern date, and subsequent to A.D. 1724.(12) It is mentioned in Lloyd's (Powel's "History of Wales," published in 1584, as being then in Merionethshire; but this is clearly an error, as it had been attached to the county of Montgomery when that

---

(6) Sir John Wynn, in his History, says—"Giraldus Cambrensis, in his 'Itinerarium Cambriæ,' sayeth that the Cantreds of Llûn and Evioneth were the possessions of Owen Gwynedd's children when he passed through Wales, and that they had two castles—the one in Carn Madrin, in Llûn, the other called Dewdraeth juxta Montana de Erryri ; which confirmeth that Ardydwy and Evioneth made but one Cantred, for Penrhyn Deudraeth, where that castle stood, is in Ardydwy."—(P. 21.) But Sir John is not altogether accurate in quoting Giraldus, for the words of that writer are :—" We continued our journey over the Traethmawr and Traeth Bachan—that is, the greater and the smaller arm of the sea, where two stone castles have newly been erected : one called Deudraeth, belonging to the sons of Conan, situated in Evionyth, towards the Northern Mountains,"—*versus* Montana Borealia, &c., &c.—Hoare's Giraldus, Vol. II., p. 82). Giraldus cannot, however, be relied upon in his topography, for he places the Dysynni between Traethmawr and the Mawddach, and the Artro between Traethmawr and Traeth bach.—Ib. p. 83). Deudraeth was no doubt then, as now, in Ardudwy. Leland, in his Itinerary, says that Ardudwy " streccith from half Traitmawr to Abermaw on the shore xii myles. All Penrine pointe is in Meirionithshire."—(Itin. Tom. V., p. 52.)

(7) Dr. Powel's Hist. of Wales, by E. Lloyd. 1584, P. 8.

(8) Llyma y modd i mesurwyd ac i rhanwyd Cantrevydd a Chymydau holl Gymru, yn amser Llywelyn ab Grufudd y Tywysawg diweddar o'r Cymry. Tair talaith a fu yn Nghymru ; un yn Aberfraw yn Môn ; a'r ail yn Ninefwr yn Neheubarth ; a'r drydedd yn Mathraval, yn Mhowys ; ac wrth Aberfraw i rhoed xv. Cantref Gwynedd, nid amgen."

(9) So called after Arwystl, one of the sons of Cunedda Wledig.

(10) Robert Vaughan, of Hengwrt, (the Antiquary), in a description of Merionethshire, writes—" We find in an old Inquisition that the land between the Rivers Dyfi and Dulas (that is, the whole parish of Llanwrin), was in times past part of the Commot of Estum Manor." The old Inquisition to which Mr. Vaughan referred was no doubt the " Extenta Com' Meryonneth" comprised in " The Record of Carnarvon," and which was said by Bishop Humphreys to have been taken Anno 7, Hen. V. No mention of Edeyrnion, or the Hamlet of Nantmor, occurs in this extent.

(11) Lhwyd's Hist. of Wales (Powel), p. 8. Parthau Cymru—Llyfr Coch o Hergest.

(12) Browne Willis, Survey of Bangor, ᵽ. 277. Le Neve's Fasti.

county was formed into Shire-ground, forty years previously. The Commote of Mowddwy did not become part of Merionethshire till it was incorporated with it by the second Statute of Wales,(13) as will hereafter appear. The Commotes of Ardudwy and Edeyrnion became portion of the county at the Conquest of Wales. The Statute of Wales, 12 Edw. I., enacts as follows :—

*Volumus etiam et Statuimus quod Vicecomites, Coronatores & Ballivi Commotorum sint in Snaudon, & terris nostris partium earundem.*

*Vicecomes de Meyronnith, sub quo Cantreda de Meironnith, Commotum de Ardudo, & Commotum de Penthlin, & Commotum de Dereynon, cum Metis & Bundis suis.*

At the time of the passing of this Act, and thenceforward till the 27th year of Hen. VIII., Gwynedd, or North Wales, consisted only of the three counties of Anglesey, Caernarvon, and Merioneth, with some outlying Cantrevydd of Flintshire, and of the subsequently formed county of Denbigh. Mowddwy continued to be part of that uncertain country known as the Marches of Wales, which was allotted and divided by the 2nd Statute of Wales. Before the passing of that Statute, but in the same year of Henry's reign, an Act(14) was passed, entitled—" For the Abuses in the Forests of Wales," which recited that divers and many forests being in Wales "and the Marches of the same as well of the inheritance and possessions of our sovereign Lord the King, as of divers others being Lords Marchers ; within which Forests certain unreasonable customs and exactions have been of long time unlawfully exacted and used," &c. It enumerates some of such exactions, and amongst others—" 3. And if any Person or Persons, not having a Token or Tokens, and not being a yearly Tributor or a Cheuser, as is aforesaid, should happen to be taken, found, or espied by any of the said Foresters, Rulers, Walkers, or Farmers, or their assigns, by the space of xxiv Foot out of the Highway, then he or they so being taken, found, or espied out of the Highway within any of the said Forests as is aforesaid, to forfeit and lose unto the said Foresters, &c., all such money or gold as should be then found upon him or them," &c. " II. And also the same Person or Persons so being taken, &c., to forfeit and lose a joint of one of his or their Hands, or else to make Fine therefore with the said Foresters, &c., at the *Will and Pleasure* of the said Foresters," &c.

The Abuses mentioned in this Statute arose in a great measure from the absence of any properly constituted legal authority with power to repress them. In the Counties, there were Sheriffs, Coroners, and Bailiffs, who held Courts and administered the law. But the Marches and lands not then assigned to any Shires were governed by officers known as Lords Marchers, who in theory were the King's Lieutenants, but in practice were semi-independent Feudatories ; and who, in consideration of levying certain subsidies for the King's Exchequer, and keeping in check the rebellious Welsh-men, were allowed to do much as they pleased. There were only four counties in the North and four in the South of Wales, and the rest of the country—the greater por-

---

(13) 27 Hen. VIII., c. 26.
(14) 27 Hen. VIII., c. 7.

tion of which was afterwards parcelled out into the counties of Denbigh, Montgomery, Monmouth, Brecknock, and Radnor—was under the government and control of the Lords Marchers. (15)   For nearly a century and a half after Edward's Conquest this state of things had been permitted to continue ; and it was reserved for the keen sense and strong will of the 8th Henry to accomplish, amongst his other great Reforms, the abolition of the barbarous customs and half independent isolation which impeded the progress of Wales—a progress which he wisely desired should proceed *pari passu* with that of the rest of his dominion.   The Preamble of the Statute by which he effected the change is very full in its statement of the reasons, and runs :—

"Albeit the Dominion, Principality, and Country of Wales justly and righteously is, and ever hath been, incorporated, &c., under the Imperial Crown of this Realm, &c., yet notwithstanding, because that in the same Country, &c., divers Rights, Usages, Laws and Customs be far discrepant from the Laws and Customs of this Realm ; and also because that the People of the same Dominion have, and do daily use, a Speech nothing like, ne consonant to the natural Mother Tongue used within this Realm ; some rude and ignorant People have made Distinction and Diversity between the King's Subjects of this Realm and his Subjects of the said Principality of Wales, &c."

By section 3 of the Statute it is also recited and enacted—" And forasmuch as there be many and divers Lordships Marchers within the said Country or Dominion of *Wales,* lying between the Shires of *England* and the Shires of the said Country, &c., of *Wales,* and being no parcel of any other Shires where the Laws and due correction is used and had, by reason whereof hath ensued, and hath been practised, &c., within and among the said Lordships and Countries to them adjoining manifold and divers detestable Murthers, brenning of Houses, Robberies, Thefts, Trespasses, Routs, Riots, unlawful Assemblies, Embraceries, Maintenances, receiving of Felons, Oppressions, Ruptures of the Peace, and manifold other Malefacts, contrary to all Laws and Justice ; and the said Offenders thereupon making their Refuge from Lordship to Lordship were and continued without punishment or correction.   2. For due Reformation whereof, and forasmuch as divers and many of the said Lordships Marchers be now in the Hands and Possession of our Sovereign Lord the King, and the smallest Number of them in the Possession of other Lords.   *It is therefore enacted, That* divers of the said Lordships Marchers shall be united, annexed, and joined to divers of the Shires of England and divers of the said Lordships Marchers shall be united, annexed, and joined to divers of the Shires of the said Country or Dominion of Wales in manner and form hereafter following ; (3) and that all the residue of the said Lordships Marchers within the said Country or Dominion of Wales shall be severed and divided into certain particular Counties or Shires, that is to say, the County or Shire of *Mon-*

---

(15) The Lords Marchers divided the lands they acquired into Manors and Lordships, and introduced gradually the customs and ordinances of the English manorial and other courts therein.   The boundaries of these Marches Lordships and Manors may be traced with greater accuracy than those of the old North Wales Hundreds, Commotes, and Parishes ; for the records of the former were preserved in the local courts, and have been handed down.

*mouth*, the County or Shire of *Brecknock*, the County or Shire of *Radnor*, the County or Shire of *Montgomery*, the County or Shire of *Denbigh*."

The Act then proceeds to define *seriatim* the Lordships, Townships, Parishes, Commotes and Cantreds assigned to each of the five new Counties, and to name the Shire-Towns of such Counties. It directed also where the Shire or County Court should be held. In Denbighshire, at Denbigh and Wrexham alternately; and in Montgomeryshire, at Montgomery the first time, and "Maghenleth" (Machynlleth) the next time, "and so to be kept in the same two Towns, *alternis vicibus*, for ever, and in none other place." This latter enactment has not been faithfully observed in its spirit, for although it had reference to the Sheriffs Courts, it no doubt also contemplated the fixing at those two towns—then the most important in the county—any Courts of Judicature which should be held in the county. At present the Courts of Assize and Quarter Sessions are held at the towns of Welshpool and Newtown alternately.

The only one of the four old counties of North Wales which received an accretion to its boundaries under this Act was Merioneth, to which was annexed [s. xix.] "the Lordship, Town, and Parish of Mouthway" [Mowddwy], "in whose possession soever it be," the latter a significant expression denoting the vagueness of its previous territorial status, and probably suggestive of some doubt whether its then Lord or possessors would assent to its incorporation with a county whose Shire-reeve would exercise jurisdiction in it. In 1555, exactly twenty years after the passing of the Act, the lawless inhabitants of Dinas Mowddwy justified this doubt by attacking and killing Lewis Owen,(16) Sheriff of the county, and one of the Barons of the Exchequer of North Wales, who had probably gone there on business connected with his office.

No alteration has been made in the boundaries of the county since the passing of this Statute, with one slight exception. By a subsequent Statute of the same reign,(17) it was enacted "that the Town or Hamlet of *Abertannad*, and all the grounds and the soil within the same, which afore this time hath been taken, reputed, and used as parcel of the said county of Merioneth, shall, from the Feast of Easter next coming, be united, annexed, and made parcel of the said county of Salop;" and it was assigned as part and parcel of the Hundred of Oswestry.

The county is bounded by Caernarvonshire on the N.W. (separated by the River Glaslyn) and N.; Denbighshire on the N.E. and E.; Montgomeryshire on the S.E.; Cardiganshire (separated by the Rivers Dovey and Estuary) on the S.; and the Irish Sea on the W.

It is 46 miles in length, and 27 in breadth.

It has an area of 602 square miles, or 385,291 acres. In point of area, it is larger than Caernarvon, Flint and Anglesey; and only one square mile less than Denbigh.

It is watered by the Dee (which has its source in it on the Garneddwen Moun-

---

(16) Lewis Owen, the Baron, was Custos Rot. for Merioneth, and twice Knight of the Shire.
(17) 34 and 35 Hen. VIII., c. 26, s. 87.

tain), Mawddach, Dysynni, Dwyryd, and other lesser rivers ; with the Rivers Glaslyn and Dovey on its northern and southern boundaries respectively.

Its general surface is very rugged and mountainous, and its geological stratification is the Silurian. (18)  The principal hills in it are Cader Idris, 2,914 feet high ; Aran Fowddwy, 2,955 feet ; Arenig Mawr, 2,809 feet ; Berwyn, 2,563 feet ; Duffwys, 2,412 feet ; Rhinog Fawr, 2,345 feet ; and Mignaint, Manod, Moelwyn, Cnycht, and others, ranging from 1,500 to 2,300.

It has between sixty and seventy lakes—the principal of which is Llyn Tegid, or Bala Lake.   This lake is the largest in Wales, and is nine miles in circumference. (19) The other chief lakes are Talyllyn, Llyn Mwnygl, Cynwch, Cregennan, Bodlin (in which Char are found), Cwmbychan, Glawlyn, Fedw, Tecwyn (2), Cwmorthin, Morwynion, Trywerin, and Llyn Arrenig.

The chief mineral product of the county is slate.   From the Festiniog Slate Quarries alone upwards of 140,000 tons were obtained in the year ending 1869, the estimated value of which was £350,000.   In addition to these, there are extensive quarries at Abercorris, Talyllyn, and in the Vale of Mawddach.   Gold has been found at many places—especially at Clogau, Cwmhesian, Gwynfynydd and Castell Carn dochan.   The mine at the first-named place was worked with much success for a few years, and yielded a large profit.   Lead, iron, and copper have also been found ; and workings in search of each of these minerals are now being prosecuted in various parts of the county.

The population in 1871 was 47,369.

The following is a table of the comparative population of the county at each of the censuses, 1801—71 :—

| Year. | | | Population. | Total increase in 70 years. |
|---|---|---|---|---|
| 1801 | ... | ... | 29,506 | |
| 1811 | ... | ... | 30,854 | |
| 1821 | ... | ... | 34,382 | |
| 1831 | ... | .. | 35,315 | |
| 1841 | ... | ... | 39,332 | 17,863. |
| 1851 | ... | ... | 38,843 | |
| 1861 | ... | ... | 38,963 | |
| 1871 | ... | ... | 47,369 | |

(18) Fuller writes :—" It is extream mountainous ; yea (if true what Giraldus Cambrensis reporteth thereof), so high the hills therein, that men may discourse one with the other on the tops thereof, and yet hardly meet (beneath in the valley) in a day's time. Yet are not the mountains altogether useless, feeding great numbers of sheep thereon. Mr. Camden takes especial notice of the beauty and comeliness of the inhabitants of this Shire."— Fuller's Eng. Worthies, Ed. 1811, p. 598.

(19) The same author, describing the "wonders" of the Shire, writes—" There is a lake in this county called in British *Lhin-tegid*, in English Pimble-Mear, which may be termed our Leman Lake, having the same work of wonder therein, though set forth by nature in a less Letter : for as Rhodanus, running through that French Lake, preserveth his stream by itself (discernible by the discolouration thereof) with the fishes peculiar thereunto, the same is here observed betwixt the River Dee and the water of the lake ; so that here is (what some cavil at in the grammar) a *conjunction disjunctive*. Let philosophers dispute what invisible partition incloseth the one severally from the other." To these notes see also Camden Britt. (Gough, 1789), Vol. II., p. 538.

It will be seen by the above table that in the year 1841 the population exceeded the number at the two following censuses. This may be accounted for by the great agricultural distress which existed in the country between the years 1847—51, and the discovery of gold in Australia, both which causes led to a large emigration—especially from the rural districts of Wales. Since 1861 the population of the county has increased, principally in the quarry district of Festiniog ; and the census of 1871 discloses a larger increase than during any former decade.

It is difficult to trace to its origin, with any degree of certainty, the formation of the various Hundreds (Cantrevydd) and Commotes (Cwmwdau). It is certain, indeed, that they have a more ancient origin than the other recognised territorial divisions. They are referred to in the Laws of Duvnwal Moelmud (Moelmutius), a British King, who flourished long before the Christian Era. Asser Menevensis, the literary guide and friend of Alfred, translated those laws at the request of the great Saxon King, and the code which the latter compiled is unquestionably indebted for many of its laws to the old British collection.[20] The minor divisions of parishes, though of much later origin, have their commencement less clearly recorded. After the erection of Ecclesiastical Sees, or Dioceses, in Wales, which took place circa A.D. 550, they were sub-divided into parishes or distinct ministerial cures. This distribution happened in Wales probably about the same time as it occurred in England, where it was brought about by the direction, as it is said, of Archbishop Honorius, circa 636.[21] Most of the parishes are called after the patrons or builders of the first churches in them, and their distinctive boundaries have been immemoriably maintained by the sure demarcation of the collection of the church's alimony of tithes.[22] The Commission issued and executed in pursuance of the 27 Hen. VIII. c. 26, for sub-dividing the country, then first formed into Shire-ground, does not appear to have touched any of the ancient parochial divisions of the old North Wales counties. The number of parishes in the county is 37 ; but of these four are partly in other counties—viz., Beddgelert, partly in Caernarvonshire, Bettws-gwerfilgoch, and Llanfihangel-glyn myfyr, partly in Denbighshire, and Mallwyd, partly in Montgomeryshire. The following table will give a comprehensive view of the Parishes, Poor Law Unions, Hundreds, gross estimated Annual Value, Area, and Population :—

[20] The Molmutian Laws are said by Hollinshed to have been translated by Alfred from the Latin of Gildas, " and mingled in his statutes."—(Holl. Chron., Vol. I., p. 451.)

[21] Hallam says that Parochial Divisions, as they now exist, did not take place, at least in some countries, till several centuries after the establishment of Christianity (Middle Ages). Blackstone, in his Commentaries, also questions Camden's accuracy in assigning the subdivision of parishes to so early a period as 630. He points out that before the time of King Edgar every man paid his tithes to what church or parish he pleased, and that the law of King Edgar, circa 970 A.D., ordered that " dentur omnes decimæ primariæ ecclesiæ ad quam parochia pertinet."—(Stephen's Blackstone, Vol. I., p. 109.)

[22] It may be questionable whether parishes were formed much earlier than the middle of the 9th century in the time of King Ethelwulf, the predecessor of Alfred, for we have an authentic record of the ordaining of Tithes by that monarch :—" A.D. 854. The same year King Ethelwulf registered a *Tenth* of his land over all his Kingdom for the honour of God and for his own everlasting salvation. The same year, also, he went to Rome with great pomp, and was resident there a twelvemonth."—Saxon Chron. (Ingram's Ed., 1823), p. 94.

| HUNDREDS. | UNIONS. | PARISHES. | Annual Value. | Area. | Population. |
|---|---|---|---|---|---|
| ARDUDWY-UWCH-ARTRO | FESTINIOG . | Festiniog . . . | 17,150 | 16,456 | 4,553 |
| | | Llanbedr . . . | 1,700 | 7,312 | 370 |
| | | Llanfair . . . | 2,120 | 5,196 | 426 |
| | | Llandanwg . . . | 2,100 | 4,964 | 739 |
| | | Llanfihangel-y-traethau | 4,010 | 7,567 | 1,687 |
| | | Llandecwyn . . | 1,883 | 6,915 | 436 |
| | | Llanfrothen . . | 3,250 | 7,482 | 830 |
| | | Maentwrog . . | 2,680 | 5,465 | 883 |
| | | Beddgelert ([23])(Hamlet of Nantmor) . . | 930 | 6,108 | 309 |
| | | Trawsfynydd . . | 5,215 | 21,950 | 1,517 |
| ESTIMANER . . | MACHYNLLETH . | Pennal . . . | 2,755 | 7,461 | 588 |
| | | Towyn . . . | 11,100 | 26,372 | 2,859 |
| . . . . | DOLGELLEY. | Talyllyn . . . | 3,877 | 15,182 | 1,284 |
| TALYBONT . . . | . . . . | Dolgelley . . . | 11,522 | 25,607 | 3,457 |
| | | Llanfachreth . . | 3,970 | 10,000 | 862 |
| | | Llangelynin . . | 4,374 | 11,004 | 891 |
| | | Llanegryn . . . | 3,565 | 6,819 | 652 |
| | | Llanfihangel-y-pennant | 1,872 | 8,321 | 368 |
| ARDUDWY-IS-ARTRO . | . . . . | Llanelltyd . . . | 2,031 | 6,736 | 465 |
| | | Llanaber . . . | 5,676 | 12,679 | 1,600 |
| | | Llanddwywe-is-y-graig. | 1,803 | } 9,348 | 264 |
| | | Llanddwywe - uwch - y-graig . . . | 413 | | 104 |
| | | Llanenddwyn . . | 3,077 | 7,777 | 891 |
| MOWDDWY . . . | . . . . . | Llanymowddwy . . | 2,502 | 15,290 | 595 |
| | | Mallwyd ([24]) . . | 3,298 | 14,556 | 938 |
| EDEIRNION . . | CORWEN . | Bettws-gwerfil-goch ([25]) | 1,020 | 2,650 | 242 |
| | | Corwen . . . | 8,688 | 12,646 | 2,042 |
| | | Gwyddelwern . . | 6,100 | 9,125 | 1,541 |
| | | Llangar . . . | 1,913 | 3,578 | 211 |
| | | Llandrillo . . . | 4,458 | 28,200 | 776 |
| | | Llansant - ffraid - glyn-dyfrdwy . . | 654 | 693 | 161 |
| | | Llanfihangel - glyn - myfyr ([26]) . . | 264 | 3,538 | 70 |
| PENLLYN . . . | BALA . . | Llanycil . . . | 8,200 | 12,868 | 2,383 |
| | | Llanfor . . . | 8,249 | 20,030 | 1,531 |
| | | Llandderfel . . | 3,966 | 7,794 | 948 |
| | | Llanuwchllyn . . | 4,620 | 12,000 | 1,145 |
| | | Llangower . . | 1,825 | 5,600 | 345 |
| | | | 152,830 | 385,291 | 38,963 |

([23]) Beddgelert parish is mostly in Caernarvonshire ; the entire parish contains 1,375 persons.

([24]) Mallwyd parish is partly in Montgomeryshire ; the entire parish contains 1,049 persons.

([25]) Bethosgwerfilgoch is partly in Denbighshire ; the entire parish contains 258 persons.

([26]) Llanfihangelglynmyfyr parish is mostly in Denbighshire ; the entire parish contains 464 persous.

The principal town of the County is Dolgelley—population, in 1861, 2,218. It is situated in the Valley of the Wnion, and is connected by Railway communication with all the other Towns of the County. The Assizes and General Quarter Sessions are held there now. Until 1869 the Sessions were held there and at Bala alternately, but in Easter of that year the holding of the Sessions was ordered in future to be at Dolgelley only. (26) The Lent Assizes were removed from Bala to Dolgelley in 1872. The town is very ancient and still possesses an old house called the "Parliament House,"(27) in which it is said Owen Glyndwr, in 1404, held a National Assembly, which, had his patriotic struggle been consecrated by success, might have gone down to History as the first great Welsh Parliament. The age of the structure does not, however, bear out this tradition.(28)

The other towns are Bala, Corwen, Barmouth, Towyn, and Aberdovey. Besides these, new towns are springing up at Blaenau Festiniog, and Penrhyndeudraeth. The ancient "County town" of Harlech is a town only in name, and has no existing sign of its title except the election of the Knight of the Shire, which still takes place

---

(26) The following Ordinance is interesting as forming the foundation of the Courts of Quarter Sessions in Wales :—

"Ad Sessionem Com̅. Merioneth tent ap^d Carn'van die Lune proxim̅. ante ff̅m̅. Sc̅e. "Marie Magdalene anno regni Henrici VIIJ^ui XXVIJ°.

"Fforasmuch as it appeareth vnto the Justice vppon complaintes made by the Kinges subiectes and Inhabitaunts of the thre Shires of the Principalitie of Northwales against the Excheators their Deputies and Ministers of the said Counties that they should cause the Kinges Subiects of the said iij shires by color of their offices f divers and sundrie times, that is to saie every xiiij daie to appere before them in Mountaynes Rocks and other desert places being distaunte frome the place or places where they Inhabite or dwell sometimes xx^ti myles sometimes xxx^ti miles more or lesse and haue no certeine knoweledge in what place or places they should or might appere to enquire for our soveraign Lord the King and for their non apparaunce do vse to assesse vppon the said Subiects divers and many great ffines and Amerceaments to their great vnquietness costes and chardges which is contrary to the Lawes and Statutes in that case ordeyned and provided. Therefore it is ordred by the said Justices that the said Excheators their deputies and ministers or any of them fromehenceforth shall not sit to enquire for o^r sou'aign Lord the Kinge by vertue of their office in any such Rocks Mountaynes or such other desert places. Nor to set to enquire so often or so many times, but y^t they from henceforth not sit but iiij^or times in the yere. That is to say once in euery quarter of the yere and in such towne and Townes place or places as the Shireff of the said Counties do comonly and severally kepe their grande Tornes. Vnlesse it be uppon diem clausit extremū to enquire for o^r soveraign Lord the King or otherwise Licensed by the Justice or Chambleyne or their Deputies for the time being, vppon paine of x^li to be leavied to the Kinges Vse of the goodes and cattells landes and teñts of such of them as shall offend or breake this ordre."—The Record of Caernarvon, Addimenta, p. 297.

(27) *I believe this to be the Cwrt Plas yn dre, the residence of Baron Owen, and doubt if any portion of it is as old as the time of Owen Glyndwr. W.

(28) Fuller, in his "English Worthies" (pp. 598-9), has the following quaint particulars relating to Dolgelley :—

"I know not whether it be worth the relating what is known for a truth of a Market Town called Dolgelthy, in this Shire, that—

"1. The Walls thereof are three miles high   =   The Mountains which surround it.
"2. Men come into it *over the Water*, but   On a fair Bridge.
"3. Go out of it under the Water   =   Falling from a rock and conveyed in a Wooden Trough (under which Travellers must make shift to pass) to drive an *Over-Shot* Mill.
"4. The Steeple thereof doth grow therein   =   The *bells* (if plural) hang on a *Yeugh Tree*."

3

here.(29)   Formerly its strong castle—the splendid ruins of which still remain—gave it great importance; but the bombardment and capture of the Castle by Cromwell's forces in 1647, and the subsequent dismantling of it by Charles II., left only the shell of the great stronghold built by Edw. I., on the site of the ancient fortress first known in Welsh history as Twr Bronwen, and afterwards as Caer Collwyn. (30)

(29) *Feb. 3, 1608.   Justices of Merionethshire to Ralph, Lord Eure, President of Wales, representing the inconvenience of holding the Sessions in different places, and requesting that they may be always held in one place, and recommend Harlech.

4 Feb., 1608.   Inhabitants of Harlech to Lord Eure, entreating him to have the Sessions brought back again to Harlech.

18 March, 1809.   Lord Eure recommends same.   Order in consequence, 22 Mar., and further reference 25 May, 1609.

(Extracts by Mr. Wynne, from Calendars of State Papers at Lower Eatington Park).

There is an original bond at Brogyntyn, from Griffith Vaughan, of Corsygedol, Esq., to Ralph, Lord Eure, Lord President of Wales, dated 25 Feb., 6 James I., for the payment of £30, conditional, on Lord Eure's getting the Great and Quarter Sessions to be held at Harlech.   Such was the open corruption of those days !   There is also a like bond, from several persons, to Sir William Maurice, of Clenenny.   W.

(30) *If I recollect, it was dismantled prior to the Restoration.   I doubt if any portion of the present building is older than the time of Edw I.   There is a letter at Brogyntyn, and copy of it at Peniarth, ordering the castle to be dismantled.  W.

# CHAPTER IV.

### LORD-LIEUTENANT AND CUSTOS ROTULORUM.

THE office of Custos, or Keeper of the Rolls of the Peace, is a very ancient one. In Wales it appears to have been established by the 34 and 35 Hen. VIII., c. 26, by which Statute it was enacted that there should be one Custos for each of the 12 counties (s. 53), and that he should be appointed together with 8 Justices of the Peace for each County, by the Lord Chancellor with the advice of the Lord President and Council of the Marches. His duties then appear to have been limited principally to the custody of the documents appertaining to the Shire. The Lords Presidents and Council exercised the privilege, which after the abolition of their office devolved upon the Custos, of recommending to the Lord Chancellor the names of those who should be inserted in the Commission of the Peace. Two years later (1545), a Statute (37 Hen. VIII., c. 1) was passed, providing for the appointment in future of all Custodes by the Sovereign under Sign Manual, without the intervention of the President and Council. The preamble of this Statute assigns as the reason for the change that ignorant persons had been appointed to this office, and also to that of Clerk of the Peace.(1) In the next Reign the appointment was again restored by Statute (3 and 4 Edw. VI., c. 1) to the Lord Chancellor, to whom "the nomination and appointing of the said office, long time before the making of the said Statute last before rehearsed, did appertain," and it continued in him till A.D. 1688, when the Statute 1 Wm. & Mary, c. 21, enacted that it should be made in manner directed by the 37 Hen. VIII. It has remained in the Sovereign by virtue of that enactment to the present day. This office is a perfectly distinct one from that of Lord-Lieutenant. Up to the latter half of the last century, it was never held by the Lord-Lieutenant.

---

(1) It appears from the recital in the preamble that "divers and sundry persons within this Realm being not learned nor yet meet ne able for lack of knowledge and Learning to occupy and exercise the said offices of Cust. Rot. and the Clerkships of the Peace, have of late years by labor, friendship and means, gotten for term of their lives, of the King's Majesty, several Grants by his Highness Letters Patents to them made of the said Clerkships of the Peace." It was therefore provided that in future, Clerks of the Peace should be "able persons instructed in the Laws of the Realm," and should be appointed by the Custos to hold their office during good behaviour for the same term as the Custos held his. By the Statute 1 Wm. & Mary, c. 21, it was enacted that the Clerk of the Peace should hold his office during good behaviour without reference to the term of office of the Custos.

But since then the two offices have been conferred upon the same person, and are now invariably held together. The office of Lord-Lieutenant was instituted in England about the year 1560. The duties were similar in many respects to those which formerly devolved upon the Comes or Earl of each County. He was the head of the military forces within the County. In Wales, the office was generally held by one and the same person for all the counties, up to the middle of the last century (1760), George, Earl of Cholmondeley, being the last who held the office for all the North Wales Counties. Until the abolition of the institution of the President and Council of the Marches, the Lord-President also held the Lieutenancy of the Welsh counties.

The vexed question of the relative precedence in the County of the Lord-Lieutenant and Sheriff has been much discussed of late years. A dictum of Blackstone, in his Commentaries, founded on an observation of Sir Edward Coke's, is relied upon in support of the theory that the Sheriff is the first man in the County. It has, however, been shown by many writers, including Sir George Young, late Garter King-at-Arms, that Sir E. Coke's observation was misapprehended by Blackstone. It is difficult to conceive that he could have intended to apply it to the Lord-Lieutenant, who occupied the position of the ancient Comes, whilst the Sheriff holds that of Vice-Comes, and is a subordinate officer, charged with the execution of the process of the Courts of Law within the County. The duties of the two offices are, in fact, perfectly distinct. The Sheriff is the Executive, within his Bailiwick, of the civil power ; whilst the Lieutenant is the head of the Military Reserve forces of the County.(2) Until 1871, all the Officers of such reserve forces were appointed by the Lord-Lieutenant ; but by the Army Regulation Act, 1871, the appointment of such officers was vested in the Crown.

It will be more convenient to prefix to the lists of Lieutenants a list of the Lords-President of Wales down to the abolition of that office in 1688.

---

(2) The power of calling into arms and mustering the population of each County, given in earlier times to the Sheriffs or Justices of the Peace, or to Special Commissioners of Array, began to be entrusted, in the reign of Mary, to a new officer, entitled the Lord-Lieutenant. This was usually a Peer, or at least a gentleman of large estate within the county, whose office gave him the command of the Militia, and rendered him the chief Vice-gerent of his sovereign, responsible for the maintenance of public order. This institution may be considered as a revival of the ancient local Earldom ; and it certainly took away from the Sheriff a great part of the dignity and importance which he had acquired since the discontinuance of that office. Yet the Lord-Lieutenant has so peculiarly military an authority, that it does not in any degree control the civil power of the Sheriff as the Executive Minister of the Law. In certain cases, such as tumultuous obstruction of legal authority, each might be said to possess an equal power, the Sheriff being still undoubtedly competent to call out the *posse comitatus* in order to enforce obedience. Practically, however, in all serious circumstances, the Lord-Lieutenant has always been reckoned the efficient and responsible guardian of public tranquillity.—Hallam's Constit. Hist., Ch. IX., p. 386.

# LORDS PRESIDENT OF WALES.[1]

## (FROM 18 EDW. IV.)

| Year. | Regnal Year. | Name. |
|---|---|---|
| 1478— 9. | 18 Edw. IV. | John Alcock, Bishop of Worcester. |
| ,, | ,, | Anthony, Earl Rivers. |
| 1501— 2. | 17 Henry VII. | William Smith, Bishop of Lincoln. |
| 1512— 3. | 4 Hen. VIII. | Geoffrey Blyth, Bishop of Coventry and Lichfield. |
| 1525— 6. | 17 ,, | John Voysey, Bishop of Exeter. |
| 1534— 5. | 26 Hen. VIII. | Roland Lee, Bishop of Coventry and Lichfield. |
| 1543— 4. | 35 ,, | Richard Sampson, Bishop of Coventry and Lichfield. |
| 1548—59. | 2 Edward VI. | John Dudley, Earl of Warwick; afterwards Duke of Northumberland. |
| 1550— 1. | 4 ,, | Sir William Herbert; afterwards Earl of Pembroke, K.G. |
| 1553— 4 | 1 Mary | Nicholas Heath, Bishop of Worcester, Lord Chancellor. |
| 1556— 7. | 3 & 4 Phil. and Mary. | William, Earl of Pembroke; reappointed on resignation of Nicholas Heath. |
| 1558— . | 5 & 6 Phil. and Mary | Gilbert Bourne, Bishop of Bath and Wells. |
| 1558— 9. | 1 Elizabeth. | Sir John Williams (afterwards John, Lord Williams, of Thame). |
| 1559—60. | 2 ,, | Sir Henry Sydney. |
| 1587— . | 29 ,, | Henry, Earl of Pembroke.[2] |
| 1602— . | 44 ,, | Edward, Lord Zouch. |
| 1609— . | 7 James I. | Ralph, Lord Eure.[3] |

---

[1] Cal. of State Papers, Domestic, 1601-3, pp. 216—19, Mr. Clive's "Documents Connected with the History of Ludlow and the Lords Marchers, 1841."

*If I recollect there is no instance when the Lord-President was not Lord-Lieutenant. See List of Lords-Lieutenant for Merionethshire, in Arch. Camb. Vol. i. I think one of them was made Lord-Lieutenant some time after he had the Patent of Lord-President. W.

[2] *Henry, Earl of Pembroke, Lord-President of the Marches, in an original document at Brogyntyn, 21 March, 1598. He died in 1601, and was succeeded in the Presidency of Wales by Edward, Lord Zouch, who was appointed King's Lieutenant in Wales, in 1603. W.

[3] *He was certainly Lord-President of Wales, and Lord-Lieutenant of the same, upon 26 July, 1609.— Original Letter at Chirk Castle. See also Note to the "Lords-Lieutenant of Merioneth," 1609, 27th May. Died at Ludlow Castle, 1st April, 1617. W.

He was appointed Lord-President of South Wales and the Marches, (Glamorgan and Monmouth excepted), on the 12th Sept., 1607, and for the Principality of Wales, on the 27th May, 1609.

| Year. | Regnal Year. | Name. |
|---|---|---|
| 1617— | 14 James I. | Thomas, Lord Gerrard. (4) |
| ,, | 15   ,, | William, Lord Compton; afterwards Earl of Northampton. |
| 1631— . | 7 Charles I. | John, Earl of Bridgewater. |
| 1660— . | 12 Charles II. | Richard, Lord Vaughan, Earl of Carberry. (5) |
| 1672— . | 24   ,, | Henry, Marquis of Worcester; afterwards Duke of Beaufort. |
| 1689— . | 1 Will. and Mary. | Charles Gerard, Earl of Macclesfield. |

(4) *He bought the Lord-Presidency, of Lord Eure, and died before the month of Oct,, in 1617.—State Papers : Commission of Lieutenancy of N. & S. Wales to him, March 7, 1617. W.

(5) For South Wales only.

# LORDS LIEUTENANT AND CUSTODES ROTULORUM(1) OF ANGLESEY.

| Name. | Appointed. |
|---|---|
| Henry, Earl of Pembroke, Lieutenant within the Principality of Wales and the Marches thereof. . . . . | 24 Feb., 1587. |
| Henry, Earl of Pembroke, Lieutenant within the Principality of Wales, and in Worcester, Monmouth, Hereford, and Salop. . | 2 Dec., „ |
| Henry, Earl of Pembroke, Lieutenant within the Principality of Wales, and in Worcester, Monmouth, Hereford, and Salop. . | 5 Aug., 1588. |
| Henry, Earl of Pembroke, Lieutenant within the Principality of Wales. . . . . . . . | 24 Sept., 1595. |
| Edward, Lord Zouch, Lieutenant within the Principality of Wales and the Marches thereof. . . . . . | 20 July, 1602. |
| Ralph, Lord Eure, Lieutenant within the Principality of Wales (Glamorgan and Monmouth excepted), the Marches thereof: and in Worcester, Hereford and Salop . . . . | 12 Sept., 1607. |
| Ralph Lord Eure, Lieutenant within the Principality of Wales (2) . | 27 May, 1609. |
| Thomas, Lord Gerrard, Lieutenant within the Principality of Wales. . . . . . . . | 7 March, 1617. |
| William, Lord Compton, Lieutenant within the Principality of Wales and the Marches thereof. . . . . | 24 Nov., „ |
| John, Earl of Bridgewater, Lieutenant within the Principality of Wales, and in Monmouth, Worcester, Hereford, and Salop. . | 11 July, 1631. |
| John Earl of Bridgewater, Lieutenant within the Principality of Wales, Monmouth, Worcester, Hereford, and Salop. . . | 12 May, 1633. |
| Algernon, Earl of Northumberland. . . Lieutenant . | 11 Feb., 1641. |
| John Bodvel, Esq. . . Custos . | 26 Aug., 1643. |
| Sir Hugh Owen, Knt. and Bart. Custos (3) | 1650. |
| Thomas Madrin, Esq. . . Custos . | 27 July, 1653. |

(1) Custodes Rotulorum were appointed by the Lord Chancellor or Keeper, 3 & 4 Edw. VI.

(2) *He died at Ludlow Castle, 1st April, 1617, but it would appear that he ceased to hold the Presidency of the Marches, with which the Lieutenancy of Wales mostly went, before his death, for amongst the State Papers is a letter dated 22 June, 1616, stating that Lord Gerard has bought the Presidency of Wales from Lord Eure. In Banks's Peerage, he is said to have died in 1618. W.

(3) *Of Orielton in Pembrokeshire, and Bodowen, Anglesey, the first Baronet of his family; died in 1670. W.

| Name. | | Appointed. |
|---|---|---|
| Robert, Lord Viscount Bulkeley.   Custos (4) | | 6 Sept., 1660. |
| Richard, Earl of Carberry.(5)   .   .   . Lieutenant | . | 22 „   „ |
| „   „   „   „   .   .   . Lieutenant | . | ? 14 July, 1662. |
| Henry, Marquis of Worcester, (afterwards Duke of Beaufort,) Lieutenant within the Principality of Wales.   .   . | . | 22 „   1672 |
| Robert, Viscount Bulkeley.    Custos . | | 7 March, 1685. |
| Henry, Duke of Beaufort, Lieutenant within the Principality of Wales and the Marches thereof; and in Gloucester, Hereford, Monmouth, &c. .   .   .   .   . | . | 28 „   „ |
| Charles, Earl of Macclesfield, Lieutenant within the Principality of Wales. .   .   .   .   .   .   . | . | 22 „   1689. |
| Nicholas Bagnall, Esq.   .   Custos . | | 8 Oct.,   „ |
| Richard, Viscount Bulkeley. .   Custos . | | 27 Feb., 1690. |
| Charles, Duke of Shrewsbury.   .   . Lieutenant | . | 31 May, 1694. |
| Charles, Earl of Macclesfield..   .   . Lieutenant | . | 10 March, 1696. |
| William, Earl of Derby.   .   .   . Lieutenant | . | 18 June, 1702. |
| Hugh, Lord Cholmondeley. .   .   . Lieutenant | . | 2 Dec.,   „ |
| Richard, Viscount Bulkeley. .   Custos (6) | | 15 Jan., 1706. |
| Hugh, Earl of Cholmondeley.   .   . Lieutenant | . | 21 Oct., 1714. |
| Owen Meyricke, Esq.   .   Custos . | | 21 Dec., 1715. |
| George, Earl of Cholmondeley.   .   . Lieutenant | . | 7 April, 1725. |
| „   „   „   „   .   .   . Lieutenant | . | 20 Sept., 1727. |
| Owen Meyricke, Esq.   .   Custos . | | 13 Nov.,   „ |
| George, Earl of Cholmondeley.   .   . Lieutenant | . | 14 June, 1733. |
| Sir Nicholas Bayley, Bart.   .   Custos (7) | | 23 „   1759. |
| „   „   „   „   . { Custos . | | 24 Nov., 1761. |
| „   „   „   „   . {   Lieutenant | . | 25 „   „ |
| Henry, Lord Paget.   . { Custos (8) | | 25 July, 1782. |
| „   „   „   . {   Lieutenant | . | 1 Aug.,   „ |

(4) *The first and Royalist Viscount Bulkeley. W.

    Sept. 21, 1648. Letters from Anglesey of the differences between Lord Bulkeley and Lord Byron that the Island is in an Uproar, and that Col. Mitton, with a strong power, is marching towards them. Whitlock's Mem., p. 333.—Oct. 2. Letters from Anglesey of the taking it by Major-General Mitton by storm; and that the Lord Byron and Lord Bulkeley were escaped by flight. id. p. 335.

    (5) Samuel Butler, the Author of "Hudibras," was Secretary to Lord Carberry, as Lord President, and was by him made Steward of Ludlow Castle.

    (6) *Richard, fourth Viscount Bulkeley, married Lady Bridget Bertie, daughter of James, first Earl of Abingdon. His son, Richard, the fifth Viscount, born 1708, married Jane, eldest daughter and heiress of Lewis Owen, of Peniarth, Esq., Custos Rotulorum for Merionethshire. He died without issue, in 1739, and his widow remarried to her near kinsman, Edward Williams, Esq., one of the younger sons of John Williams, of Chester and Bodelwyddan, Esq.; she died in 1765. There are portraits of Lord and Lady Bulkeley, in their coronation robes, at Baronhill and Peniarth. W.

    (7) *Father of Henry, first Earl of Uxbridge, of his family. W.

    (8) *Afterwards first Earl of Uxbridge. W.

| Name. | | Appointed. |
|---|---|---|
| Henry William, Earl of Uxbridge. (9) | Lieutenant | 21 April, 1812. |
| „ „ „ „ | Custos | 2 May, „ |
| „ „ Marquis of Anglesey. | Custos | 18 Sept., 1830. |
| „ „ „ „ | Lieutenant | 20 Nov., „ |
| „ „ „ „ | Lieutenant | 18 „ 1837. |
| „ „ „ „ | Custos | 22 „ „ |
| Henry, Marquis of Anglesey. | Custos (10) | 15 May, 1854. |
| „ „ „ „ | Lieutenant | 18 „ „ |
| The Hon. William Owen Stanley, M.P. (11) . . | Lieutenant | 2 March, 1869. |
| „ „ „ „ | Custos | 4 „ „ |

(9) ✳Afterwards the gallant Marquis of Anglesey. W.

(10) ✳Second Marquis of Anglesey. W.

(11) See Members for Beaumaris.

# LORDS-LIEUTENANT AND CUSTODES ROTULORUM OF CAERNARVONSHIRE.

(FOR LORDS-LIEUTENANT OF CAERNARVON FROM 1587—1733, SEE ANGLESEY.)

| Name. | | | Appointed |
|---|---|---|---|
| Thomas Mostyn, of Mostyn and Gloddaith, Esq. | Custos | | 2 July, 1596. |
| Philip, Lord of Pembroke and Montgomery, nominated by the House of Commons to be Lieutenant of Wilts, Caernarvon, and Merioneth. | | | 11 Feb., 1642. |
| Griffith Jones, of Castellmarch, Esq. | Custos | | Sept., 1650. |
| John Carter, Esq. | Custos | | 1 May, 1651. |
| William Lloyd, of Bodfan, Esq. | Custos | | 25 June, 1656. |
| John Carter, Esq. | Custos | | 4 July, „ |
| Sir Richard Wynn, Bart. | Custos | | 6 Sept., 1660. |
| Sir Roger Mostyn, Bart. | Custos | | 5 Dec., 1674. |
| Richard Bulkeley, Esq. | Custos | | 3 May, 1679. |
| „ „ „ | Custos | | 7 March, 1685. |
| Edward Russell, Esq., (afterwards Lord Edward Russell) | Custos | | 8 Oct., 1689. |
| Lord Edward Russell. (1) | Custos | | 16 July, 1702. |
| Peregrine, Lord Willoughby d'Eresby. | Custos | | 1 Dec., 1714. |
| Sir William Yonge. (2) | Custos | | 28 June, 1739. |
| Sir John Wynn, Bart. | Custos | | 10 April, 1756. |
| „ „ „ „ | Custos | | 28 April, 1761. |
| Thomas Wynn, Esq. (3) | | Lieutenant | 4 July, „ |
| Sir Thomas Wynn, Bart. | Custos | | 1 March, 1773. |
| Thomas James, Lord Viscount Bulkeley. (4) | | Lieutenant | 27 Dec., 1781. |
| „ „ „ „ „ | Custos | | 23 Jan., 1782. |

---

(1) *Of Penrhyn, in right of his wife Frances, daughter and heiress of Sir Robert Williams, of Penrhyn, Bart., and relict of Robert Lloyd, Esq., of Esclusham and Dulassey, in the Counties of Denbigh and Caernarvon. Lord Edward was a younger son of the first Duke of Bedford, and brother of the celebrated William, Lord Russell.  W.

(2) *Owner of one moiety of Penrhyn.   He was one of the Lords Commissioners of the Treasury.  W.

(3) *Thomas Wynn, Esq., of Glynllifon and Bodean, afterwards Lord Newborough.  W.

(4) *Seventh and last Viscount ; died in 1822.  W.

| Name. | | Appointed. |
|---|---|---|
| Thomas Assheton Smith, Esq. | ⎰ Custos . | . 10 July, 1822. |
| „    „    „    „ | ⎱ . Lieutenant . 18   „    „ |  |
| Peter Robert, Lord Gwydir. (5) | ⎰ Custos . | . 20 Aug., 1828. |
| „    „    „    „ | ⎱ . Lieutenant . 25 Nov.,  „ |  |
| Peter Robert, Lord Willoughby d'Eresby. | ⎰ Custos . | . 18 Sept., 1830. |
| „   „   „   „   „ | ⎱ . Lieutenant . 2 Dec.   „ |  |
| „   „   „   „   „ | ⎰ . Lieutenant . 18 Nov., 1837. |  |
| „   „   „   „   „ | ⎱ Custos . | . 28   „    „ |
| Sir Richard Bulkeley Williams Bulkeley, Bart. | ⎰ Custos . | . 27 Feb., 1851. |
| „    „    „    „    „ | ⎱ . Lieutenant . 7 March, „ |  |
| Edward Gordon, Lord Penryhn. | ⎰ Custos . | . 13 Sept., 1866. |
| „    „    „    „ | ⎱ . Lieutenant . 14   „    „ |  |

(5) *Peter Robert, Lord Gwydir, afterwards Lord Willoughby d'Eresby. I have heard him say that he had "the wreck of four estates;" a valuable wreck, too, if he meant Grimsthorpe, Willoughby, Gwydir, and Drummond Castle! W.

# LORDS-LIEUTENANT AND CUSTODES ROTULORUM OF MERIONETH.

(FOR LORDS-LIEUTENANT OF MERIONETHSHIRE FROM 1587—1733, SEE ANGLESEY.)

| Name. | | Appointed. |
|---|---|---|
| Lewis Owen, of Dolgelly, Esq. [Baron Owen] (1) | Custos | 1553. |
| Ellis Price, of Plasiolyn, LL.D. (2) | Custos | 1576. |
| Thomas Middleton, Esq. | Custos | 24 July, 1599. |
| Hugh Nanney, of Nanney, Esq. (3) | Custos | 164— |
| Philip, Earl of Pembroke and Montgomery, nominated by the House of Commons to be Lieutenant of Wilts, Merioneth, and Caernarvon . | | 11 Feb., 1642. |
| Owen Salisbury, Esq. | Custos | 1650. |
| Sir Thomas Middleton, Knt. | Custos | 31 Aug., 1660. |
| Sir John Owen, Knt. (4) | Custos | 22 July, 1663. |
| William Owen, Esq. | Custos | 11 „ 1666. |
| Sir John Glynne, Knt. | Custos | 25 March, 1678. |
| Sir John Wynne, Knt. and Bart. | Custos | 3 April, 1685. |
| William, Marquis of Powis. | Custos | 14 „ 1688. |
| Sir William Williams, Knt. and Bart., (5) "one of the King's Council Learned in the Law." | Custos | 8 Oct., 1689. |

(1) *On the 23rd of April, he was Custos Rotulorum. He was murdered in Oct. 1555. W.

(2) *About January, 1576, his name occurs as Custos Rot. for Merionethshire. Add. MS. Brit. Mus. No. 14893. W.

(3) *Died in 1647. He is stated to have been Lieutenant and Custos Rot. for Merionethshire. I doubt his having held the former office, though a contemporary elegy is quoted as the authority. W.

(4) June 10th, 1648. Col. Carter and Lieut.-Col. Twisselden marched towards Caernarvon, to relieve Col. Mason and Col. Mitton, besieged in Caernarvon Castle by Sir John Owen; but the latter drew off some Horse and Foot, and met the Parliament forces near Bangor, where he was defeated. "Capt. Taylor, singly encountering Sir John Owen, after he had broken his sword upon his head, closed with him, dismounted him and took him prisoner, and his party immediately fled." Order by Parliament for £200 for Capt. Taylor, and gratuities for divers others.—Whitelock's Mem., p. 307. July 26th. Sir John Owen was sent to Windsor Castle, on a charge of High Treason and murder against him for the business of North Wales.—Id. p. 319. Nov. 10th. Vote that Lords Goring, Capel, &c., and Sir John Owen, shall be banished out of the kingdom. Id. p. 343. The sentence does not appear to have been carried out, as the following entry occurs in Evelyn's Diary:—"1649, June 13th. I din'd with my worthy friend, Sir John Owen, newly freed from sentence of death among the Lords that suffered."—Evelyn's Mem., p. 237.

(5) *The first Baronet of the Williams-Wynn family. He was Speaker of the House of Commons in 1679-80, and died in 1700. W.

In the Patent Roll it is entered as "Williams Williams, Esq."

| Name. | | | Appointed. |
|---|---|---|---|
| Sir John Wynne, Bart. (6) | . Custos . | | . 19 March, 1690. |
| Edward Vaughan, Esq. | . Custos . | | . 7 Jan., 1711. |
| Lewis Owen, Esq. (7) | . Custos . | | . 17 Dec., 1722. |
| „        „        „ | . Custos . | | . 10 Jan., 1728. |
| William Vaughan, Esq. | . Custos . | | . 2 Aug., 1731. |
| „        „        „ (8) | . { Custos . | | . 28 April, 1761. |
| „        „        „ | . { | . Lieutenant | . 26   „   1762. |
| Sir Watkin Williams Wynn, Bart. | . { Custos . | | . 8 June, 1775. |
| „    „    „    „    „ | . { | . Lieutenant (9) | . 10   „     „ |
| Watkin Williams, Esq. (10) | . { | . Lieutenant | . 27 Aug., 1789. |
| „        „        „ | . { Custos . | | . 4 Sept.,  „ |
| Sir Watkin Williams Wynn, Bart. | . { | . Lieutenant | . 4 Dec., 1793. |
| „    „    „    „    „ | . { Custos . | | . 28   „     „ |
| „    „    „    „    „ | . { | . Lieutenant | . 29   „   1830. |
| „    „    „    „    „ | . { Custos . | | . 7 Feb., 1831. |
| „    „    „    „    „ | . { Custos . | | . 28 Nov., 1837. |
| „    „    „    „    „ | . { | . Lieutenant (11) | . 29   „     „ |
| { The Honorable Edward Mostyn Lloyd Mostyn, (afterwards Lord Mostyn). | { Custos . | | } . 25 Jan., 1840. |
| | { | . Lieutenant } | |

(6) *Sir John Wynn, of Watstay, which name he changed to Wynnstay. He died in 1719, aged 91, leaving his large estates to his kinsman, Watkin Williams, Esq., grandson and eventually successor in the Baronetcy and estates of Sir William Williams mentioned above. Mr. Williams assumed the additional surname of Wynn, and the present Sir Watkin Williams Wynn, Bart., is his representative, and third in descent from him. W.

(7) *Of Peniarth ; died in Dec. 1729. W.

(8) *Of Corsygedol. W.

The Letters Patent of the 14th June, 7 George II. (1733), appointing George, Earl of Cholmondeley, Lieutenant, were revoked as to the County of Merioneth, and William Vaughan appointed, as above.

(9) April 21, 1775. "I consent to Sir Watkin Williams " (Wynn) " being Lieutenant of Merioneth, if he means to be grateful ; otherwise, favours granted to persons in opposition is not very political."—Donne's Letters of Geo. III. to Lord North. Vol. i., p. 245.

(10) *Of Penbedw, co. Denbigh, first cousin, (his uncle's son), to the preceding Lieutenant. He was also Lieutenant for the County of Denbigh, Constable of the Castle of Flint, and M.P. at one time for Montgomeryshire, afterwards for many years for the Flint Boroughs. Mr. Williams was owner of Dugoed and other property in the parish of Mallwyd, and co. of Merioneth. W.

(11) Also Lieutenant of Denbigh.

# CHAPTER V.

## SHERIFFS. (1)

THIS ancient office, one of great dignity and importance, was first created by King Alfred. The name is a compound, derived from the Saxon words "Shire" and "Reeve,"—a Governor. Ingulphus of Croyland, who wrote in the tenth Century, says of Alfred :—"He also divided the Governors of the Provinces, before called Lieutenants, into two departments, Judges, now called Justices, and Sheriffs who still retain their name."(2)   The Latin name by which he was known and called in our ancient Statutes, Records, and Accounts, was Vice-comes.

Sheriffs were formerly chosen by the Inhabitants of the several Counties, and it was ordained by the Statute 28 Edw. I. c. 8, that the people should have elections of Sheriffs in every shire where the shrievalty was not of inheritance.   The reason for these popular elections is assigned in the same Statute, c. 13 : "That the Commons of the Shire might choose such as shall not be a burthen to them, and such as shall not lodge too oft in one place, nor with poor persons, or men of religion."   These elections, growing tumultuous, were put an end to in the following reign—the Statute 9 Edw. II. enacting that the Sheriffs should from thenceforth be assigned by the Chancellor, Treasurer and the Judges, as being persons in whom the same trust might with confidence be reposed.   The powers and duties of a Sheriff are various :—They are as a Judge of the County or Sheriff's Court ; as Keeper of the King's Peace, with power to raise a Posse Comitatus ; as a Ministerial Officer of the Superior Courts of Justice, and, as such, the officer to wait upon and guard Her Majesty's Judges when they come into his County to hold Courts of Oyer and Terminer and General Gaol Delivery : and as the King's Bailiff, having custody of the County Gaol.(3)

---

(1) "Expect not my description should conform this principality to England in presenting the respective Sheriffs with their Arms.   For as to heraldry, I confess myself luscum in Angliâ, cœcum in Walliâ.   Besides, I question whether our rules in blazonry, calculated for the east, will serve on the west of Severn? and suspect that my venial mistakes may meet with mortal anger.

"I am also sensible of the prodigious antiquity of Welsh pedigrees ; so that what Zalmana said of the Israelites slain by him at Tabor, 'Each of these resembleth the children of a King ;' all the gentry here derive themselves from a prince at least.   I quit, therefore, the Catalogue of Sheriffs to abler pens." Fuller's Worthies. Vol. iii., p. 511.

(2) Camd. Brit. cxxxi.   Hallam disputes this, and states that Sheriffs were known long previously, and were mentioned in the laws of Ina.

(3) Stephen's Blackstone, Vol. iii. p. 25, et seq., which see for a fuller description of the duties.

It does not appear that our Welsh princes ever established this Saxon office, as no mention can be found of a Sheriff of a Welsh County till the Statute of Rhuddlan, (12 Edw. I.). By that Act, Edward assimilated the administration of the Welsh Counties to the form which existed in England. The same wise Prince, anxious to conciliate his newly conquered subjects, appointed Welshmen to the office; and the names appear to indicate that they continued to be appointed during the three following reigns, and until the Rebellion of Owen Glyndwr early in the 15th century. Owing to that Rebellion, Henry IV. caused severe penal Statutes to be passed, which enacted that no Welshman should be chosen Citizen or Burgess of any City, Borough, or Market Town, nor be appointed to any office of Mayor, Bailiff, Chamberlain, &c.;— that no Welshman should be made Justice, Chamberlain, Chancellor, &c. of a Castle; —Receiver, Escheator, &c., nor other Officer or Keeper of Records, &c. (4) These prohibitions were re-enacted by his son Henry V., and continued to be acted upon until the Welsh Harry Tudor ascended the English Throne, A.D. 1485, when Welshmen were once more admitted to a share in the privileges and responsibilities of office.

The limitation of the time during which the office might be held was fixed by the Act 28 Edw. III. c. 7, which enacted "that the Sheriffs of the Counties shall be removed every year out of their offices, so that no Sheriff that hath been in his office by a year shall abide in the same office the year next following; and that no Commission be made to him thereof or renewed for the same year following." This enactment was repeated by the Statutes 14 and 42 of the same reign, and the 23 Henry VI. c. 7. (5) Notwithstanding these provisions the Patent Rolls and Ministers Accounts shew that during the reigns of all the Kings from Edward III. to Henry VIII. the Sheriffs in Wales were more frequently appointed, and held their offices, for life, than for the time limited by Statute. It was not till the passing of the Statute 27 Henry VIII. c. 26, that the provision re-enacted by that Statute limiting the term of office to one year, began to be regularly observed. By that Statute and the 34 and 35 of the same reign (c. 61) it was provided that the Sheriffs should be nominated in each year from and after the Feast of All Saints. The Statute 1 Wm. & Mary c. 27, which abolished the Courts of the Lords President and Council of the Marches of Wales, provided for the annual nomination by the Justices of the Great Sessions of three substantial persons for each Shire in their respective Circuits to be Sheriffs of the same, and lists were accordingly submitted to the King in Council, as the Judges' are at present. The nominations under that Statute continued to be made by such Justices till the abolition of the Welsh Judicature in 1830. (6) Since that date the Sheriffs of Wales, like the English

---

(4) 2 Hen. IV., c. xx.; 4 Hen. IV., cc. xxxii, xxxiii.

(5) By the Statute 9 Henry V. it was however provided, that in consequence of the insufficiency of competent persons to fill the said office, the King might during four years thereafter assign Sheriffs to the office to continue for more than one year.

(6) 1 Will. IV. c. 70.

Sheriffs, have been nominated by the Judges in the Court of Exchequer, yearly, on the morrow of St. Martin's, (7) from six names delivered to them by the outgoing Sheriffs for every County at the Summer Assizes; and the list so nominated by the Judges, which consists of three for each County, is submitted to the Privy Council. At the end of January, or the beginning of February, the Sovereign in Council pricks the name of the Sheriff from the Judges' list, and he is thereupon appointed by Sign Manual. This ceremony of pricking is supposed to be a relic of the lack-learning days when royal hands were not taught to write.

The qualification for the office appears to have been first fixed by the Statute 9 Edw. II. s. 2, by which it was enacted that none should be sheriff except he have sufficient land within the same shire where he should be sheriff, to answer the King and his people; and that none who is steward or bailiff to a great lord shall be made sheriff except he be out of service, &c. This provision requiring a land qualification within the County, was re-enacted by the 5 Edw. III. c. 4., and subsequent Statutes.

The Act 1 William & Mary, c. 27, requires that he shall be a "substantial person;" and such only is the qualification in the present day, without reference to the nature or situation of the qualifying property.

"The vast expense which custom had introduced in serving the office of High Sheriff was grown such a burden to the subject, that it was enacted by Statute 13 & 14 Car. II. c. 21, that no Sheriff (except of London, Westmoreland, and towns which are counties of themselves,) should keep any table at the assizes, except for his own family, or give any presents to the judges or their servants, or have more than forty men in livery; yet for the sake of safety and decency he may not have less than twenty men in England and twelve in Wales, upon forfeiture, in any of these cases, of £200."—(Stephen's Blackstone.)

The twelve men referred to have always been known as Javelin-men, from their carrying long Pikes (Halberds), or Javelins. Where the Sheriffs have been land-owners of sufficient territorial extent, it has been customary for them to put twelve of their tenants in livery and make them Javelin-men. Since the establishment of the rural Police Force in 1857, the custom of employing twelve officers of the Force in lieu of Javelin-men, has been creeping into vogue and now very generally obtains. The expense to the Sheriff is thus much lessened, and the efficiency of his attendants is largely increased. (8)

The following is a copy of the Oath taken by Sheriffs in the time of Elizabeth:—

"I Jeuan lloyde do vtt'lye testyfye and declare in my consience that the Quenes

---

(7) Altered from the Feast of All Saints, by the Act of 2 Will. IV. for shortening Michaelmas Term.

(8) The following extract from Evelyn's Memoirs throws some light upon the magnificence of an English sheriff's retinue, early in the seventeenth century. "1634.—My father was appointed Sheriff of Surrey and Sussex, before they were disjoyned. He had 116 servants in liverys, everyone livery'd in greene satin doublets; divers gentlemen and persons of quality waited on him in the same garbe and habit, which at that time (when 30 or 40 was the usual retinue of the High Sheriff) was esteem'd a great matter."—(Vol. I., p. 4.)

hyghnes is the onlye suꝑme goůner of this Raylme and of all other her hyghnes dominyons and countryes aswell in all spirituall thyng's or causes as temporall, and that no forrayn prynce, ꝑson, prelate, state or potentate hath or ought to haue any Jurisdiccōn power supioritye ꝑhemynence or auctoritye eccłiastical or sꝓtuall Wythin this Reylme and therfore I do vtterlye renounce and forsake all forrayn [iurisdic]cōns, powers, supiorityes and auctorityes and do ꝑmyse that from hensfourth I shall beare fayth and trewe alegeannce to the Quenes hyghnes her heyres and lawfull successours  And to my power shall assiste and defende all iurisdiccōns priuilegis ꝑhemynencys and auctorityes grauntyd or belongyng to the Quenes hyghnes her heyres and successours or vnytyd and annexed to the ymperiall Crowne of this Raylme so helpe me God and by the content's of this boke."

# SHERIFFS OF ANGLESEY.

## (FROM 12 EDW. I. TO 32 HEN. VIII.)

| Anno Dom. | | Regnal Year. | | | Name. | | Appointed. |
|---|---|---|---|---|---|---|---|
| 1284 | — (1) | 12 to —. | | Edw. I. | Roger de Puylesdon or Pywelesdon(2) [was Sheriff in the 20th year.] | ... | 20 March. |
| 1307 | — 13 | 1 to 6. | | Edw. II.? | Griffith ap Owen. | ... | |
| 1308-9 | — | 2 „ —. | | „ | Henry de Dynynton.(3) | ... | |
| 1309-10 | — | 3 „ —. | | „ | Madoc Thloyd [Llwyd] | ... | |
| 1316 | — 27 | 10 „ 20. | | „ | Anian de Jevan. | ... | |
| 1327 | — | 1 „ —. | | Edw. III. | Gilbert de Ellesfeld. | ... | |
| 1332 | — 5 | 6 „ 8. | | „ | John de Sapy. | ... | |
| 1334 | — 50 | 8 „ 24. | | „ | William Trussell. | ... | |
| 1350 | — 3 | 24 „ 27. | | „ | William de Ellerton. | ... | 1 Oct. |
| 1353 | — 5 | 27 „ 29. | | „ | Thomas de Harebergh, or Harlebergh. | ... | „ |
| 1355 | — 8 | 29 „ 32. | | „ | Griffith ap Madoc Glodeigh [Gloddaeth]. | ... | „ for 3 years. |
| ?1358 | — 61 | ?32 „ 35. | | „ | William Walton. | ... | |
| 1363 | — 4 | 37 „ 38. (4) | | „ | Ralph de Alrewych, or Allerwych. | ... | |
| 1376 | — 85 | 50 Edw. III. to 8 Ric. II. | | | Richard Pykemere. | ... | |
| 1386 | — 7 | 10 to 11. | | Ric. II. | Richard de Golden. | ... | |
| 1387 | — 8 | 11 „ 12. | | „ | Richard Pikemere.(5) | ... | |
| 1391 | — 6 | 15 „ 19. | | „ | Adam le Clerc, or Clerk. | | |
| 1396 | — 9 | 19 „ 22. | | „ | Wyllym ap Griffith ap Willym. | ... | 14 or 15 Jan. |
| 1407 | — 9 | 9 „ 10. | | Hen. IV. | Ralph de Barton. (6) | ... | |

(1) Those dates only are given which have been taken from the Minister's Accounts, &c., as few entries are found of the date of appointment in the reigns of Edw. I. II. and III. and Ric. II.

(2) Ayloffe, p. 89. See Notes to Sheriffs of Caernarvon.

(3) Record of Caernarvon, p. 225.      (4) Was Sheriff in these years, *vide* Minister's Accounts.

(5) Probably he continued in office until Clerk was appointed.

(6) He was Sheriff probably during the whole of Hen. IV.'s reign. He is mentioned in the Minister's Account for the above years.

| Anno Dom. | Regnal Year. | | Name. | Appointed. |
|---|---|---|---|---|
| 1413 — 15 | 1 to 2. | Hen. V. | Ralph de Barton. | |
| 1415 — 16 | 2 „ 3. | „ | Richard del Wode. ... | 1 March. |
| ?1416 — ?18 | ?3 „ ?6. | „ | John Walsh. | |
| 1418 — ?22 | 6 „ 9. | „ | Roger Strangways(7)... | 4 Nov. |
| 1425 — 6 | 3 and 4. | Hen VI. | John Stanley. ... | 2 Feb. |
| 1437 — ?60 | 16 to 38. | „ | John Stanley. ... | 28 Dec. |
| 1464 — 83 | 4 „ 22. | Edw. IV. | Sir Thomas Mont-gomery, Knt. ... | 30 July, for life. |
| 1483 — 5 | 1 and 2. | Ric. III. | Sir Richard Hudleston, Knt. ... | 28 Nov., for life. |
| 1483 — | 2 „ 3. | „ | Robert Chamberlain, Knt. of the Royal Body. ... | 10 Feb., for life. |
| 1485 —1504} or 5 | 1 to 20.? | Hen. VII. | Res ap Llewelyn ap Hulkyn. ... | 20 Sept. |
| 1504 or 5—27 { | 19 or 20 Hen.VII.,(8) } to 18 Hen. VIII. | | Owen Holande. ... | 2 March, for life. |
| 1527 — 34 | 18 to 25. | Hen VIII. | Robert Seymer, Esq. ... | 12 Jan., for life. |
| 1534 — 40 | 25 „ 32. | „ | William ap Robert ap Meredith. ... | 27 Jan., for life. |
| 1540 — 1 | 32 and 33. | „ | Roland Griffith, Esq. ... | 18 Nov., for life. |

(FROM 33 HEN. VIII.)

## HENRY VIII.

| Anno Dom. | Regnal Year. | | Name. | Appointed. |
|---|---|---|---|---|
| ?1541— 2 | 33 & 34 | | Sir Richard Bulkeley, Knt. . . . | |
| 1542— 3 | 34 „ 5 | | John ap Res ap Llewelyn ap Hulkyn, Esq. | 22 Nov. |
| 1543— 4 | 35 „ 6 | | Richard (9) Bulkeley, Esq. . . . | 23 „ |
| 1544— 5 | 36 „ 7 | | Ruthergh (Rhydderch) ap David, Esq. . | 16 „ |
| 1545— 7 | 37 „ 8 | | Richard Hampton, Esq. . . . . | 22 „ |

(7) There can be no doubt that he remained in office until Stanley was appointed.
(8) Some Rolls give the 19th, others the 20th year.       (9) William, in Mona Antiqua.

5—2

## EDWARD VI.

| Anno Dom. | Regnal Year. | Name. | Appointed. |
|---|---|---|---|
| 1547 | I | Sir Richard Bulkeley, Knt. . . . | 29 Jan. |
| 1547—8 | I & 2 | Roland Gruffith, Esq. . . . . | 27 Nov. |
| 1548—9 | 2 „ 3 | William Lewes, Esq. . . . . | 3 Dec. |
| 1549—50 | 3 „ 4 | David ap Richard ap David ap Gwilim, Esq. . . . . . . | |
| 1550— 1 | 4 „ 5 | Hugh Peke, Esq. . . . . | |
| 1551— 2 | 5 „ 6 | Sir Richard Bulkeley, Knt. . . . | |
| 1552— 3 | 6 „ 7 | Rowland Griffith, Esq. (10) . . . | |

## MARY AND PHILIP AND MARY.

| 1553 | I | Rees Thomas, Esq. . . . . | 6 July. |
|---|---|---|---|
| 1553—4 | { I & I & / 2 P. & M. } | Thomas Mostyn, Esq. . . . . | |
| 1554—5 | { I and 2— / 2 „ 3 } | John ap Rice ap Llewelyn ap Hulkyn, Esq. | |
| 1555—6 | { 2 „ 3— / 3 „ 4 } | Thomas Williams, Esq. . . . | |
| 1556—7 | { 3 „ 4— / 4 „ 5 } | Robert Bulkeley, Esq. . . . | |
| 1557—8 | { 4 „ 5— / 5 „ 6 } | William Lewes, Esq. . . . | |

*The Cross † inserted in the margin denotes that the name is taken from Rowland's Mona Antiqua.*

## ELIZABETH.

| 1558— 9 | I | Lewis ap Owen ap Merycke, Esq. . . |
|---|---|---|
| 1559—60 | 2 and 3 | Sir Nicholas Bagnall, Knt. . . . |
| 1560— 1 | 3 „ 4 | Sir Richard Bulkeley, Knt. . . . |
| 1561— 2 | 4 „ 5 | Maurice Griffith, of Porthamel, (11) Esq. . |
| 1562— 3 | 5 „ 6 | Owen ap Hugh, gent. . . . |
| 1563— 4 | 6 „ 7 | Rice Thomas, Esq. . . . . |
| 1564— 5 | 7 „ 8 | Sir Nicholas Bagnall, Knt. (12) . . |
| †1565— 6 | 8 „ 9 | John Lewis, of Presaddfed, Esq. . . |
| 1566— 7 | 9 „ 10 | David ap Rees ap David ap Gwilim, Esq. |
| 1567— 8 | 10 „ 11 | Richard White, Esq. . . . |
| 1568— 9 | 11 „ 12 | Roland Bulkeley, Esq. . . . |
| 1569—70 | 12 „ 13 | Sir Richard Bulkeley, Knt. . . . |
| †1570— 1 | 13 „ 14 | Lewis Owen ap Meurick, of Frondêg, Esq. |
| 1571— 2 | 14 „ 15 | William Lewes, Esq. . . . |
| 1572— 3 | 15 „ 16 | Richard Owen, Esq. . . . |

(10) Either died during office, or was superseded.    (11) Plasnewydd, in Mona Antiqua.
(12) Richard Owen, in Mona Antiqua.

| Anno Dom. | Regnal Year. | Name. | Appointed. |
|---|---|---|---|
| 1573— 4 | 16 & 17 | John Wynne, Esq. . . . . . | |
| 1574— 5 | 17 „ 18 | Thomas Mostyn, Esq. . . . . | |
| †1575—6 | 18 „ 19 | Edward Conway, of Bodtryddan, Esq. . | |
| †1576—7 | 19 „ 20 | Owen Wood, of Rhosmor, Esq. . . | |
| †1577—8 | 20 „ 1 | Dr. Ellis Price, of Plas Iolyn. . . | |
| †1578—9 | 21 „ 2 | William Thomas, of Aber, Esq. . . | |
| 1579—80 | 22 „ 3 | Owen ap Hugh, Esq. . . . . | 30 Nov. |
| 1580— 1 | 23 „ 4 | Hugh Hughes, of Porthamel, (13) Esq. . | 21 „ |
| 1581— 2 | 24 „ 5 | John Griffith, Esq. . . . . | |
| 1582— 3 | 25 „ 6 | Richard White, Esq. . . . . | |
| 1583— 4 | 26 „ 7 | Thomas Glynne, Esq. . . . . | |
| 1584— 5 | 27 „ 8 | Maurice Kyffyn, Esq. . . . . | 19 Nov. |
| 1585— 6 | 28 „ 9 | Dr. Ellis Price. . . . . | 2 Dec. |
| 1586— 7 | 39 „ 30 | John Griffith, Esq. . . . . | |
| 1587— 8 | 30 „ 1 | Thomas Mostyn, of Mostyn, Esq. . . | 4 Dec. |
| 1588— 9 | 31 „ 2 | Richard White, Esq. . . , . | |
| 1589—90 | 32 „ 3 | Roger Mostyn, of Beaumaris, Esq. . . | 13 Dec. |
| 1590— 1 | 33 „ 4 | Owen Holland, Esq. . . . . | 24 Nov. |
| 1591— 2 | 34 „ 5 | Hugh Hughes, Esq. . . . . | |
| 1592— 3 | 35 „ 6 | John Griffith, Esq. . . . . | 4 Dec. |
| 1593— 4 | 36 „ 7 | Richard White, of Llanvaes, (14) Esq. . | 26 Nov. |
| 1594— 5 | 37 „ 8 | Peter Lloyd, of Gwaredog, Esq. . . | 18 „ |
| 1595— 6 | 38 „ 9 | Arthur Bulkeley, Esq. . . . . | 27 „ |
| 1596— 7 | 39 „ 40 | William Glynne, of Llewar,(15) Caernar-. von, Esq. . . . . . | 22 „ |
| 1597— 8 | 40 „ 1 | Richard Bulkeley, of Porthamel, Esq. . | 25 „ |
| 1598— 9 | 41 „ 2 | Owen Holland, of Berw, Esq. . . | 28 „ |
| 1599—1600 | 42 „ 3 | Hugh Hughes, of Porthamel, Esq. (16) . | 2 Dec. |
| 1600— 1 | 43 „ 4 | Thomas Glynne, of Glynllivon, Caernarvon, Esq. . . . . . . . | 24 Nov. |
| 1601— 2 | 44 „ 5 | Richard Bulkeley, of Porthamel, Esq. . | 2 Dec. |
| 1602— 3 | 45 | Pierce Lloyd, of Gwaredog, Esq. (17) . | 7 Dec. |

# JAMES I.

| | | | |
|---|---|---|---|
| 1603 | 1 | Pierce Lloyd, of Gwaredog, Esq. . . | |
| 1603— 4 | 1 & 2 | William Lewis, of Chwayne, Esq. . . | 1 Dec. |
| 1604— 5 | 2 „ 3 | William Griffiths, of Trevarthen, Esq. . | 5 Nov. |

(13) Plas Coch.      (14) Monachlog.      (15) Glynllifon.      (16) Plas Coch.      (17) Lligwy.

*The names at the foot of this page are those given in Mona Antiqua.*

| Anno Dom. | Regnal Year. | Name. | Appointed. |
|-----------|--------------|-------|------------|
| 1605— 6 | 3 & 4 | John Lewes, Esq.    .    .    .    . | |
| 1606— 7 | 4 „ 5 | Sir Richard Gwynne, of Hirdrefaig, Knt. (18) | 17 Nov. |
| 1607— 8 | 5 „ 6 | Sir Hugh Owen, Knt. | |
| 1608— 9 | 6 „ 7 | Thomas Holland, Esq.    .    .    . | 10 Nov. |
| 1609—10 | 7 „ 8 | William Owen, Esq.    .    .    . | |
| 1610—11 | 8 „ 9 | John Bodvel, Esq.    .    .    . | |
| 1611—12 | 9 „ 10 | Pierce Lloyd, Esq.    .    .    . | 12 Nov. |
| 1612—13 | 10 „ 11 | John Edwards, Esq.    .    .    . | 16 Nov. |
| 1613—14 | 11 „ 12 | Owen Woode, Esq.    .    .    . | |
| 1614—15 | 12 „ 13 | Richard Merrick, Esq.    .    .    . | |
| 1615—16 | 13 „ 14 | Hugh Lewes, Esq.    .    .    . | |
| 1616—17 | 14 „ 15 | Reece Williams, Esq. (19) .    .    . | |
| 1617—18 | 15 „ 16 | John Lewes, Esq.    .    .    . | |
| 1618—19 | 16 „ 17 | Sir William Glynne, Knt.    .    . | 9 Nov. |
| 1619—20 | 17 „ 18 | Henry Lloyde, Esq.    .    .    . | |
| 1620— 1 | 18 „ 19 | Hugh Wynne, Esq.    .    .    . | |
| 1621— 2 | 19 „ 20 | Sir Thomas Holland, Knt.    .    . | |
| 1622— 3 | 20 „ 1 | Richard Owen, of Penmynydd, Esq.    . | 7 Nov. |
| 1623— 4 | 21 „ 2 | John Bodychan, junior, Esq. .    .    . | 7 Nov. |
| 1624— 5 | 22 „ 3 | William Thomas, Esq. .    .    .    . | |

## CHARLES I.

| | | | |
|-----------|--------------|-------|------------|
| 1625 | 1 | William Thomas, Esq.    .    .    . | |
| 1625— 6 | 1 & 2 | William Griffith, Esq.    .    .    . | |
| 1626— 7 | 2 „ 3 | Hugh Morgan, Esq.    .    .    . | |
| 1627— 8 | 3 „ 4 | Edward Wynne, Esq.    .    .    . | |
| 1628— 9 | 4 „ 5 | Richard Glynne, Esq. (20) .    .    . | |
| 16-9—30 | 5 „ 6 | Thomas Glyn or Gwynne, Esq.    .    . | |
| 1630— 1 | 6 „ 7 | Henry Lloyd, Esq. (21) .    .    . | |
| 1631— 2 | 7 „ 8 | Thomas Chedle, Esq.    .    .    . | |
| †1632— 3 | 8 „ 9 | William Owen, of Frondêg, Esq.    . | |
| †1633— 4 | 9 „ 10 | Hugh Owen, of Bodowen, Esq.    . | |
| †1634— 5 | 10 „ 11 | Robert Wynne of Tre'rgof, Esq.    . | |
| 1635— 6 | 11 „ 12 | Edward Wynne, Esq.    .    .    . | |
| 1636— 7 | 12 „ 13 | William Buckley, Esq.    .    .    . | |
| †1637— 8 | 13 „ 14 | Pierce Lloyd, of Lligwy, Esq.    . | |
| †1638— 9 | 14 „ 15 | Richard Bulkeley, of Porthamel, Esq.    . | |

---

(18) Richard Glynn, of Glynllifon.                    (19) Richard.
(20) Edward Wynne, of Bodewryd, Esq.        (21) William Robinson, of Monachdy, Esq.

*The names at the foot of this page are those given in Mona Antiqua.*

## WILLIAM III.

| Anno Dom. | Regnal Year. | Name. | Appointed. |
|---|---|---|---|
| 1694— 5 | 6 & 7 | John Thomas, Esq. . . . . | |
| 1695— 6 | 7 „ 8 | Henry White, of the Fryers, Esq. . . | ? 7 Dec. |
| 1696— 7 | 8 „ 9 | Hugh Wynne, of Tredewith, Esq. . . | ? 5 „ |
| 1697— 8 | 9 „ 10 | William Griffith, of Careglwyd, Esq. . | 23 „ |
| 1698— 9 | 10 „ 11 | Pierce Lloyd, Esq. . . . . | ? 24 „ |
| 1699—1700 | 11 „ 12 | Francis Edwards, Esq. . . . . | ? 18 Nov. |
| 1700— 2 | 12 „ 13 | John Williams, Esq. . . . . | ? 1 Dec. |
| 1702 | 13 „ 14 | John Wynn, Esq. . . . . | 4 Jan. |

## ANNE.

| 1702 | 1 | John Wynn, Esq. . . . . . | |
| 1702— 3 | 1 & 2 | Robert Owen, Esq. . . . . | ? 5 Dec. |
| 1703— 4 | 2 | William Robinson, Esq. . . . . | ? 4 „ |
| 1704 | 2 | William Morgan, Esq. . . . . | ? 15 Jan. |
| 1704 | 2 „ 3 | William Owen, Esq. . . . . | ? 22 „ |
| 1704— 5 | 3 „ 4 | Hugh Wynn, of Cromlech, Esq. . . | ? 19 Dec. |
| 1705— 6 | 4 „ 5 | Owen Merrick, Esq. . . . . | ? 5 „ |
| 1706— 7 | 5 „ 6 | Owen Roberts, Esq. . . . . | ? 7 „ |
| 1707— 8 | 6 „ 7 | John Sparrow, Esq. . . . . | 18 „ |
| 1708— 9 | 7 | John Morrice, Esq. . . . . | ? 27 Nov. |
| 1709 | 7 „ 8 | John Griffith, Esq. . . . . | 27 Jan. |
| 1709—10 | 8 „ 9 | William Lewis, Esq. . . . . | 1 Dec. |
| 1710—11 | 9 „ 10 | John Morrice, Esq. . . . . | 24 Nov. |
| 1711—12 | 10 | William Robinson, Esq. . . . | 13 Dec. |
| 1712 | 10 „ 11 | William Roberts, Esq. . . . . | 12 Jan. |
| 1712—13 | 11 „ 12 | Thomas Roberts, Esq. . . . . | 11 Dec. |
| 1713 | 12 | Edward Bayly, of Plasnewydd, Esq. . | 30 Nov. |
| 1713—14 | 12 „ 13 | William Lewis, of Llysdulas, Esq. . | 13 Dec. |

## GEORGE I.

| 1714 | 1 | William Lewis, of Llysdulas, Esq. . . | |
| 1714—15 | 1 & 2 | William Bulkeley, Esq. . . . | 6 Dec. |
| 1715—16 | 2 „ 3 | Maurice Williams, Esq. . . . | 5 „ |
| 1716—17 | 3 „ 4 | Edward Bayly, of Plasnewydd, Esq. . | 5 „ |
| 1717—18 | 4 „ 5 | William Bodvele, of Beaumaris, Esq. . | 21 „ |
| 1718—20 | 5 „ 6 | Hugh Hughes, of Plascoch, Esq. . | 21 „ |
| 1720— 1 | 6 „ 7 | Rice Thomas, of Kemmes, Esq. . | 7 Jan. |

| Anno Dom. | Regnal Year. | Name. | Appointed. |
|---|---|---|---|
| 1721 | 7 & 8 | Thomas Lloyd, of Llanydan, Esq. | 14 Jan. |
| 1721— 2 | 8 „ 9 | Richard Hampton, of Beaumaris, Esq. | 14 Dec. |
| 1722— 4 | 9 „ 10 | William Owen, of Penrhos, Esq. | 11 „ |
| 1724 | 10 „ 11 | John Griffith, of Carreglwyd, Esq. | 7 Jan. |
| 1724— 6 | 11 „ 12 | John Owen, of Presaddfed, Esq. | 22 Dec. |
| 1726 | 12 „ 13 | Thomas Rowlands, of Caerau, Esq. | 13 Jan. |
| 1726— 7 | 13 | Henry Morgan, of Henblas, Esq. | 29 Nov. |

# GEORGE II.

| Anno Dom. | Regnal Year. | Name. | Appointed. |
|---|---|---|---|
| 1727 | 1 | Henry Morgan, of Henblas, Esq. | |
| 1727— 8 | 1 & 2 | Robert Morris, of Celliniog, Esq. | 14 Dec. |
| 1728— 9 | 2 „ 3 | John Williams, of Trearddur, Esq. | 18 „ |
| 1729—30 | 3 „ 4 | Henry Williams, of Llangoed, Esq. | 18 „ |
| 1730— 1 | 4 „ 5 | Henry Powell, of Llangefni, Esq. | 14 „ |
| 1731— 2 | 5 „ 6 | Robert Hampton, of Henllys, Esq. | 9 „ |
| 1732— 3 | 6 „ 7 | William Evans, of Treveilyr, Esq. | 14 „ |
| 1733— 4 | 7 „ 8 | Robert Bulkeley, of Gronant, Esq. | 20 „ |
| 1734— 5 | 8 | Humphry Roberts, of Llanbeulan, Esq. | 19 „ |
| 1735 | 8 „ 9 | Richard Lloyd, of Rhosbeiro, Esq. | 9 Feb. |
| 1735— 7 | 9 „ 10 | Richard Roberts, of Bodsyran, Esq. | 18 Dec. |
| 1737— 8 | 10 „ 11 | Edmond Meyrick, of Trefriw, Esq. | 19 Jan. |
| 1738 | 11 | William Robinson, of Monachdû, Esq. | 12 „ |
| 1738 | 11 „ 12 | William Roberts, of Bodear, Esq. | 15 Feb. |
| 1738— 9 | 12 „ 13 | Robert Williams, of Penmynydd, Esq. | 21 Dec. |
| 1739—40 | 13 „ 14 | William Owen, of Pencraig, Esq. | 27 „ |
| 1740— 1 | 14 „ 15 | Rice Williams, of Quirt, Esq. | 24 „ |
| 1741— 3 | 15 „ 16 | Hugh Jones, of Gymmunod, Esq. | 31 „ |
| 1743— 4 | 16 „ 17 | Hugh Williams, of Pentir, Esq. | 19 Jan. |
| 1744— 5 | 17 „ 18 | Richard Hughes, of Castellor, Esq. | 5 „ |
| 1745— 6 | 18 „ 19 | John Nangle, of Llwydiarth, Esq. | 10 „ |
| 1746 | 19 | Edward Williams, of Plas Tirion, Esq. | 16 „ |
| 1746— 7 | 19 „ 20 | Henry Williams, of Plas Tirion, Esq. | 27 Feb. |
| 1747— 8 | 20 „ 1 | William Thomas, of Cemmais, Esq. | 15 Jan. |
| 1748— 9 | 21 „ 2 | William Lewis, of Llandyfnan, Esq. | 14 „ |
| 1749—50 | 22 „ 3 | Owen Wynn, of Penheskin, Esq. | 11 „ |
| 1750 | 23 | Charles Allanson, of Dreiniog, Esq. | 17 „ |
| 1750 | 23 „ 4 | John Jones, of Henllyn, Esq. | 21 „ |
| 1750— 2 | 24 „ 5 | John Lloyd, of Hirdrefaig, Esq. | 6 Dec. |
| 1752— 3 | 25 „ 6 | Charles Evans, of Trefeilir, Esq. | 14 Jan. |

| Anno Dom. | Regnal Year. | Name. | Appointed. |
|---|---|---|---|
| 1753— 4 | 26 & 27 | Bodychan Sparrow, of Bodychan, Esq. | 7 Feb. |
| 1754— 5 | 27 „ 8 | Richard Hughes, of Bodwyn, Esq. | 31 Jan. |
| 1755— 6 | 28 „ 9 | Hugh Davis, of Brynharddyn, Esq. | 29 „ |
| 1756— 7 | 29 „ 30 | Charles Allanson, of Dreiniog, Esq. | 27 „ |
| 1757 | 30 | John Rowland, of Porthlongdu, Esq. | 4 Feb. |
| 1757 | 30 | Owen Pritchard, of Beaumaris, Esq. | 16 „ |
| 1757— 8 | 30 „ 1 | John Rowland, of Porthlongdu, Esq. | 1 Mar. |
| 1758 | 31 | Edward Owen, of Pen Rhos, Esq. | 27 Jan. |
| 1758— 9 | 31 „ 2 | John Griffith, of Garreg-lwyd, Esq. | 16 Feb. |
| 1759—60 | 32 „ 3 | Robert Owen, of Penrhos, Esq. | 2 „ |
| 1760 | 33 „ 4 | Robert Lloyd, of Tregaian, Esq. | 1 „ |

## GEORGE III.

| | | | |
|---|---|---|---|
| 1760— 1 | 1 | Robert Lloyd, of Tregaian, Esq. | |
| 1761— 2 | 1 & 2 | Francis Lloyd, of Monachdû, Esq. | 16 Feb. |
| 1762— 3 | 2 „ 3 | Hugh Barlow, of Pen Rhos, Esq. | 15 „ |
| 1763— 4 | 3 „ 4 | Felix Feast, of Bodliw, Esq. | 4 „ |
| 1764— 5 | 4 „ 5 | William Lewis, of Lanvihangel, Esq. | 10 „ |
| 1765— 6 | 5 „ 6 | Herbert Jones, of Llynon, Esq. | 1 „ |
| 1766— 7 | 6 „ 7 | Hugh Williams, of Tû fry, Esq. | 17 „ |
| 1767— 8 | 7 „ 8 | Hugh Williams, of Cromlech, Esq. | 13 „ |
| 1768— 9 | 8 „ 9 | William Hughes, of Plâscoch, Esq. | 15 Jan. |
| 1769—70 | 9 „ 10 | William Smith, of Dreiniog, Esq. | 27 „ |
| 1770— 1 | 10 „ 11 | John Hampton Jones, of Henllys, Esq. | 9 Feb. |
| 1771— 2 | 11 „ 12 | Paul Panton, of Plâs Gwyn, Esq. | 6 „ |
| 1772— 3 | 12 „ 13 | John Jones, of Penrhos Brodwen, Esq. | 17 „ |
| 1773 | 13 | Hugh Wynne Jones, of Tre Ewarth, Esq. | 8 „ |
| 1773— 4 | 13 „ 14 | Henry Sparrow, of Red Hill, Esq. | 10 „ |
| 1774— 5 | 14 „ 15 | Owen Putland Meyricke, of Bodorgan, Esq. | 7 „ |
| 1775— 6 | 15 „ 16 | William Lloyd, of Llwydiarth, Esq. | 6 „ |
| 1776— 7 | 16 „ 17 | Hugh Hughes, of Bodwyn, Esq. | 5 „ |
| 1777— 8 | 17 „ 18 | Rice Thomas, of Cemmes, Esq. | 31 Jan. |
| 1778— 9 | 18 „ 19 | Owen Jones, of Penrhos-brodwen, and of Coed Helen, Caernarvon, Esq. | 28 „ |
| 1779—80 | 19 „ 20 | William Peacock, of Llanedwen, Esq. | 1 Feb. |
| 1780— 1 | 20 „ 1 | Holland Griffith, of Carreglwyd, Esq. | 2 „ |
| 1781— 2 | 21 „ 2 | John Bodychan Sparrow, of Redhill, Esq. | 5 „ |
| 1782 | 22 | Morgan Jones, of Skerries, Esq. | 1 Jan. |
| 1782— 3 | 22 „ 3 | William Vickar, of Llanfawr, Esq. | 4 March. |

6—2

| Anno Dom. | | Regnal Year. | | | Name. | Appointed. |
|---|---|---|---|---|---|---|
| 1783— | 4 | 23 & 24 | | | Morgan Jones, of Skerries, Esq. | 10 Feb. |
| 1784— | 5 | 24 „ | 5 | | Thomas Assheton Smith, of Trefarthyn, and of Vaenol, Caernarvon, Esq. | 11 „ |
| 1785— | 6 | 25 „ | 6 | | Richard Lloyd, of Monachdû, Esq. | 7 „ |
| 1786 | | 26 | | | Arthur Owen, of Bodowyr Issa, Esq. | 13 „ |
| 1786— | 7 | 26 „ | 7 | | William Pritchard of Trescawen, Esq. | 22 March. |
| 1787— | 8 | 27 „ | 8 | | John Griffin Lewis, of Tryselwyn, Esq. | 12 Feb. |
| 1788— | 9 | 28 „ | 9 | | Henry Pritchard, of Trescawen, Esq. | 8 „ |
| 1789— | 90 | 29 „ | 30 | | John Williams, of Nantannog, Esq. (27) | 29 April. |
| 1790— | 1 | 30 „ | 1 | | Thomas Williams, of Lanedan, Esq. | 29 Jan. |
| 1791— | 2 | 31 „ | 2 | | Herbert Jones, of Llynnon, Esq. | 4 Feb. |
| 1792— | 3 | 32 „ | 3 | | Hugh Price, of Wern, Esq. | 3 „ |
| 1793— | 4 | 33 „ | 4 | | Evan Lloyd, of Maes-y-Porth, Esq. | 6 „ |
| 1794— | 5 | 34 „ | 5 | | Hugh Jones, of Carrog, Esq. | 5 „ |
| 1795— | 6 | 35 „ | 6 | | John Bulkeley, of Presaddfed, Esq. | 11 „ |
| 1796— | 7 | 36 „ | 7 | | John Morris Conway, of Celleniog, Esq. | 5 „ |
| 1797— | 8 | 37 „ | 8 | | Richard Jones, of Tros-y-Marian, and Bodtryddan, Flintshire, Esq. | 1 „ |
| 1798— | 9 | 38 „ | 9 | | William Evans, of Glenalaw, Esq. | 7 „ |
| 1799— | 1800 | 39 „ | 40 | | Hugh Wynne, of Beaumaris, Esq. | 1 „ |
| 1800 | | 40 | | | John Price, of Wern, Esq. | 5 „ |
| 1800 | | 40 | | | Evan Hughes, of Gwdryn, Esq. | 21 „ |
| 1800— | 1 | 40 „ | 1 | | William Harvey, of Park, Esq. | 5 March. |
| 1801— | 2 | 41 „ | 2 | | John Price, of Wern, Esq. | 11 Feb. |
| 1802 | | 42 | | | William Bulkeley Hughes, of Brynddu, Esq. | 10 „ |
| 1802— | 3 | 42 „ | 3 | | Gwyllim Lloyd Wardle, of Cefn Coch, Esq. | 10 March. |
| 1803— | 4 | 43 „ | 4 | | William Bulkeley Hughes, of Plas Coch, Esq. | 3 Feb. |
| 1804 | | 44 | | | Thomas Parry Jones, of Cefn Coch, and Madryn, Caernarvon, Esq. | 1 „ |
| 1804— | 5 | 44 „ | 5 | | Charles Evans, of Trefeilir, Esq. | 27 June. |
| 1805— | 6 | 45 „ | 6 | | John Williams, of Treban, Esq. | 6 Feb. |
| 1806— | 7 | 46 „ | 7 | | Sir Hugh Owen, of Bodowen, Bart. | 1 „ |
| 1807— | 8 | 47 „ | 8 | | Paul Panton, of Plas Gwyn, Esq. | 4 „ |
| 1808 | | 48 | | | Edward Jones, of Cromlech, Esq. | 3 „ |
| 1808— | 9 | 48 „ | 9 | | John Jones, of Penrhos Brodwen, Esq. | 24 „ |

(27) At this date (29th April) it was entered as *William* Williams, which the King i Council altered on the 28th May, to *John* Williams.

| Anno Dom. | Regnal Year. | Name. | Appointed. |
|---|---|---|---|
| 1809—10 | 49 & 50 | Sir John Thomas Stanley, of Bodewryd, Bart. . . . . . | 6 Feb. |
| 1810—11 | 50 „ 1 | Hugh Evans, of Henblas, Esq. . . | 31 Jan. |
| 1811—12 | 51 „ 2 | Henry Williams, of Trearddur, Esq. . | 8 Feb. |
| 1812—13 | 52 „ 3 | Hugh Bulkeley Owen, of Coedanna, Esq. | 24 Jan. |
| 1813—14 | 53 „ 4 | John Hampton Hampton, of Henllys, Esq. | 10 Feb. |
| 1814—15 | 54 „ 5 | George Francis Barlow, of Tynyllwyn, Esq. | 4 Feb. |
| 1815—16 | 55 „ 6 | Robert Hughes, of Plasyn Llangoed, Esq. | 13 „ |
| 1816 | 56 | Robert Bulkeley, of Gronant, Esq. . | 12 „ |
| 1816—17 | 56 „ 7 | John Price, of Plas Llanfaelog, Esq. . | 9 March. |
| 1817—18 | 57 „ 8 | Rice Thomas, of Cemaes, Esq. . . | 12 Feb. |
| 1818—19 | 58 „ 9 | John Price, of Cadnant, Esq. . . | 10 „ |
| 1819—20 | 59 „ 60 | William Pritchard Lloyd, of Llwydiarth, Esq., | 10 „ |

## GEORGE IV.

| | | | |
|---|---|---|---|
| 1820 | 1 | William Pritchard Lloyd, of Llwydiarth, Esq. | |
| 1820— 1 | 1 & 2 | Robert Lloyd, of Tregauan, Esq. . . | 12 Feb. |
| 1821— 2 | 2 „ 3 | James Webster, of Derry, Esq. . . | 6 „ |
| 1822— 3 | 3 „ 4 | William Wynne Sparrow, of Tynewydd, Esq. | 4 „ |
| 1823— 4 | 4 „ 5 | Jones Panton, of Plas-gwyn, Esq. . . | 31 Jan. |
| 1824— 5 | 5 „ 6 | John Owen, of Trehwfa, Esq. . . | 31 „ |
| 1825— 6 | 6 „ 7 | Thomas Meyrick, of Cefncoch, Esq. . | 2 Feb. |
| 1826— 7 | 7 „ 8 | Hugh Davies Griffith, (28) of Caerhûn, Esq. | 30 Jan. |
| 1827 | 8 | Richard Bulkeley Williams Bulkeley, of Baron-hill, Esq. (29) . . . . | 5 Feb. |
| 1827— 8 | 8 „ 9 | Owen John Augustus Fuller Meyrick, of Bodorgan, Esq. . . . . | 14 March. |
| 1828— 9 | 9 „ 10 | Jones Panton, of Llanddyfnan, Esq. . | 13 Feb. |
| 1829—30 | 10 „ 11 | Henry Prichard, of Madyn, Esq. . . | 11 „ |
| 1830 | 11 | Thomas Williams, of Glanrafon, Esq. . | 2 „ |

## WILLIAM IV.

| | | | |
|---|---|---|---|
| 1830— 1 | 1 | Thomas Williams, of Glanrafon, Esq. . | |
| 1831— 2 | 1 & 2 | Owen Owen, of Llanfigael, Esq. . . | 31 Jan. |
| 1832— 3 | 2 „ 3 | Sir John Williams, of Bodelwyddan, (30) Bart. | 6 Feb. |
| 1833— 4 | 3 „ 4 | Charles Henry Evans, of Henblas, Esq. . | 4 „ |

(28) Amended by the King in Council, (the 15 Feb.) from Griffith*s* to Griffit*h*.
(29) Afterwards Sir Richard.
(30) Amended by the King in Council (the 22 Feb.) from Tyfry to Bodelwyddan.

| Anno Dom. | Regnal Year. | Name. | Appointed. |
|---|---|---|---|
| 1834— 5 | 4 & 5 | James King, of Presaddfed, Esq. . . | 3 Feb. |
| 1835— 6 | 5 „ 6 | William Hughes, of Plas Llandyfrydog, Esq. | 7 „ |
| 1836— 7 | 6 „ 7 | Richard Lloyd Edwards, of Monachdu, and Nanhoron, Caernarvon, Esq. . . | 3 „ |
| 1837 | 7 | Hugh Beaver, of Glyn Garth, Esq. . . | 28 Jan. |

## VICTORIA.

| | | | |
|---|---|---|---|
| 1837— 8 | 1 | Hugh Beaver, of Glyn Garth, Esq. . | |
| 1838— 9 | 1 & 2 | William Barton Panton, of Garreglwyd, Esq. | 1 Feb. |
| 1839—40 | 2 „ 3 | James Greenfield, of Rhyddgaer, Esq. . | 4 „ |
| 1840— 1 | 3 „ 4 | Major-General Sir Love Parry Jones Parry, of Madryn, K.H. . . . | 29 Jan. |
| 1841— 2 | 4 „ 5 | Richard Trygarn Griffith, of Carreglwyd, Esq. | 5 Feb. |
| 1842— 3 | 5 „ 6 | John Sanderson, of Aberbraint, Esq. . | 2 „ |
| 1843— 4 | 6 „ 7 | Owen Roberts, of Tynewydd, Esq. . | 1 „ |
| 1844— 5 | 7 „ 8 | Edmund Edward Meyrick, of Cefncoch, Esq. | 31 Jan. |
| 1845— 6 | 8 „ 9 | Robert Jones Hughes, of Plas Llangoed, Esq. . . . . . . | 3 Feb. |
| 1846— 7 | 9 „ 10 | John Lewis Hampton Lewis, of Henllys, Esq. . . . . . . | 30 Jan. |
| 1847— 8 | 10 „ 11 | The Rt. Hon. Spencer Bulkeley, Lord Newborough, of Treiddon, and of Glynllifon, Caernarvon . . . | 4 Feb. |
| 1848— 9 | 11 „ 12 | Sir Harry Dent Goring, of Trysglwyn, Bart. | 11 „ |
| 1849—50 | 12 „ 13 | Stephen Roose, of Tan-y-lan, Esq. . . | 13 „ |
| 1850— 1 | 13 „ 14 | Richard Griffith, of Bodowyr-isaf, Esq. (31) | 5 „ |
| 1851— 2 | 14 „ 15 | Thomas Owen, of Tyddyn Glan-y-mor, Esq. . . . . . . | 11 „ |
| 1852 | 15 | Evan Lloyd, of Maes-y-porth, Esq. (32) . | 2 „ |
| 1852— 3 | 15 „ 16 | Rice Roberts, of Tal-y-Llyn, Esq. . | 1 July. |
| 1853— 4 | 16 „ 17 | Richard Williams Prichard, of Erianell, Esq. . . . . . . | 7 Feb. |
| 1854— 5 | 17 „ 18 | Robert Brisco Owen, of Haulfre, near Beaumaris, Esq. . . . . | 30 Jan. |
| 1855— 6 | 18 „ 19 | Hugh Robert Hughes, of Bodrwyn, and of Kinmel, Esq. . . . . . | 8 Feb. |

(31) A Merchant and Alderman of Liverpool.      (32) Died during his year of office.

| Anno Dom. | Regnal Year. | Name. | Appointed. |
|---|---|---|---|
| 1856— 7 | 19 & 20 | John Jacob, of Llanfawr, Esq. | 30 Jan. |
| 1857— 8 | 20 „ 1 | John Thomas Roberts, of Ucheldre, Esq. | 2 Feb. |
| 1858— 9 | 21 „ 2 | Richard Davies, of Bwlch-y-fen, Esq.(33) . | 3 „ |
| 1859—60 | 22 „ 3 | Henry Owen Williams, of Trearddur, Esq. | 2 „ |
| 1860— 1 | 23 „ 4 | George Richard Griffith, of Pencraig, Esq. | 23 Jan. |
| 1861— 2 | 24 „ 5 | William Bulkeley Hughes, of Plas Coch, Esq. (34) | 4 Feb. |
| 1862— 3 | 25 „ 6 | Robert Davies, of Bwlchfen, Esq. (35) | 5 „ |
| 1863— 4 | 26 „ 7 | Robert Lloyd Jones Parry, of Tregaian, Esq. | 3 Feb. |
| 1864— 5 | 27 „ 8 | William Massey, of Cornelyn, Esq. . | 3 „ |
| 1865— 6 | 28 „ 9 | George Higgins, of Red Hill, Esq. . | 4 „ |
| 1866— 7 | 29 „ 30 | The Hon. Henry Warrender Fitzmaurice, of Trergof. | 3 „ |
| 1867— 8 | 30 „ 1 | William James Griffith, of Bodowyr, Isaf, Esq. (36) | 2 „ |
| 1868— 9 | 31 „ 2 | Henry Lambert, of Tan-y-Graig, Esq. . | 30 Jan. |
| 1869—70 | 32 „ 3 | Thomas Lewis Hampton, of Henllys, Esq. | 4 Feb. |
| 1870— 1 | 33 „ 4 | Sir Richard Bulkeley Williams Bulkeley, of Baron Hill, Bart. | 5 „ |
| 1871 | 34 | John Jones, of Tre-anna, Esq.(37) | 8 „ |
| 1871— 2 | 34 „ 5 | John Wynne Paynter, of Maes-y-llwyn, Esq. | 24 March. |
| 1872 | 35 | William Williams, of Tyddyn Mawr, Esq. | 5 Feb. |
| 1872— 3 | 35 „ 6 | William Duff Assheton Smith, of Trefarthin, and of Vaenol, Caernarvon, Esq. | 21 „ |

(33) Afterward M.P. for the County.   (34) M.P. for Caernarvon Boroughs.   (35) Brother of the Sheriff of 1858.
(36) Son of the Sheriff of 1850.   A Major of Volunteers in Liverpool   Altered by the Queen in Council, the 26 Feb., from William Griffiths of Bodowyr, to William *James* Griffith of Bodowyr, *Isaf.*
(37) Died during office.

# SHERIFFS OF CAERNARVON.

## EDWARD I.

| Anno Dom. | Regnal Year. | Name. | Appointed. |
|---|---|---|---|
| 1284—95 | 12—23 | Richard de Pulesdon, or Pyuldeson. (1) | 18 Oct. |
| 1295—99 | 23—27 | Robert de London. | 16 Sept. |
| 1299—1307 | 28—35 | Henry de Dynynton. (2) | |

## EDWARD II.

| | | | |
|---|---|---|---|
| 1307 | 1 | Henry de Dynynton. | |
| 1308—9 or 10 | 1— 3 | Griffith ap Rees, or Rys. (3) | |
| 1309 or 10—15 | 3— 8 | William Troutwyn, or Trumwyn. | |
| 1315—16 | 8— 9 | Richard Casteleyn. (4) | 4 May. |
| 1316 | 9—10 | John de Maners. | 27 June. |
| 1316—21 | 10—15 | John de Sapy, or Sapi. | 8 Aug. |
| 1321—25 | 15—19 | Giles de Bello Campo. | 12 Oct. |
| 1325—26 | 19—20 | Madoc Gloddaith. (5) | 9 Nov. |
| 1326—27 | 20 | Thomas Ate, or Ace. | |

## EDWARD III.

| | | | |
|---|---|---|---|
| 1327 | 1 | Thomas Ate, or Ace. | |
| 1327—29 | 1— 3 | Giles de Bello Campo. | 25 March. |
| 1329—31 | 3— 5 | Thomas Ate, or Ace. (6) | 17 Sept. |
| 1331— 2 | 5— 6 | ,,      ,,      ,, (7) | 7 Feb. |
| 1332—37 | 6—11? | Howel ap Henry. | |
| 1337— | 11 | Stephen de Pulton, or Polton, (Puleston)? | 27 Dec. |

(1) His brother Roger was at the same time Sheriff of Anglesey. The latter was in 1294 directed to levy the subsidy for the French War, which so offended the Welshmen that they rebelled, and took Sir Roger, whom they hanged, and afterwards beheaded. Dr. Powel's "Hist. of Wales," p. 380.

*As far as I can make out from the pedigree of the Puleston family, Richard was son of Roger de Pulesdon (Puleston). The Tax here referred to was of a fifteenth. I find from Carte's "Hist. of England," vol. ii, p. 236, that it "was levied in Wales in 1294," but its collection must have commenced in 1293. See Ayloffe's "Rotuli Wallie," December 29 (1293), p. 99. Puleston's murder must have taken place after 18 January, 1294, for on that day he witnesses at Emral,—being then a Knight,—a deed to which Richard de Puleston is a party. W.

The following entry is taken from Ayloffe's "Rot. Wall.," p. 101, 14 Edw. I. "De concedendo £40 Ricardo de Pyulesdon, vicecomiti de Kaernarvon ad sustentationem suam in officio una cum arreragiis suis a retro."

(2) Dynynton is mentioned as Sheriff in the Chamberlain's Accounts for the 6 & 7 years of Edward, Prince of Wales (1306-7): also in the first half year of Edw. II. (1307).

(3) *Griffith ap Rees, I have little doubt was the celebrated Sir Griffith Lloyd, who brought to King Edward I. the intelligence of the birth of Edward of Caernarvon. He is said to have been Knighted, but it could not have been till afterwards. See Ayloffe's "Rot. Wall.," p. 93. He was Knighted in 20 Edw. II. W.

He was Sheriff of Merioneth in 1314-17 and 1321-7.

(4) Died 26 June, 1316.   (5) Appointed for one year.   (6) Appointed for life.   (7) Appointed for 10 years.

| Anno Dom. | Regnal Year. | Name. | | | | | Appointed. |
|---|---|---|---|---|---|---|---|
| 1339—45 | 13—19 | Richard, Earl of Arundel. | . | . | . | | 12 July. |
| 1345— 6 | 19—20 | Edward de St. John. | . | . | . | . | |
| 1347— 8 | 21— 2 | Eignion ap Philip. | . | . | . | . | |
| [1348—50?] | 22— 4 | Robert de Holewell. | . | . | . | . | |
| 1350— 1 | 24— 5 | Robert de Parys. (8) . | . | . | . | . | |
| 1351— 9 | 25—33 | Eignion ap Griffith. (9) | . | . | . | . | 1 Oct. |
| 1359—60 | 33— 4 | Thomas de Middelton. | . | . | . | . | |
| | | Ade Hayne. . | . | . | . | } | temp. Edw. III. |
| | | John Stircheley. . | . | . | . | } | |
| 1376— 7 | 50— 1 | Hugh Coly. . | . | . | . | . | |

## RICHARD II.

| | | | | | | | |
|---|---|---|---|---|---|---|---|
| 1377— 8 | 1 | Hugh Coly. . | . | . | . | . | |
| 1378—82 | 1— 6? | William de Hunton, or Huntyndon. | . | | | | 23 May. |
| 1382— 5 | ?6— 9? | Thomas de Wodelef. | . | . | . | . | |
| 1385—90 | ?9—14? | Jevan ap Eignion ap Griffith. (10) | . | | | | |
| 1390— 5 | ?14—19 | Hugh Coly. . | . | . | . | . | |
| 1395— 9 | 19—22? | Richard de Pykemere, or Pekemere. | . | | | | 1 Oct. |
| 1399 | 22 or 23 | John ap Howell. . | . | . | . | . | |

## HENRY IV.

| | | | | | | | |
|---|---|---|---|---|---|---|---|
| 1399—1407? | 1— 8 | John ap Howell. (11) . | . | . | . | . | |
| 1407 | 8 | Reginald Bayldon. (12) | . | . | . | . | 24 May. |
| 1407— 8 | 9—10 | John Salshall. (13) | . | . | . | . | |
| 1408— 9 | 10—11 | Robert Fenrether. | . | . | . | . | |
| 1410—11 | 12—13 | Thomas Camvill. | . | . | . | . | |
| 1411—13 | 13—14 | Hugh Huls, or Holes. | . | . | . | . | |

---

(8) *Robert de Parys was Chamberlain of North Wales in the year ending at Mich. 1 Hen. IV.  W.

(9) *Eignion ap Griffith of Chwilog? was Sheriff and Farmer of the office of Sheriff of Caernarvon in 28-29 Edw. III. (1354-6).  Abstracts of ancient records in Hengwrt MSS.  He was appointed Sheriff for 3 years upon 1 Oct. 25 Edw. III. (1351).  He renders his account to same day, 26 Edw. III.  Ministers' Accounts for Caernarvon for year ending at Mich. 26 Edw. III. and 10 of the principality of Prince Edward.  W.

(10) *In a roll of Ministers' Accounts for the year ending at Mich. 22 Ric. II. (1398), I find " Jevan ap Eignion nuper vicecomes de Caernarvon " was in arrear 46ˡⁱ. 6ˢ. viijᵈ.  W.

(11) The Roll on which this name occurs is dated 23 Ric. II. to 1 Hen. IV.

(12) *Doubtless the same person as was Sheriff of Merioneth in 11 Ric. II  W.

   (In the Merioneth List he is called " Robert Balden.")

(13) *I have little doubt that this is the same person as John  Salghall, who was Constable of the Castle o Harlech.  W.

## HENRY V.

| Anno Dom. | Regnal Year. | Name. | Appointed. |
|---|---|---|---|
| 1413 | 1 | Hugh Huls, or Holes. | |
| 1413—22 | 1—10 | Nicholas Saxton. (14) | 26 Oct. or Dec. |

## HENRY VI.

| | | | |
|---|---|---|---|
| 1422—37 | 1—15 | Nicholas Saxton. | |
| 1437—60 | 15—39? | John Hiende, or Hynde. | 25 Jan. |

## EDWARD IV.

| | | | |
|---|---|---|---|
| 1461—73 | 1—13 | Sir Henry Bolde, Knt. (15) | 23 Sept. |
| 1473—83 | 13—23 | Anthony, Earl of Rivers. (16) | 30 Aug. |

## RICHARD III.

| | | | |
|---|---|---|---|
| 1483— 4 | 1 | Anthony, Earl Rivers. | |
| 1484— 5 | 1— 3 | Thomas Tunstall, Esq. (17) | 12 Feb. |

## HENRY VII.

| | | | |
|---|---|---|---|
| 1485—1500 | 1—15 | William ap Griffith ap Robyn. (18) | 24 Sept. |
| 1500— 9 | 15—24 { | Sir Hugh Vaughan, Knt. | 26 March } |
| 1505— 6 | 21—22 { | Ralph Birkenhead, Esq. (19) | 1 Oct. } |

## HENRY VIII.

| | | | |
|---|---|---|---|
| 1509—27 | 1—19 | Sir Hugh Vaughan, Knt. | |
| 1527—40? | 19—32 | Sir Richard Bulkeley, Knt. | 3 Dec. |
| ?1540— 1 | 32— 3 | Edmund Lloyd, of Glynllivon. (20) | |
| 1541 | 33 | Griffith ap Robert Vaughan, Esq. (21) | 1 July. |

---

(14) In some Rolls his appointment is dated 26 Oct., and in others 26 Dec., 1 Hen. V. (1413).

(15) *He was Sheriff at Mich., 13 Edw. IV., having been appointed for life.   W.

(16) *Anthony, Earl Rivers, K.G., was brother to Elizabeth, Queen of Edw. IV.   The shrievalty of Caernarvonshire must have been a profitable office, as one of this family was appointed to it.   W.

    Was killed at the Battle of St. Auban, in France, 1488.

(17) *He was appointed Constable of the Castle of Conway upon 30 Nov., 1 Ric. III. (1483).   W.

(18) *Of Cochwillan.   There is a receipt at Peniarth, dated 6 Sept., 9 Hen. VII. from William Griffith, Esq., Sheriff of Caernarvonshire, to Madoc Vickan (Vychan) ap Rees ap Hoell, for payment of a Relief upon the death of Meredith ap Res ap Atha, of the Ville of Aberkin.   W.

(19) Vaughan and Birkenhead must have served cojointly in 1505-6 ; for in the Minister's Rolls from 1506-27, the Patent of the 26 March, 15 Hen. VII., is continually recited.   Birkenhead was afterwards Knighted, and made Chamberlain of North Wales.   He lived at Dolwyddelan Castle, and his Executors sold the Lease of the same to Meredydd ap Jevan, ancestor of the Wynns of Gwydir.   A son or brother of his was Prothonotary and Clerk of the Crown for the Co. of Flint in 1542, and is mentioned by name (John Brekenhead) in the Stat. 34 & 35 Hen. VIII. c. 26. s. 44.

(20) *Ancestor in the direct male line of the Glynnes of Glynllifon, now of Hawarden Castle.   W.

    He died during his year of office.

(21) *Of Talhenbont, now Plashen, grandfather to the Sheriff for 1600-1.   W.

| Anno Dom. | Regnal Year. | Name. | Appointed. |
|---|---|---|---|
| 1541— 2 | 33 & 4 | William Griffith, alias Williams, Esq. . | 23 Nov. |
| 1542— 3 | 34— 5 | Sir Richard Bulkeley, Knt. . . . | 22 „ |
| 1543— 4 | 35— 6 | John Puleston, Esq. . . . . | 23 „ |
| 1544— 5 | 36— 7 | John Wyn ap Meredith, of Gwydyr, Esq. (22) | 16 „ |
| 1545— 7 | 37— 8 | Hugh Peak, of Conway, Esq. . . . | 22 „ |

## EDWARD VI.

| | | | |
|---|---|---|---|
| 1547 | I | William Williams, of Cochwillan, Esq. . | 29 Jan. |
| 1547— 8 | I— 2 | Griffith ap William Madoc, of Llwyndy-rus, Esq. . . . . . | 27 Nov. |
| 1548— 9 | 2— 3 | John Roberts, of Castellmarch, Esq. (23) . | |
| 1549—50 | 3— 4 | Sir Richard Bulkeley, Knt. . . . | 12 Nov. |
| 1550— I | 4— 5 | John Wynne ap Hewe, of Bodvel, Esq. (24) | 11 „ |
| 1551— 2 | 5— 6 | Hugh Peeke, Esq. . . . . . | 11 „ |
| 1552— 3 | 6— 7 | William ap William, of Cochwillan, Esq. (25) | |

## MARY AND PHILIP AND MARY,

| | | | |
|---|---|---|---|
| 1553 | I | William ap William, of Cochwillan, Esq. | |
| 1553— 4 | 1 & 1 & 2 P. & M. | Griffith ap William Madoc, Esq. (26) . . | |
| 1554— 5 | 1 & 2 / 2 „ 3 | Morrice Wynne, of Gwydir, Esq. (27) . | |
| 1555— 6 | 2 „ 3 / 3 „ 4 | Griffith Davies, of Caernarvon, Esq. . | 14 Nov. |
| 1556— 7 | 3 „ 4 / 4 „ 5 | John Wynne ap Meredith, of Gwydir, Esq. (28) | |
| 1557— 8 | 4 „ 5 / 5 „ 6 | Sir Richard Bulkeley, Knt. (29) . . | 16 Nov. |

## ELIZABETH.

| | | | |
|---|---|---|---|
| 1558— 9 | I | Ellis Price, of Plasiolyn. (30) . . . | 23 Nov. |

(22) Father of Maurice Wynn, and grandfather of Sir John Wynn, the Historian. He died in 1553 (Hist. of Gwydir Family).

(23) *John ap Robert ap Llewellyn Ithel, of Castellmarch, Esq., ancestor in a direct line, and in the fourth degree to the Sheriff for 1663-4. W.

(24) *He was Standard-bearer at the Battle of Norwich in 1549, to John, Earl of Warwick, afterwards Duke of Northumberland. See Additions to 4to. Hist. of the Gwydir Family, Ruthin, 1827, p. 120. W.

(25) *His Will is dated 22 June, 1558, and was proved 3 June, 1559. The celebrated Lord Keeper Williams, Archbishop of York, was his great-grandson. W.

(26) *Of Llwyndyrus(?), ancestor to the Edwards, of Nanhoron. W.

(27) *Eldest son and successor of the Sheriff for 1544-5, and 1556-7. He died 10 Aug., 1580, and there was an inscription to his memory in the Gwydir Chapel at Llanrwst, but it has disappeared. W.

(28) He died 9 July, 1559.

(29) *See "Pennant's Tour," ed. 1784, 4to. vol. 2, p. 175. W.

(30) *See "Pennant's Tour," ed. 1784, 4to. vol. 2, p. 338. W.

| Anno Dom. | Regnal Year. | Name. | Appointed. |
|---|---|---|---|
| 1559—60 | 2 & 3 | John Wynne ap Hugh, of Bodvel, Esq. | |
| 1560— 1 | 3 „ 4 | Robert Pugh, (or ap Hugh,) of Penrhyn-creuddyn, Esq. | |
| 1561— 2 | 4 „ 5 | William Glynn, of Glynllivon, Esq. | |
| 1562— 3 | 5 „ 6 | William Griffith, Esq. (31) | |
| 1563— 4 | 6 „ 7 | Griffith Glynn, of Pwllheli, Esq. (32) | |
| 1564— 5 | 7 „ 8 | Griffith Davies, of Caernarvon, Esq. | |
| 1565— 6 | 8 „ 9 | Sir William Herbert, of Swansea, Knt. | |
| 1566— 7 | 9 „ 10 | { Sir Richard Griffith, of Penrhyn, Knt. (33) / William Mostyn, of Mostyn, Esq. | |
| 1567— 8 | 10 „ 11 | Thomas Owen, of Plasdu, Esq. | |
| 1568— 9 | 11 „ 12 | Maurice Wynne, of Gwydir, Esq. | |
| 1569—70 | 12 „ 13 | Edward Williams, of Maes-y-castell, Esq. (34) | |
| 1570— 1 | 13 „ 14 | William Williams, of Cochwillan, Esq. (35) | |
| 1571— 2 | 14 „ 15 | Richard Mosten, of Bodysgallen, Esq. | |
| 1572— 3 | 15 „ 16 | Griffith Davies, of Caernarvon, Esq. | |
| 1573— 4 | 16 „ 17 | Rece Thomas, of Caernarvon, Esq. (36) | |
| 1574— 5 | 17 „ 18 | Rowland Puleston, of Caernarvon, Esq. | |
| 1575— 6 | 18 „ 19 | Richard Peak, of Conway, Esq. | |
| 1576— 7 | 19 „ 20 | Edward Conwey, of Bryneirin, Esq. | |
| 1577— 8 | 20 „ 1 | Richard Peake, Esq. | |
| 1578— 9 | 21 „ 2 | Richard Vaughan, of Llwyndyrus, Esq. (37) | |
| 1579—80 | 22 „ 3 | Maurice Kyffin, of Maenan, Esq. | 30 Nov. |
| 1580— 1 | 23 „ 4 | William Thomas, of Caernarvon, Esq. (38) | 21 „ |
| 1581— 2 | 24 „ 5 | William Morris, (or Maurice,) of Cleneney, Esq. (39) | |

(31) *Of Caernarvon. His tomb remains in Llanrug Church. W.

(32) *There is an elegy upon him by the poet, Sion Philip, in Hengwrt MS., 362A. W.

(33) *Sir Rees Griffith, of Penrhyn, Knt. He repaired and ornamented the house at Penrhyn, as appeared by his name over the fire-place in the old Hall there: R. G. K.G. 1575. W.

(34) *He was the fourth son of William Williams, of Cochwillan, Esq. W.

(35) *Elder brother of the Sheriff for the preceding year. W.

(36) *Ancestor to the Thomas, of Coedhelen family. W.

(37) *And Corsygedol: died about 1588. His mother Gwen, dau. of Griffith ap William Lloyd, was heiress of Llwyndyrus. W.

(38) *Eldest son of the Sheriff for 1573-4. Was slain in Flanders in 1586. W.

(39) *Afterwards Sir William Maurice of Cleneney and Porkington. He was a personal friend of James I., and it was at Sir William's suggestion, the King assumed the title of "King of Great Britain." I extract the following from the copy of a letter at Porkington, dated 6 Feb., 1603, from Mrs. Ann Wynn Brynker to her brother Sir William Maurice.—"methinks you should desier his Majesty to speake to my Lord Chaunceller and my Lo. president to use you well & to shewe you some favoure thereby, for the great service that you have done in her Majesty's raigne, being Knight of the shire so manie yeers, & attendinge upon the Parlament so due-lie and truelie as you have done: By reson alsoe that you are his godfather and intiteled his highnes Kinge of

| Anno Dom. | Regnal Year. | Name. | Appointed. |
|---|---|---|---|
| 1582— 3 | 25 & 26 | John Griffith, of Caernarvon, Esq. . . | 5 Dec. ? |
| 1583— 4 | 26 „ 7 | Thomas Mostyn, of Mostyn, Esq. . . | 9 „ |
| 1584— 5 | 27 „ 8 | John ap Hugh ap Richard, of Bodurda, Esq. | 19 Nov. |
| 1585— 6 | 28 „ 9 | John Vaughan, of Penmachno, Esq. (40) . | 2 Dec. |
| 1586— 7 | 29 „ 30 | Thomas Madrin, of Madryn, Esq. . . | |
| 1587— 8 | 30 „ 1 | John Wynn, of Gwydir, Esq. (41) . . | 4 Dec. |
| 1588— 9 | 31 „ 2 | Hugh Gwynne Bodvel, of Bodvel, Esq. . | 25 Nov. |
| 1589—90 | 32 „ 3 | Griffith ap John ap Griffith, of Llyn, Esq. | 13 Dec. |
| 1590— 1 | 33 „ 4 | Robert Wynne, of Conwey, Esq. (42) . | 24 Nov. |
| 1591— 2 | 34 „ 5 | William Williams, of Cochwillan, Esq. . | |
| 1592— 3 | 35 „ 6 | Rowland Puleston, Esq, . . . . | 4 Dec. |
| 1593— 4 | 36 „ 7 | Richard Gwynne, of Caernarvon, Esq. . | 26 Nov. |
| 1594— 5 | 37 „ 8 | Robert Wynne Bryncker, of Bryncker, Esq. | 18 „ |
| 1595— 6 | 38 „ 9 | William Morrice ap Ellis, of Clene-ney, Esq. (43) . . . . . | 27 „ |
| 1596— 7 | 39 „ 40 | Hugh Gwinne, of Bodvel, Esq. . . | 22 „ |
| 1597— 8 | 40 „ 1 | Thomas Vaughan, of Pantglas, Esq. . | 25 „ |
| 1598— 9 | 41 „ 2 | William Williams, of Vaynol, Esq. . . | 28 „ |
| 1599—1600 | 42 „ 3 | Hugh Gwynne, of Pennarth, Esq. . . | 2 Dec. |
| 1600— 1 | 43 „ 4 | Richard Vaughan, of Plashen, Esq. (44) . | 24 Nov. |
| 1601— 2 | 44 „ 5 | Maurice Lewes, of Festiniog, Esq. (45) . | 2 Dec. |
| 1602— 3 | 45 | John Wynn, of Gwydir, Esq. (46) . . | 7 „ |

## JAMES I.

| | | | |
|---|---|---|---|
| 1603 | 1 | John Wynn, of Gwydir, Esq. . . . | |
| 1603— 4 | 1 & 2 | John Griffith, of Llyn, Esq. . . . | 1 Dec. |
| 1604— 5 | 2 „ 3 | Robert Madrin, of Madrin, Esq. . . | 5 Nov. |
| 1605— 6 | 3 „ 4 | Hugh Bodwrda, Esq. . . . . | |
| 1606— 7 | 4 „ 5 | William Williams, of Vaynol, Esq. . . | 17 Nov. |
| 1607— 8 | 5 „ 6 | Sir William Thomas, Knt. . . . | 9 Dec. |

Great Britaine. Let his Majesty therefore speake in your behalfe a word or to (two), or els you will favour the worst otherwise : be not abashed to speake with his highnes at this time, & desier his highnes that you maie be dealt w<sup>th</sup>all, and to find such favour at his majesty's hand as Queene Elizabeth did before him."  See more upon this subject in the Printed Calendar of State Papers, A.D. 1603-10, p. 338.  One of the printed " Broadsides " whereby the King assumed the title of King of Great Britain, is at Peniarth.  W.

(40) *He was one of the Queen's Footmen.  W.

(41) The Historian of the Gwydir Family, and afterwards Knight and Baronet.

(42) *Son of John Wynn ap Meredith, and uncle of Sir John Wynne.  W.

(43) Afterwards Knighted.

(44) *He died between 29 April, 1605, and 7 May, 1606.  His daughter and heiress, Ann, was wife of William Vaughan, of Corsygedol, Esq.  W.

(45) *Of Pengwern, Festiniog.  He died in 1606.  W.

(46) *There is a letter at Porkington, from " John Wynn, of Gwydir, Sheriff," dated 7 Dec., 1603.  W.

| Anno Dom. | Regnal Year. | Name. | Appointed. |
|---|---|---|---|
| 1608— 9 | 6 & 7 | Thomas Bodvel, of Bodvel, Esq. . . | 10 Nov. |
| 1609—10 | 7 „ 8 | Robert Richard, of Conway, Esq. (47) . | |
| 1610—11 | 8 „ 9 | Sir William Glynn, Knt. . . . . | |
| 1611 | 9 | William Glynne, of Penllechog, Esq. . | |
| 1611—12 | 9 „ 10 | William Humfrey, of Pantdu, Esq. (48) . | 12 Nov. |
| 1612—13 | 10 „ 11 | William Vaughan, of Plashên, Esq. . | 16 „ |
| 1613—14 | 11 „ 12 | Humfrey Meredith, of Clynnog, Esq. . | |
| 1614—15 | 12 „ 13 | Griffith Hughes, of Cefn Llanvair, Esq. . | |
| 1615—16 | 13 „ 14 | William Griffith, of Caernarvon, Esq. . | |
| 1616—17 | 14 „ 15 | Simon Williams, of Wig, Esq. . . | |
| 1617—18 | 15 „ 16 | John Griffith, of Lleyn, Esq. (49) . . | |
| 1618—19 | 16 „ 17 | John Wynne, of Penllech, Esq. . . | 9 Nov. |
| 1619—20 | 17 „ 18 | Robert Wynne, of Llanddeiniolen, Esq. (50) | |
| 1620— 1 | 18 „ 19 | Robert Owen, of Ystumcegid, Esq. . . | |
| 1621— 2 | 19 „ 20 | Thomas Glynne, of Glyn-Llivon, Esq. . | |
| 1622— 3 | 20 „ 1 | Sir John Bodvill, Knt. . . . . | 7 Nov. |
| 1623— 4 | 21 „ 2 | Ellis Brynkir, of Brynkir, Esq. . . . | 7 „ |
| 1624— 5 | 22 „ 3 | Richard Evans, of Elernion, Esq. (51) . | |

## CHARLES I.

| | | | |
|---|---|---|---|
| 1625 | 1 | Richard Evans, of Elernion, Esq. . . | |
| 1625— 6 | 1 & 2 | Sir Thomas Williams, of Vaynol, Bart. (52) | |
| 1626— 7 | 2 „ 3 | Thomas Glynne, of Nantle, Esq. . | 6 Nov. |
| 1627— 8 | 3 „ 4 | John Vaughan, of Pantglas, Esq. . | |
| 1628— 9 | 4 „ 5 | Henry Humfreis, of Pwllheli, Esq. . | 9 Dec. |
| 1629—30 | 5 „ 6 | John Bodwrda, Esq. . . . . | 10 Nov. |
| 1630— 1 | 6 „ 7 | John Owen, of Cleneney, Esq. (53) . . | |
| 1631— 2 | 7 „ 8 | William Vaughan, of Plashen, Esq. . | |

(47) * ? Prichard. W.

He died during his year of office.

(48) *There is a very curious letter at Porkington, from this William Humffreys, ordering clothes for himself as Sheriff, and for his men. I have a copy of it. The apparel appears to have been rather magnificent, "some colored sattan cutt with a diamond pink, a fayer cloche (cloak) ether [side] lined before with velvett, and a fayer gould and silver bottom hanging dowen further." This was to be for himself. He orders also, "a dozen liveries cloches, one robe for a foot-boy, 13 hats and fether." He says his bidding (building?) "hath empty my purse whoully." This letter is dated June 10, without the year. W.

(49) *John Griffith, junior. W.

(50) *And of Glascoed. W.

(51) *His daughter and heiress, Margaret, married William Glynne, of Brynygwdion, the Sheriff for 1633-4. Richard Evans' wife was, Mary, daughter of Robert Wynn Brynker, of Brynkir, Esq., and he died about the year 1630. There is an elegy upon him in Hengwrt MS., 362A. W.

(52) *His Patent bears date 13 Nov. 1625. Gr. Bodurda was his Under-Sheriff. W.

(53) *Afterwards the celebrated Sir John Owen, Knt. W.

| Anno Dom. | Regnal Year. | Name. | Appointed. |
|---|---|---|---|
| 1632— 3 | 8 & 9 | Griffith Madrin, of Madryn, Esq. | |
| 1633— 4 | 9 „ 10 | William Glynne, of Elernion, Esq. (54) | |
| 1634— 5 | 10 „ 11 | John Wynne, of Conway, Esq. | |
| 1635— 6 | 11 „ 12 | Evan Wynne, of Saethon, Esq. | |
| 1636— 7 | 12 „ 13 | William Lewis Anwyl, of Park, Esq. (55) | |
| 1637— 8 | 13 „ 14 | William Thomas, of Aber, Esq. (56) | |
| 1638— 9 | 14 „ 15 | William Hookes, Esq. | |
| 1639—40 | 15 „ 16 | Sir William Williams, of Vaynol, Bart. | |
| 1640— 1 | 16 „ 17 | James Brynkir, of Brynkir, Esq. | |
| 1641— 2 | 17 „ 18 | Thomas Chedle, of Beaumaris, Esq. | |
| 1642— 3 | 18 „ 19 | Thomas Madryn, of Madryn, Esq. | Nov. |
| 1643— 4 | 19 „ 20 | Robert Jones, of Castell-march, Esq. | |
| 1644— 5 | 20 „ 1 | Sir John Owen, of Cleneney. (57) | |
| 1645— 6 | 21 „ 2 | Richard Wynne, of Glasynfryn, Esq. | |
| 1646 | 22 | Thomas Williams, Esq. (58) | 22 July. |
| 1646— 7 | | | |
| 1647— 8 | 23 „ 4 | William Lloyd, of Plashen, Esq. (59) | 17 Nov. |
| ?1648— 9 | 24 | Thomas Madryn, Esq. (60) | |

## THE COMMONWEALTH AND CHARLES II.

| | | | |
|---|---|---|---|
| 1649 | | Thomas Madryn, Esq. | |
| 1649—50 | | John Carter. | 9 Oct. |
| 1650 | | John Carter, of Kinmel, Esq. | 13 Feb. |
| 1650— 1 | | Griffith Williams, of Penrhyn, Esq. | 7 Nov. |
| 1651— 2 | | Henry Williams, of Maesycastell, Esq. | 4 „ |
| 1652— 3 | | Sir Owen Wynn, of Gwydir, Bart. (61) | 12 „ |
| 1653— 4 | | Sir William Williams, of Vaynol, Bart. | 10 „ |

(51) *And of Brynygwdion. (See Note 51.) He married Margaret, daughter and heiress of Richard Evans, Esq., the Sheriff for 1624-5. W.

(55) *His Will is dated in Dec. 1641, and he died soon afterwards, the representative of one of the oldest families, and owner of one of the largest estates in the county of Merioneth. W.

(56) *Afterwards Sir William Thomas, Knt., eldest son and successor to the Sheriff for 1580-1. W.

(57) *Sir John was grandson and heir through his mother to the Sheriff for 1581-2. There is a letter addressed by John, Lord Byron, to Sir John as Sheriff, dated 2d Oct. 1645. Orig. at Porkington. W.

(58) Of Dinas. He was appointed and nominated to be Sheriff by the House of Commons, on 22d July, 1646, (Journals House of Commons, vol. 4, p. 622), which appointment was sent to the House of Lords for their Lordships' concurrence, on the 24th July, 1646, (Jo. Ho. Com., vol. 4, p. 625). Doubtless he continued in office until William Lloyd was appointed on the 17th Nov. 1647.

(59) He was killed in a skirmish near Caernarvon, by Sir John Owen, during his year of office, and was succeeded in office by Thomas Madryn. He was a son of the "House of Bodidris," and married Miss Vaughan, the heiress of Plashên. (Vaughan MSS., Mostyn Collection.)

(60) *It is proved by a contemporary deed that he was Sheriff in October, 1649. W.

(61) *He died in 1658, aged 68. W.

| Anno Dom. | Regnal Year. | Name. | Appointed. |
|---|---|---|---|
| 1654— 5 | | Edward Williams, of Wig, Esq. (62) . | Nov. |
| 1655— 6 | | William Vaughan, of Plashen, Esq. (63) . | ,, |
| 1656— 7 | | Richard Anwyl, of Hafod dwyryd, Esq. . | |
| 1657— 8 | | Richard Wynne, of Gwydir, Esq. (64) . | |
| 1658— 9 | | John Williams, of Meillionydd, Esq. (65) . | |
| 1659—60 | | John Williams, Esq.    ,, | |
| 1660— 1 | 12 & 13 | ,,    ,,    ,,    ,, | |
| ?1661 | 13 | William Griffith, of Lleyn, Esq.   .   , | |
| 1661— 2 | 13 ,, 14 | Sir Griffith Williams, of Penrhyn, Bart. . | |
| 1662— 3 | 14 ,, 15 | Richard Kyffin, of Maenan, Esq.   .   . | |
| 1663— 4 | 15 ,, 16 | Griffith Jones, of Castellmarch, Esq. (66) . | |
| 1664— 5 | 16 ,, 17 | Richard Glyn, of Elernion, Esq. (67) .   . | |
| 1665— 6 | 17 ,, 18 | Thomas Madrin, Esq.   .   .   . | 12 Nov. |
| 1666— 7 | 18 ,, 19 | Sir Roger Mostyn, Knt. and Bart. .   . | 7 ,, |
| 1667— 8 | 19 ,, 20 | William Lloyd, of Bodfan, Esq.   .   . | 6 ,, |
| 1668— 9 | 20 ,, 1 | John Glynne, of Glynllivon, Esq. .   . | 6 ,, |
| 1669—70 | 21 ,, 2 | Sir Robert Williams, of Penrhyn, Bart. (68) | 8 ,, |
| 1670— 1 | 22 ,, 3 | Evan Lloyd, of Hafod Lwyfog, Esq.   . | 5 ,, |
| 1671— 2 | 23 ,, 4 | William Winne, of Glan yr Avon, Esq. . | 6 ,, |
| 1672— 3 | 24 ,, 5 | Robert Williams, Esq.   .   .   . | 7 ,, |
| ?1673 | 25 | William Wynn, of Llanwnda, Esq. (69) . | |
| 1673— 4 | 25 ,, 6 | William Griffith, of Madryn-isa, Esq.   . | 10 ,, |
| 1674— 5 | 26 ,, 7 | Sir John Wynne, Knt. and Bart. (70)   . | 18 ,, |

(62) *His sister and heiress, Grace, was wife of Sir Owen Wynn, of Gwydir, Bart., who was Sheriff in 1652-3. W.

(63) *And of Corsygedol. W.

(64) *Afterwards Sir Richard. His daughter and heiress, Mary, marrying Robert, thirteenth Lord Willoughby d'Eresby, afterwards first Duke of Ancaster, conveyed the Gwydir estates into that family. She died in 1689. W.

(65) *Elder brother of the Sheriff for 1680-1. W.

(66) *There is a very good picture, supposed to be of him, at Rhiwlas. I believe it was through a branch of this family that the Prices obtained their Caernarvonshire estate ; but this Griffith Jones left only two daughters, one of whom married Sir William Williams, of Vaynol, Bart., the other, first Sir William's brother, and afterwards Thomas Bulkeley. W.

(67) *Eldest son and successor of the Sheriff for 1633-4. The present Sheriff married and left issue, who all died childless, and the Elernion, Penllechog and Brynygwdion estates eventually centred in Catherine, wife of William Wynne, of Wern, Esq., daughter of Richard Glynne's sister Elizabeth, by her husband, Gabriel Goodman, of Beaumaris ; second son of Hugh Goodman, of Bodedern, in Anglesey, by Ann, daughter of Richard Meyrick, of Bodorgan. W.

(68) *There is a very good picture of him at Hawarden Castle. W.

(69) *The heiress of this family married to Richard Garnons, of Pantdu, and they were the parents of the late much respected Richard Garnons, Esq., of Caernarvon. W.

(70) *Of Wynnstay in Denbighshire, the last Baronet of the Gwydir line. He died in 1719, aged 96, leaving his estates to his kinsman Watkin Williams, eldest son of Sir William Williams of Llanvorda, Bart., who assumed the additional surname of Wynn, and was eventually the first Sir Watkin Williams Wynn, Bart. W.

| Anno Dom. | Regnal Year. | Name. | Appointed. |
|---|---|---|---|
| 1675— 6 | 27 & 28 | Owen Wynne, of Ystumkegid, Esq. (71) . | 11 Nov. |
| 1676 | 28 | Griffith Winne, of Pen-y-Berth, Esq. (72) . | 9 „ |
| 1676— 7 | 28 | Holland Williams, Esq. (73) . . . | 26 „ |
| 1677 | 28 „ 9 | Richard Wynne, of Glasynfryn, Esq. . | 10 Jan. |
| 1677— 8 | 29 „ 30 | Griffith Vaughan, of Corsygedol, Esq. . | 15 Nov. |
| 1678— 9 | 30 „ 1 | Thomas Wynne, of Glasgoed, Esq. (74) . | — „ ? |
| 1679—80 | 31 „ 2 | Robert Coytmore, of Tymawr, Esq. . . | 13 „ |
| ?1680 | 32 | William Lloyd, of Hafodlwyfog, Esq. . | ——— |
| 1680— 1 | 32 „ 3 | Edward Williams, of Meillionydd, Esq. (75) | 4 „ |
| 1681— 2 | 33 „ 4 | William Arthur, of Vaynol, Esq. . . | 16 „ |
| 1682 | 34 | Owen Jones, Esq. . . . . | 22 „ |
| 1682— 3 | 34 „ 5 | George Twisleton, Esq. (76) . . . | 4 Dec. |
| 1683— 4 | 35 „ 6 | Robert Coytmore, Esq. . . . | 19 Nov. |
| 1684— 5 | 36 „ 7 | Love Parry, of Cefn-Llanfair, Esq. . . | 24 „ |

## JAMES II.

| | | | |
|---|---|---|---|
| 1685 | 1 | Love Parry, of Cefn-Llanfair, Esq. . | |
| 1685— 6 | 1 „ 2 | William Wynne, of Wern, Esq. (77) . | 26 Nov. |
| 1686— 7 | 2 „ 3 | Hugh Bodurda, Esq. . . . . | 25 „ |
| 1687— 8 | 3 | William Pugh, of Penrhyn, Esq. . . | 29 Dec. |
| 1688 | 3 | Honble. Thomas Bulkeley, of Dinas. . | [5—9] Jan. |
| 1688 | 4 | John Rowlands, of Conway, Esq. (78) . | [15—17] Nov. |

## WILLIAM & MARY.

| | | | |
|---|---|---|---|
| 1688— 9 | 1 | John Rowlands, of Conway, Esq. . . | |
| 1689 | 1 | Thomas Mostyn, Esq. . . . . | 16 March. |
| 1689 | 1 | Owen Wynne, of Peny Bryn, Esq. . . | 10 April. |

(71) *And of Glynn, in Merionethshire, elder brother of the Sheriff for 1685-6. He died in Dec., 1682. W.

(72) *He married Margaret Ellis, heiress of Ystymllyn, and died in 1719. W.

(73) *He died in Dec., 1680, or Jan., 1681, in his 40th year. W.

(74) *He married Mary, daughter and heiress of Robert Jones, third son of Sir William Jones, of Castellmarch, Knt. W.

(75) *He was drowned in the River Ffriwlyd, in Nov., 1697. Third in descent from him was Ann, daughter of Edward Williams of Meillionydd, and of Ystymcolwyn, co. Montgomery : who was wife of Robert Howel Vaughan, of Nannau and Hengwrt, the first Baronet of that family.

(76) *Of Lleuar. He was a Colonel in the Parliamentary Army, and Governor of Denbigh Castle. His wife was Mary Glynne, heiress of Lleuar, daughter of William Glynne, Esq. : she died in June, 1676. Col. Twisleton died in June, 1697. The Glynnes of Lleuar and Elernion were different branches of the same family. W.

He defeated and took prisoner Sir J. Owen, of Clenenney. Buried at Clynnog-fawr. Was son-in-law to William Glynne of Elernion, who was Sheriff in 1633-4.

(77) *Younger brother to the Sheriff for 1675-6; obtained the Wern estate by marrying his cousin, Frances Jones, the heiress of it. He died in Dec., 1700. W.

(78) *He married a sister of Sir Robert Owen of Porkington, M.P. for the co. Merioneth, and afterwards for the Caernarvon Boroughs. W.

| Anno Dom. | Regnal Year. | Name. | Appointed. |
|---|---|---|---|
| 1689—90 | 1 & 2 | Samuel Hanson, of Bodvel, Esq. | 14 Nov. |
| 1690— 1 | 2 „ 3 | David Parry, of Brinne Milinian, Esq. | 27 „ |
| ?1691 | 3 | Hugh Lewis, of Pontnewydd, Esq. | ———— |
| 1691— 2 | 3 „ 4 | David Parry, of Llwyn-ynn, Esq. | 21 Dec. |
| 1692— 3 | 4 „ 5 | John Rowlands, of Caernarvon, Esq. | 17 Nov. |
| 1693— 4 | 5 „ 6 | John Thomas, of Aber, Esq. | 16 „ |
| 1694 | 6 | Richard Madryn, Esq. | 6 „ |

## WILLIAM III.

| | | | |
|---|---|---|---|
| 1694— 5 | 6 „ 7 | Richard Madryn, Esq. | |
| 1695— 6 | 7 „ 8 | James Brinker, Esq. (79) | 5 Dec. |
| 1696— 7 | 8 „ 9 | Richard Edwards, of Nanhoron, Esq. | 3 „ |
| 1697— 8 | 9 „ 10 | Henry Vaughan, of Pantglas, Esq. | 23 „ |
| 1698 | 10 | Richard Vaughan, of Corsygedol and Plashen, Esq. (80) | 12 „ |
| 1698— 9 | 10 „ 11 | Edward Holland, of Conway, Esq. | [22—26] Dec. |
| 1699—1700 | 11 „ 12 | Pierce Lloyd, of Llanidan, Esq. (81) | 23 Nov. |
| 1700 | 12 | Sir Roger Mostyn. (82) | 28 „ |
| 1700— 1 | 12 „ 13 | Edward Holland, Esq. | 12 Dec. |
| 1702 | 13 „ 14 | Arthur Williams, of Meillionydd, Esq. (83) | 1 Jan. |

## QUEEN ANNE.

| | | | |
|---|---|---|---|
| 1702 | 1 | Arthur Williams, of Meillionydd, Esq. | |
| 1702 | 1 | Maurice Jones, Esq. | 3 Dec. |
| 1702 | 1 | John Thomas, Esq. | 10 „ |
| 1702— 3 | 1 „ 2 | Simon Foulkes (or Folkes), of Bodvil, Esq. | 27 „ |
| 1703 | 2 | Lloyd Bodvel, Esq. | 2 „ |
| 1703— 4 | 2 | Griffith Wynne, Esq. (84) | 18 „ |
| 1704 | 2 „ 3 | Lloyd Bodvel, Esq. | 13 Feb. |
| 1704— 5 | 3 „ 4 | Thomas Roberts, of Bryn-y-neuodd, Esq.(85) | 18 Dec. |

(79) *Of Brynkir. There is a portrait of him at Peniarth. W.

(80) Mr. Wynne states that "Richard Vaughan was certainly Sheriff in some part of 1699," but I cannot find any entry of the name, though he may very possibly have served during 1699.

(81) Pierce Lloyd made the Parliamentary Return for the Knight of the Shire, which is dated 18 Jan., 12 William III., (1701); Edward Holland should have made it, having been appointed Sheriff on the 12 Dec., 1700.

(82) *Of Mostyn, the third Baronet of his family, was Paymaster of the Marine Forces to Queen Anne, and afterwards a Teller of the Exchequer. He married the Lady Essex, daughter of Daniel, Earl of Nottingham, and died 5 May, 1739. W.

(83) *Eldest son and successor of the Sheriff for 1680-1. He was born 28 April, 1681, and married Meryel, daughter and heiress of Lumley Williams, Esq., of Ystymcolwyn, co. Montgomery. She was born 27 Sept., 1684. W.

(84) *Of Bodvean; father of the Sheriff for 1712: died 21 Sept. 1680. W.

(85) *The heiress of this family, Mary, daughter and heiress of Humphrey Roberts, Esq., married in the year 1751, Robert Wynne, of Garthmeilio and Cwmmein, in the co. of Denbigh and Merioneth. W.

| Anno Dom. | Regnal Year. | Name. | Appointed. |
|---|---|---|---|
| 1705— 6 | 4 & 5 | Richard Owen, of Peniarth, Esq. . . | 3 Dec. |
| 1706— 7 | 5 „ 6 | Sir William Williams, Bart. (86) . . | 5 „ |
| 1707— 8 | 6 „ 7 | Sir Griffith Williams, Bart. (87) . . | 18 „ |
| 1708 | 7 | Sir Bourchier Wray, Bart. . . . | 25 Nov. |
| 1708— 9 | 7 „ 8 | George Coitmore (or Coytmer), Esq. . | 3 Dec. |
| 1709—10 | 8 „ 9 | John Griffith, of Aber, Esq. . . . | 1 „ |
| 1710—11 | 9 „ 10 | Roger Price, of Plasdu, Esq. (88) . | 24 Nov. |
| 1711—12 | 10 | Thomas Ellis, Esq. . . . . | 13 Dec. |
| 1712 | 10 | William Owen, Esq. . . . . | 12 Jan. |
| 1712 | 10 „ 11 | Thomas Wynne, of Bodvean, Esq. (89) . | 21 „ |
| 1712—13 | 11 „ 12 | Hugh Davies, of Caerhûn, Esq. . . | 11 Dec. |
| 1713—14 | 12 „ 13 | Thomas Ellis, of Wern, Esq. (90) . . | 30 Nov. |

## GEORGE I.

| Anno Dom. | Regnal Year. | Name. | Appointed. |
|---|---|---|---|
| 1714 | 1 | Thomas Ellis, of Wern, Esq. . . . | |
| 1714—15 | 1 & 2 | Timothy Edwards, of Nanhoron, Esq. . | 6 Dec. |
| 1715—16 | 2 „ 3 | Lewis Owen, of Peniarth, Esq. (91) . . | 5 „ |
| 1716—17 | 3 | Maurice Williams, of Glascoed, Esq. . | 6 „ |
| 1717 | 3 „ 4 | John Wynne, of the Abbey, Esq. (92) . | 10 Jan. |
| 1717—18 | 4 „ 5 | William Wynne, of Wern, Esq. (93) . | 21 Dec. |
| 1718—20 | 5 „ 6 | William Bodvel, of Madryn, Esq. . | 21 „ |
| 1720— 1 | 6 „ 7 | Edward Bayley, of Gorswen, Esq. (94) . | 7 Jan. |
| 1721 | 7 „ 8 | Hugh Lewis, of Pont-Newydd, Esq. . | 14 „ |
| 1721— 2 | 8 „ 9 | Love Parry, of Cefn-Llanfair, Esq. . | 14 Dec. |
| 1722— 4 | 9 „ 10 | Thomas Rowlands, of Nant, Esq. . . | 11 „ |
| 1724 | 10 | William Brynkir, of Treborth, Esq. (95) . | 7 Jan. |
| 1724 | 10 „ 11 | William Wynne, of Llanwnda, Esq. . | 29 „ |
| 1724— 6 | 11 „ 12 | William Brynkir, of Treborth, Esq. . | 10 Dec. |

(86) *Of Llanvorda, eldest son and successor of the Rt. Hon. William Williams, Speaker of the House of Commons in 1679-80. The above Sheriff was father to the first Sir Watkin Williams Wynn, Bart. W.

(87) *The last Sir William Williams, of Vaynol, Bart., left his estates to Sir Bourchier Wrey, and Chichester Wrey, for life, and afterwards to King William III., who gave them to the ancestor of the Assheton Smith family, who was Speaker of the House of Commons. W.

(88) *And of Rhiwlas, Merionethshire. W.

(89) *Thomas Wynn, created a Baronet 25 Oct., 1742. He was grandfather to Sir Thomas Wynn, created Lord Newborough in 1776. See note 8. W.

(90) * ?Wernfawr. W.

(91) *Son and successor to the Sheriff for 1705-6. He was Custos Rotulorum of Merioneth, and died in Dec., 1729. W.

(92) *Eldest son of the Sheriff for 1712. W.

(93) *Only son and successor of the Sheriff for 1685-6. He died in 1721. W.

(94) *Of Plasnewydd (Anglesey), in Mr. Wynne's List. W.

(95) *And of Brynkir. He married Catherine Fletcher, heiress of Treborth?, near Bangor, and secondly the relict of Sir Clobery Holte, Bart. of Aston, co. Warwick. W.

| Anno Dom. | Regnal Year. | Name. | Appointed. |
|---|---|---|---|
| 1726 | 12 & 13 | Humphry Roberts, of Bryn-y-Neuodd, Esq. (96) . . . . . | 13 Jan. |
| 1726— 7 | 13 | Hugh Winne, of Cromlech, Esq. . . | 29 Nov. |

## GEORGE II.

| Anno Dom. | Regnal Year. | Name. | Appointed. |
|---|---|---|---|
| 1727 | 1 | Hugh Winne, of Cromlech, Esq. . . | |
| 1727— 8 | 1 „ 2 | William Wynne, of Plas-yn-Llanvair, Esq. | 14 Dec. |
| 1728— 9 | 2 „ 3 | Izacheus Hughes, of Trevan, Esq. (97) . | 18 „ |
| 1729—30 | 3 „ 4 | Maurice Wynne, of Peny-bryn, Esq. . | 18 „ |
| 1730— 1 | 4 „ 5 | William Buttler, of Llysvaen, Esq. . . | 14 „ |
| 1731— 2 | 5 „ 6 | William Price, of Penmorva, Esq. (98) . | 9 „ |
| 1732— 3 | 6 „ 7 | John Wynne, of Glyn-llivon, Esq. (99) . | 14 „ |
| 1733— 4 | 7 „ 8 | John Griffith, of Caernarvon, Esq. . | 20 „ |
| 1734— 5 | 8 | Humphrey Meredith, of Pengwern, Esq. | 19 „ |
| 1735 | 8 „ 9 | William Wynne, of Wern, Esq. (100) . | 9 Jan. |
| 1735— 7 | 9 „ 10 | Humphrey Owen, of Bodidda, Esq. . | 18 Dec. |
| 1737— 8 | 10 „ 11 | George Devereux, of Saython, Esq. . | — Jan. |
| 1738 | 11 „ 12 | Humphrey Meredith, of Pengwern, Esq. | 12 „ |
| 1738— 9 | 12 „ 13 | John Lloyd, of Tyddynbychan, Esq. . | 21 Dec. |
| 1739—40 | 13 „ 14 | Rice Williams, of Glanyrafon, Esq. . | 27 „ |
| 1740— 2 | 14 „ 15 | John Owen, of Castellmai, Esq. . . | 24 „ |
| 1742— 3 | 15 „ 16 | Hugh Williams, of Pentir, Esq. . . | — Jan. |
| 1743— 4 | 16 „ 17 | Edward Philip Pugh, of Penrhyn, Esq.(101) | 19 „ |
| 1744— 5 | 17 „ 18 | William Brynker, the younger, of Brynker, Esq. (102) . . . . | 5 „ |
| 1745— 6 | 18 „ 19 | John Hoare, of Conway, Esq. . . | 10 „ |
| 1746— 7 | 19 „ 20 | William Thomas, of Coedhelen, Esq. . | 16 „ |
| 1747— 8 | 20 „ 21 | Robert Parry, of Mellionen, Esq. (103) . | 15 „ |
| 1748 | 21 | John Salusbury, of Bodvel, Esq. (104) . | 16 „ |
| 1748— 9 | 21 „ 22 | Christopher Buttler, of Llysffaen, Esq. . | 13 Feb. |

(96) See note 85.                                    (97) *Zaccheus.  W.

(98) *And of Rhiwlas, Merionethshire, Sheriff of that County in 1731.  He married Mary, daughter of Price, Viscount Hereford.  William Price was eldest son and successor of the Sheriff for 1710-11, by Martha, daughter of Robert Viscount Bulkeley,  W.

(99) *Afterwards Sir John Wynn, Bart., father of Thomas, first Lord Newborough.  W.

(100) *Only son and successor of the Sheriff for 1717-18.  Mr. Wynne died in 1766.  W.

(101) *His daughter and heiress married Col. Glynne Wynn, brother of the first Lord Newborough.  W.

(102) *He appears to have been "dangerously ill" in June, 1744.  W.

(103) *Ancestor to the late Richard Parry, Esq., of Llwynyn, near Ruthin.  W.

(104) *The celebrated Mrs. Piozzi was born at Bodvel, and her maiden name was Salusbury.  John Salusbury was probably her father,  W.

| Anno Dom. | Regnal Year. | Name. | Appointed. |
|---|---|---|---|
| 1749—50 | 22 & 23 | Charles Allenson, of Vaenol, Esq. (105) . | 11 Jan. |
| 1750 | 23 „ 24 | Owen Holland, of Conway, Esq. . . | 17 „ |
| 1750— 2 | 24 „ 25 | Charles Evans, of Vaenol, Esq. . . | 6 Dec. |
| 1752— 3 | 25 „ 26 | John Lloyd, of Berth-Aur, Esq. . . | 14 Jan. |
| 1753— 4 | 26 „ 27 | Owen Hughes, of Trefan, Esq. . . | „ |
| 1754— 5 | 27 „ 28 | Hugh Davies, of Caerhûn, Esq. . . | „ |
| 1755 | 28 | Richard Lloyd, of Tan-y-bryn, Esq. . | 29 „ |
| 1755— 6 | 28 „ 29 | William Stodart, of Deganwy, Esq. . | 6 Feb. |
| 1756 | 29 | William Owen, of Cleneney, Esq. (106) . | 27 Jan. |
| 1756— 7 | 29 „ 30 | Owen Wynn, of Penbryn, Esq. . . | 17 Feb. |
| 1757— 8 | 30 „ 31 | Robert Wynne, of Llanerch (Garthewin), Esq. . . . . . | Jan. |
| 1758— 9 | 31 „ 32 | Zacheus Jones, of Aber-y-Pwll, Esq. . | „ |
| 1759—60 | 32 „ 33 | William Smith, of Vaenol, Esq. (107) . | „ |
| 1760 | 33 „ 34 | Richard Lloyd, of Ty-newydd, Esq. . | Feb. |

## GEORGE III.

| Anno Dom. | Regnal Year. | Name. | Appointed. |
|---|---|---|---|
| 1760— 1 | 1 | Richard Lloyd, of Ty-newydd, Esq. . | |
| 1761— 2 | 1 „ 2 | Robert Wynn, of Varchwel, Esq. . . | 16 Feb. |
| 1762— 3 | 2 „ 3 | Hugh Hughes, of Bodvan, Esq. . . | 15 „ |
| 1763— 4 | 3 „ 4 | Love Parry, of Wernfawr, Esq. . . | 4 „ |
| 1764— 5 | 4 „ 5 | John Griffith, of Try-garn, Esq. . . | 10 „ |
| 1765— 6 | 5 „ 6 | John Griffith, of Cefn-Amwlch, Esq. . | 1 „ |
| 1766— 7 | 6 „ 7 | Hugh Williams, of Pentir, Esq. . . | 17 „ |
| 1767— 8 | 7 „ 8 | Edward Lloyd, of Llangelynin, Esq. . | 13 „ |
| 1768— 9 | 8 „ 9 | Robert Howel Vaughan, of Meillionydd, Esq. (108) . . . . . | 15 Jan. |
| 1769—70 | 9 „ 10 | Robert Godolphin Owen, of Cleneney, Esq. (109) . . . . . | 27 „ |
| 1770— 1 | 10 „ 11 | William Archer, of Llechan, Esq. . . | 9 Feb. |
| 1771— 2 | 11 „ 12 | Rice Thomas, of Coed Helen, Esq. . | 6 „ |
| 1772— 3 | 12 „ 13 | Richard Parry, of Meillionen, Esq. . | 17 „ |
| 1773— 4 | 13 „ 14 | Ralph Griffith, of Caerhûn, Esq. . . | 8 „ |

(105) *If I recollect, there is a monument to him in Bangor Cathedral.  W.

(106) *Grandfather, through her mother, to the late Mrs. Ormsby Gore, of Porkington, Clenenney, and Glynn. He married Mary, sister and sole heir at law, of Francis, the last Lord Godolphin, of Helston, and died in 1766. W.

(107) *See note 87.

(108) *Afterwards Sir Robert Howel Vaughan, Bart.  W.

(109) *Eldest son and successor to the Sheriff for 1756. Mr. R. G. Owen died without issue, and his large estates passed to his two sisters.  Margaret, the eldest, was wife of Owen Ormsby, Esq., of Willowbrook, co. Sligo, and Ellen, the youngest, died unmarried.  See note 128. W.

| Anno Dom. | Regnal Year. | Name. | Appointed. |
|---|---|---|---|
| 1774 | 14 & 15 | Thomas Assheton Smith, of Vaneol, Esq. (110) | 7 Feb. |
| 1774— 5 | 15 | Hugh Ellis, Esq. (111)      .      .      .      . | |
| 1775— 6 | 15 „ 16 | William Stodart, of Deganwy, Esq. .      . | 6 „ |
| 1776— 7 | 16 „ 17 | James Coytmore Pugh, of Penrhyn, Esq. . | 5 „ |
| 1777— 8 | 17 „ 18 | Hugh Griffith, of Brynodol, Esq.      .      . | 31 Jan. |
| 1778— 9 | 18 „ 19 | John Rowlands, of Bodadan, Esq.      .      . | 28 „ |
| 1779—80 | 19 „ 20 | Terence Prendergast, of Marle, Esq. (112) . | 1 Feb. |
| 1780— 1 | 20 „ 1 | Robert Lloyd, of Gwnnis, Esq.      .      . | 2 „ |
| 1781— 2 | 21 „ 2 | Edward Carreg, of Carreg, Esq.      .      . | 5 „ |
| 1782— 3 | 22 „ 3 | Richard Pennant, of Penrhyn, Esq. (113) . | 1 Jan. |
| 1783— 4 | 23 „ 4 | Thomas Assheton Smith, of Vaenol, Esq. | 10 Feb. |
| 1784— 5 | 24 „ 5 | Robert Wynne, of Llanerch, Esq. (114)   . | 11 „ |
| 1785— 6 | 25 „ 6 | John Jones, of Brynhir, Esq. .      .      . | 7 „ |
| 1786— 7 | 26 „ 7 | John Griffith, of Tryfan, Esq. .      .      . | 13 „ |
| 1787 | 27 | David Jones, of Cefn-Coed, Esq.      .      . | 12 „ |
| 1787— 8 | 27 „ 8 | John Lloyd, of Gesail Gyfarch, Esq.      . | 12 Mar. |
| 1788 | 28 | John Holland, of Teyrdan, Esq.      .      . | 8 Feb. |
| 1788— 9 | 28 „ 9 | William Peacock, of Ty-yn-y-Cae, Esq.   . | 27 „ |
| 1789—90 | 29 „ 30 | William Hughes, of Nantcall, Esq.      .      . | 29 April. |
| 1790— 1 | 30 „ 1 | Robert Lloyd, of Gesail Gyfarch, Esq.   . | 29 Jan. |
| 1791— 2 | 31 „ 2 | Thomas Lloyd, of Hendre-fenws, Esq.   . | 4 Feb. |
| 1792— 3 | 32 „ 3 | Edward Lloyd, of Ty-Mawr, Esq.      .      . | 3 „ |
| 1793 | 33 | Richard Lloyd, of Trallwyn, Esq. (115)   . | 6 „ |
| 1793— 4 | 33 „ 4 | William Owen, of Pencraig, Esq.      .      . | 16 „ |
| 1794— 5 | 34 „ 5 | Richard Lloyd, of Tref-beblig, Esq.      . | 5 „ |
| 1795 | 35 | William Lloyd, of Penmachno, Esq.      . | 11 „ |
| 1795— 6 | 35 „ 6 | William Jones, of Bodfawr, Esq.      .      . | 6 March. |
| 1796— 7 | 36 „ 7 | William John Lenthall, of Mainan, Esq. . | 5 Feb. |
| 1797— 8 | 37 „ 8 | Sir Edward Price Lloyd, of Pant-glas, Bart. (116)    .      .      .      .      .      . | 1 „ |

(110) Died during his year of office (in Nov. or Dec.).

(111) Hugh Ellis was Deputy to Thomas Assheton Smith, and acted as Sheriff upon the decease of the said T. A. Smith.   See Notes to the List of the M.P.'s for Caernarvon.

(112) *Second husband of Anne Lady Prendergast, widow of the Rt. Hon. Sir Thomas Prendergast, Bart., and daughter and sole heiress of Sir Griffith Williams, of Marle, Bart., who is said to have owned one-third of the county of Caernarvon.   Lady Prendergast, the heiress of these great estates, and of Park, Plasnewydd, Llwyn, &c., in Merionethshire, was Maid of Honour to Caroline, Queen of George II. ; but all the large possessions of her family were dissipated during her lifetime, and it is said that she wandered about as a common beggar, and died in the poor-house at Whitchurch, near Denbigh.   W.

(113) *Afterwards Lord Penrhyn.   W.          (114) *And of Garthewin, Denbighshire.   W.

(115) Died during his year of office, and was succeeded by William Owen.

(116) *Afterwards created Lord Mostyn.   W.

| Anno Dom. | Regnal Year. | Name. | Appointed. |
|---|---|---|---|
| 1798— 9 | 38 & 39 | Sir Thomas Mostyn, of Gloddaeth, Bart. (117) | 7 Feb. |
| 1799—1800 | 39 „ 40 | Evan Lloyd, of Porth-yr-Aur, Esq. . . | 1 „ |
| 1800 | 40 | Evan Prichard, of Tynewydd, Esq. . . | 5 „ |
| 1800 | 40 | Rice Edwards, of Porthyregwl, Esq. (118) . | 21 „ |
| 1800— 1 | 40 „ 41 | Rowland Jones, of Wergloddfawr (Broom Hall), Esq. (119) . . . . . | 14 March. |
| 1801— 2 | 41 „ 2 | William Hervey, of Bodvel, Esq. . . | 11 Feb. |
| 1802— 3 | 42 „ 3 | Robert William Wynne, of Llannerch, Esq. (120) . . . . . . | 10 „ |
| 1803— 4 | 43 „ 4 | Gwyllym Lloyd Wardle, of Wern-Fawr, Esq. (121) . . . . . . | 3 „ |
| 1804— 5 | 44 „ 5 | Owen Molineux Wynn, of Penmachno, Esq. (122) . . . . . . | 1 „ |
| 1805— 6 | 45 „ 6 | Richard Garnons, of Pantdu, Esq. (123) . | 6 „ |
| 1806— 7 | 46 „ 7 | William Williams, of Llangwstenin, Esq. . | 1 „ |
| 1807— 8 | 47 „ 8 | Hugh Rowlands, of Bodaden, Esq. . . | 4 „ |
| 1808— 9 | 48 „ 9 | Robert Thomas Carreg, of Carreg, Esq. . | 3 „ |
| 1809 | 49 | Thomas Parry Jones Parry, of Madryn, Esq. . . . . . . | 6 „ |
| 1809—10 | 49 „ 50 | William Griffith, of Bodegroes, Esq. . | 15 Mar. |
| 1810—11 | 50 „ 1 | Humphry Rowland Jones, of Ystymllyn, Esq. . . . . . . | 31 Jan. |
| 1811—12 | 51 „ 2 | Thomas Parry Jones Parry, of Madryn, Esq. . . . . . . | 8 Feb. |
| 1812 | 52 | The Honble. Peter Robert Drummond Burrel, of Gwydir (124) . . . | 24 Jan. |
| 1812—13 | 52 „ 3 | George Thomas Smith, of Pendyffryn, Esq. | 4 Mar. |
| 1813—14 | 53 „ 4 | John Griffith, of Llanfair, Esq. . . | 13 Feb. |
| 1814—15 | 54 „ 5 | Charles Wynne Griffith Wynne, of Cefn Amwlch, Esq. (125). . . . . | 4 „ |

(117) *The last Baronet of the Mostyn of Mostyn family. · He died in April, 1831. W.

(118) He died during his year of office.

(119) The sale of his valuable collection of objects of vertu, &c., after his death in 1850, will long be remembered.

(120) *Eldest son and successor of the Sheriff for 1784-5. W.

(121) *The celebrated Colonel Wardle ; famous for the charges which he brought against Frederick, Duke of York, for mal-administration in his office of Commander-in-Chief. W.

(122) *And of Pengwern, Merionethshire. W.

(123) *A gentleman very generally respected. He resided at Caernarvon and at Colomendy, near Mold. W.

(124) *Afterwards Lord Willoughby d'Eresby, and Lord Lieutenant for the County. W.

(125) *He afterwards represented the County in Parliament; and his son the Boroughs. W.

| Anno Dom. | Regnal Year. | Name. | Appointed. |
|---|---|---|---|
| 1815—16 | 55 & 56 | William Gryffyd Oakeley, of Bachysaint, Esq. (126) . . . . . . | 13 Feb. |
| 1816—17 | 56 „ 7 | Thomas Burrow, of Bennarth, Esq. . . | 12 „ |
| 1817 | 57 | Daniel Vawdrey, of Plasgwynnant, Esq. . | 12 „ |
| 1817—18 | 57 „ 8 | John Lloyd, of Trallwyn, Esq. . . | 1 Mar. |
| 1818—19 | 58 „ 9 | Thomas Jones, of Bryntirion, Esq. . . | 10 Feb. |
| 1819—20 | 59 „ 60 | George Hay Dawkins Pennant, of Penrhyn Castle, Esq. (127) . . . . . | 10 „ |

## GEORGE IV.

| | | | |
|---|---|---|---|
| 1820 | 1 | George Hay Dawkins Pennant, of Penrhyn Castle, Esq. . . . . | |
| 1820— 1 | 1 „ 2 | William Ormsby Gore, of Clenenney, Esq. (128) . . . . . . | 12 Feb. |
| 1821— 2 | 2 „ 3 | Joseph Huddart, of Brynkir, Esq. (129) . | 6 „ |
| 1822— 3 | 3 „ 4 | William Lloyd Caldecot, of the Cottage, Esq. | 4 „ |
| 1823— 4 | 4 „ 5 | William Turner, of Carreg-fawr, Esq. . | 31 Jan. |
| 1824— 5 | 5 „ 6 | Sir David Erskine, of Plas Isa, Bart. . | 31 „ |
| 1825— 6 | 6 „ 7 | Hugh Davies Griffith, of Caerhûn, Esq. . | 2 Feb. |
| 1826— 7 | 7 „ 8 | Kyffin John William Lenthall, of Maenan, Esq. . . . . . . | 30 Jan. |
| 1827— 8 | 8 „ 9 | William Glynn Griffith, of Bodegroes, Esq. | 5 Feb. |
| 1828— 9 | 9 „ 10 | Richard Watkin Price, of Bronygader, Esq. (130) . . . . . . | 13 „ |
| 1829 | 10 | Thomas Lloyd, of Glangwna, Esq. (131) . | 12 „ |
| 1829—30 | 10 „ 11 | Daniel Vawdrey, of Plasgwynant, Esq. . | 25 „ |
| 1830 | 11 | John Williams, of Bryntirion, Esq. . | 2 Feb. |

(126) *And of Tanybwlch, co. Merioneth ; died in Oct. 1835. W.

(127) *Succeeded by bequest to the great estates of Penrhyn, on the death of Susannah Anne, Lady Penrhyn, widow of the Sheriff for 1782-3. W.

(128) *He married Mary Jane, only child and heiress of Owen Ormsby, Esq., of Porkington in Shropshire, Clenenney, and Glynn ; and of Willowbrook, co. Sligo. Mr. Ormsby Gore represented in one Parliament the Caernarvonshire Boroughs, and was afterwards, for many years, one of the representatives for North Shropshire. He died in 1860. See Note 109. W.

(129) In some Records he is erroneously called John. He was knighted in 1821, during his year of office, when George IV. visited the county.

*He was purchaser of the ancient estates of Wern and Brynkir, in the parishes of Penmorva and Llanvihangel y Pennant. W.

In the Parliamentary Return for the Borough of Caernarvon, (dated 12 Jan., 1823), Sir Joseph Huddart, Knt., makes the same as Sheriff, but I cannot find any entry of his appointment for that date.

(130) *And of Rhiwlas, Merionethshire. W.

(131) Died during his year of office.

## WILLIAM IV.

| Anno Dom. | Regnal Year. | | Name. | Appointed. |
|---|---|---|---|---|
| 1830— 1 | 1 | | John Williams, of Bryntirion, Esq. . . | |
| 1831— 2 | 1 & 2 | | Rice Thomas, of Coedhelen, Esq. . . | 31 Jan. |
| 1832— 3 | 2 „ | 3 | John Rowlands, of Plastirion, Esq. . . | 6 Feb. |
| 1833— 4 | 3 „ | 4 | David Price Downes, of Hendre-rhys-gethin, Esq. . . . . . . | 4 „ |
| 1834— 5 | 4 „ | 5 | Richard Lloyd Edwards, of Nanhoron, Esq. (132) . . . . . | 3 „ |
| 1835— 6 | 5 „ | 6 | John Morgan, of Weeg, Esq. . . . | 7 „ |
| 1836— 7 | 6 „ | 7 | Thomas Parry Jones Parry, of Aber-du-nant, Esq. (133) . . . . | 3 „ |
| 1837 | 7 | | The Honble. Thomas Pryce Lloyd, of Plashen . . . . . . . | 28 Jan. |

## QUEEN VICTORIA.

| Anno Dom. | Regnal Year. | | Name. | Appointed. |
|---|---|---|---|---|
| 1837— 8 | 1 | | The Honble. Thomas Pryce Lloyd, of Plashen. (134) . . . . . | |
| 1838— 9 | 1 „ | 2 | Sir Richard Bulkeley Williams Bulkeley, of Plas-y-nant, Bart. (135) . . . | 1 Feb. |
| 1839—40 | 2 „ | 3 | John Williams, of Hendregadno, Esq. (136) | 4 „ |
| 1840— 1 | 3 „ | 4 | The Honble. Edward Mostyn Lloyd Mostyn, of Plas Hên. (137) . . . . | 29 Jan. |
| 1841— 2 | 4 „ | 5 | David White Griffith, of Hafodydd-Brithion, Esq. . . . . . . | 5 Feb. |
| 1842— 3 | 5 „ | 6 | John Griffith Watkins, of Plas Llanfair, Esq. . . . . . . . | 2 „ |
| 1843— 4 | 6 „ | 7 | David Jones, of Bodfan, Esq. . . . | 1 „ |
| 1844— 5 | 7 „ | 8 | John Price, of Garth y Glo, Esq. . . | 31 Jan. |
| 1845— 6 | 8 „ | 9 | „    „    „    „    „ (continued) | |
| 1846— 7 | 9 „ | 10 | Charles Henry Evans, of Pont-newydd, Esq. | 30 „ |

---

(132) *Present representative of one of the oldest families in this County.   W.

(133) *One of the younger sons of the Sheriff for 1811-12.   W.

(134) *Youngest son of Edward Pryce, first Lord Mostyn.   W.

(135) *Should be Sir R. B. Williams Bulkeley, and of Baronhill, Anglesey, inheritor of the ancient Baronetc of Williams of Penrhyn, and owner of the estates of the Bulkeley family, by the bequest of Thomas James, the seventh and last Viscount Bulkeley, his father's brother, half-blood.   W.

(136) Better known as of Tuhwntirbwlch, Portmadoc.

(137) *Now second Lord Mostyn, Lord Lieutenant of Merionethshire.   W.

| Anno Dom. | Regnal Year. | Name. | Appointed. |
|---|---|---|---|
| 1847— 8 | 10 & 11 | Thomas Wright, of Derwenfawr, Esq. | 4 Feb. |
| 1848— 9 | 11 „ 12 | George Augustus Huddart, of Brynkir, Esq. (138) | 11 „ |
| 1849—50 | 12 „ 13 | Samuel Owen Priestley, of Trefan, Esq. | 13 „ |
| 1850— 1 | 13 „ 14 | Isaac Walker, of Hendre-gadredd, Esq. | 5 „ |
| 1851— 2 | 14 „ 15 | John Williams, of Hafodyllan, Esq. | 11 „ |
| 1852 | 15 | Martin Williams, of Penamser, Esq. (139) | 2 „ |
| 1852— 3 | 15 „ 16 | George Hammond Whalley, of Plas Madoc, Ruabon, Esq. (140) | 5 Mar. |
| 1853— 4 | 16 „ 17 | Robert Vaughan Wynne Williams, of Llandudno, Esq. | 7 Feb. |
| 1854— 5 | 17 „ 18 | Thomas Love Duncombe Jones Parry, of Madryn, Esq. (141) | 30 Jan. |
| 1855— 6 | 18 „ 19 | Samuel Duckinfield Darbishire, of Pendyffryn, Esq. | 8 Feb. |
| 1856— 7 | 19 „ 20 | Lieutenant-Colonel John Macdonald, of Plas-ucha Dwygyfylchwy | 30 Jan. |
| 1857— 8 | 20 „ 1 | James Edwards, of Benarth, Esq., M.D. | 2 Feb. |
| 1858— 9 | 21 „ 2 | John Nanney, of Maesy-neuodd, Merionethshire, Esq. | 3 „ |
| 1859—60 | 22 „ 3 | John Lloyd Jones, of Broom Hall, Esq. | 2 „ |
| 1860— 1 | 23 „ 4 | John Whitehead Greaves, of Tanyrallt, Esq. | 23 Jan. |
| 1861— 2 | 24 „ 5 | Henry McKellar, of Sygun-fawr, Esq. | 4 Feb. |
| 1862— 3 | 25 „ 6 | David Williams, of Castle Deudraeth, Esq. (142) | 5 „ |
| 1863— 4 | 26 „ 7 | John Platt, of Bryn-y-neuodd, Esq. | 3 „ |
| 1864— 5 | 27 „ 8 | Griffith Humphreys Owen, of Ymwlch, Esq. | 3 „ |
| 1865— 6 | 28 „ 9 | Charles Millar, of Penrhos, Esq. | 4 „ |

(138) *Son and successor of the Sheriff for 1821-2.   W.

(139) *And of Bryngwyn, Montgomeryshire.   Was trustee of the Madocks estates in this county; and married Mary, youngest daughter of John Edward Madocks, Esq., of Fron iw, co. Denbigh, and niece of the well-known founder of Tremadoc.   W.

He was excused on the ground of non-residence and having no property within the county in which he had a beneficial interest.

(140) The well-known Member for Peterborough.

(141) *Grandson and inheritor of the estates of the Sheriff for 1811-12 ; eldest son and successor of the late General Sir Love Parry, K. H.   W.

Afterwards Member for the County.

(142) Sheriff of Merioneth, 1861-2, and Member for that County 1868-9.

| Anno Dom. | Regnal Year. | Name. | Appointed. |
|---|---|---|---|
| 1866— 7 | 29 & 30 | John Dicken Whitehead, of Glangwna, Esq. . . . . . . | 3 Feb. |
| 1867— 8 | 30 „ 1 | Abram Jones Williams, of Gelliwig, Esq. (143) | 2 „ |
| 1868— 9 | 31 „ 2 | Robert Sorton Parry, of Tan-y-Graig, Esq. | 30 Jan. |
| 1869—70 | 32 „ 3 | Rice William Thomas, of Coed Helen, Esq. (144) . . . . . . | 4 Feb. |
| 1870— 1 | 33 „ 4 | Hugh John Ellis Nanney, of Plas-hen, Esq. | 5 „ |
| 1871— 2 | 34 „ 5 | John Griffith Wynn Griffith, of Llanfair, Esq. | 8 „ |
| 1872— 3 | 35 „ 6 | Owen Evans, of Broom Hall, Esq. . . | 5 „ |

(143) Younger brother of Sheriff for 1862-63. Married (1853) Sarah, daughter of Lt.-Genl. Sir Love Parry, of Madryn.

(144) *Grand-nephew (his sister's grandson) and successor of Coedhelen to the Sheriff for 1831-2. W,

9 — 2

# SHERIFFS FOR THE COUNTY OF MERIONETH.

## EDWARD I.

| Anno Dom. | Regnal Year. | Name. | Appointed. |
|---|---|---|---|
| 1292— 3 | 21 | Robert de Staundon . . . . | 23 March. (1) |
| 1293— 4 | 22 | Robert Fitz Walter . . . . | |
| 1294— 5 | 23 | Robert de Staundon . . . . | |
| 1295— 6 | 24 | Robert de Eccleshale . . . . | |
| 1300— 1 | 29 | Griffin (Gruffydd) ap David . . . | |
| 1304— 5 | 33 | Robert de Eccleshale . . . | |
| 1306— 7 | 35 | Jevan ap Howel . . . . | |

## EDWARD II.

| | | | |
|---|---|---|---|
| 1307—10 | 1 | Jevan ap Howel (2) . . . | |
| 1310—13 | 4 | Griffin, son of William de la Pole . | 6 Dec. |
| 1313—14 | 7 | Robert de Eccleshale, or Egleshale . | 17 Sept. |
| 1314 | 8 | Griffin (Gruffydd) ap Rees . . . | 2 Aug. |
| 1316—17 | 10 | John Cam, (or John de Cam) (3) . . | |
| 1321 | 15 | Griffin (Gruffydd) ap Rees (4) . . | 16 Nov. |

## EDWARD III.

| | | | |
|---|---|---|---|
| 1327— | 1 | Griffin (Gruffydd) ap Rees . . . | |
| 1327— 8 | 2 | Edmund Haclut (Hakeluyt) . . . | |
| 1331 | 5 | Richard de Holand . . . . | 29 Feb. |
| 1332 | 6 | Robert de Middleton . . . . | 28 Jan. |

---

(1) "De concedendo Roberto de Staundon officium Vicecomitis Comitatus Merioneth, pro quo £40 singulis annis percipiet ad Scaccarium regis de Kaernarvan."—Ayloffe's Rot. Wall. p. 90.

(2) Eccleshale was Sheriff during the time Jevan ap Howel was in office. *(Where two Sheriffs occur at the same time, I suspect that one was sometimes "Farmer" of the office). Howel was of Evioneth, and of the tribe of Collwyn, ancestor to many of the principal families of Caernarvonshire, amongst them the Wynns of Bodvean, now Lord Newborough. W.

(3) Griffith ap Rees and John Cam were Sheriffs at the same time.

(4) *In a Return to a Precept of 20 Edw. II. (1326-7), for the election of Representatives in Parliament for the County of Merioneth—which precept is addressed to the Sheriff—he is styled Griffith ap Rees, Knight. I have little doubt that this was the celebrated Sir Griffith Lloyd, of Dinorwig, whose father's name was Rees. Sir Griffith Lloyd brought to Edw. I. the intelligence of Queen Eleanor's accouchement at Caernarvon   W.

| Anno Dom. | Regnal Year. | Name. | Appointed. |
|---|---|---|---|
| 1332 | 6 | Walter de Manny (5) . . . . . | 29 Dec. |
| 1347— | 21— | Mewrig Maelan . . . . |  |

Griffith ap Llewelin ap Kenric    ⎫
  of Corsygedol (6)   .  .   ⎪
Eignion ap Ithel  .   .   .   ⎬ temp. Edw. III.
Eignion ap Griffith ap Llew   ⎪ and Ric. II.
  ap Kenric  .   .   .   ⎪
Richard Mascy (7) .   .   .  ⎭

## RICHARD II.

| | | | |
|---|---|---|---|
| 1387— 8 | 11—12 | Richard Balden (8) . . . . . |  |
| 1391— 2 | 15 | Viviam, or Viviann, le Colyer, jun. (9) . | 28 Oct. |

## HENRY IV.

| | | | |
|---|---|---|---|
| ?1399— | 1 | Eignion ap Ithel ap Gwrgenu (10) . . |  |

## HENRY V.

| | | | |
|---|---|---|---|
| 1413—20 | 1 | Thomas Strange. (11) . . . . | 6 July. |

## HENRY VI.

| | | | |
|---|---|---|---|
| 1423—30 | 1 | Robert Orell . . . . . | 6 March. |
| 1430— 2 | 8 | Thomas Dankynson . . . . | 27 „ |
| 1432—60 ? | 11 | Thomas Burneby ⎫ . . . . . | 25 Dec. |
| 1434— 5 |  | John Hampton (12) ⎬ |  |
| 1453—60 ? | 31 | Thomas Parker ⎭ . . . . | 5 June. |

(5) He was knighted, and created a Baron during his tenure of office; also a Knight of the Garter; died 1372. His under-Sheriff was Eignion ap Griffith ap Llewelyn ap Ken, afterwards Sheriff of the county. It is, however, somewhat doubtful whether he was Sheriff. He accounted as such but may have done so for his father.

(6) *At Mich. 16 Ric. II., Eignion ap Gruffydd ap Llewelyn makes a payment of viijˢ· viijᵈ·, which, in the Roll, appears "de arreragüs vicecomitis Co."—Roll at Peniarth. Griffith ap Llewellyn ap Kenric was ancestor to the Vaughans of Corsygedol, and in the 15th degree to W. W. E. Wynne, Esq., of Peniarth, both in a direct line. He was great-grandson to Osborn, called in the Welsh pedigrees "Osborn Wyddel," a cadet of the great house of the Geraldines of Desmond. This Osborn settled in Merionethshire about the middle of the 13th century, and was assessed in the parish of Llanaber, towards the tax of a Fifteenth, levied in Wales in 1293 or 1294. Griffith ap Llewelyn ap Kenric was Sheriff or "Farmer" of the Shrievalty in 46 Edw. III., and in a Roll of Ministers' accounts for the year ending at Mich. 1392, he is referred to as "modo Vicecomes." He died about 1399. W.

(7) *Called also "Dycon le Mascy." W.

(8) This name is entered on a Roll of Accounts for the 11th year of Ric. II.

(9) *Of Harlech. He was appointed Sheriff 28th October, 1391; his Shrievalty to date from the preceding Michaelmas. W.

(10) *Of Rhiwaedog, Esquire of the Body to John of Gaunt, Duke of Lancaster. He died Sheriff for the County between 25th January and 29th September, 1400. W.

(11) There is no doubt that he continued to be Sheriff until the end of the reign of Hen. V.

(12) In the Ministers' Accounts, where Hampton's name occurs, blanks were left for the date in the Patent ap-

## EDWARD IV.

| Anno Dom. | Regnal Year. | Name. | Appointed. |
|---|---|---|---|
| 1461—83 | 1—23 | Roger Kenaston, or Kynaston, Esq. (13) . | 23 Sept. |

## RICHARD III.

| | | | |
|---|---|---|---|
| 1483— 5 | 1— 3 | Roger Kynaston, Esq. . . . . | 5 March. |

## HENRY VII.

| | | | |
|---|---|---|---|
| 1485 | 1 | Roger Kynaston, Esq. . . . . | |
| 1485—1509 | 1—24 | Peter (or Piers) Stanley, Esq. . . . | 23 Sept. |

## HENRY VIII.

| | | | |
|---|---|---|---|
| 1509—20 | 1—12 | Peter (or Piers) Stanley, Esq. . . . | |
| 1520— 8 | 12—20 | John Scudamore, Esq. (14) . . . | 5 July. |
| 1528—36 | 20—28 | William Brereton, Esq. ⎱ (15) . . | 22 June. |
| 1533—40 | 25—32 | John Puleston, Esq. . ⎰ . . | 25 May. |
| 1540— 1 | 32—33 | Elie [Ellis] ap Morise, of Cleneney, Esq. (16) | 18 Nov. |
| 1541— 2 | 33—34 | Jaynkyn [Jenkin] Vaughan, Esq. (17) . | 23 ,, |
| 1542— 3 | 34—35 | John Powys, Esq. (18) . . . . | 22 ,, |
| 1543— 4 | 35—36 | Robert Salysburye, Esq. (19) . . . | 23 ,, |
| 1544— 5 | 36—37 | Edward Stanley, Esq. (20) . . . | 16 ,, |
| 1545— 7 | 37—38 | Lewis Owen, Esq. . . . . . | 16 ,, |

## EDWARD VI.

| | | | |
|---|---|---|---|
| 1547 | 1 | Richard Mitton, or Mytton, Esq. (21) . | 29 Jan. |
| 1547— 8 | 1 ,, 2 | Rees Vaughan, of Corsygedol, Esq. (22) . | 27 Nov. |
| 1548— 9 | 2 ,, 3 | Robert Salesbury, Esq. . . . . | 3 Dec. |

---

pointing him ; and in the Accounts of Burneby to 38 Hen. VI. the Patent of 25th Dec., 11 Hen. VI. is always recited : Burneby and Hampton must therefore have been Sheriffs at the same time. Again, in the Chamberlain's Account for North Wales, 38 Hen. VI., No 49, I find Burneby and Parker appointed by Letters Patent dated 5th June, 31 Hen. VI., for life.

(13) *Of Hordley, Shropshire, afterwards knighted. He was owner of Vegla, in the parish of Llangelynin. W.
      Was appointed Constable of Harleigh Castle 15th Dec., 1 Ric. III., and was confirmed in the offices of Sheriff and Escheator for Merioneth (granted to him for life by Edward IV.), 5th March, 1 Ric. III.

(14) *Humphrey ap Howel of Ynysmaengwyn, witnesses a Deed as Sheriff, dated 6th Sept., 13 Hen. VIII. He was probably "farmer" of the office under John Scudamore. W.

(15) Brereton and Puleston served the office of Sheriff cojointly, from the 25 May, 25—28 Hen. VIII.

(16) *Ancestor to the Maurices of that place. See 1590-1. W.

(17) *Of Caethle, in the parish of Towyn. W.

(18) *Of Kymmer, now Vaner, grantee or lessee of the dissolved monastery there. W.

(19) *Of Rûg. W.                                                   (20) *Of Harlech. W.

(21) *Lord of the Lordship or Manor of Mowddwy. W.

(22) *Fifth in lineal descent from Griffith ap Llewelyn ap Kenric. See Note 6 W.

| Anno Dom. | Regnal Year. | | Name. | Appointed. |
|---|---|---|---|---|
| 1549—50 | 3 & 4 | | John David Lloid, of Ceiswyn, Esq. | 12 Nov. |
| 1550— 1 | 4 „ 5 | | John ap Howell [ap Hugh], Esq. (23) | 11 „ |
| 1551— 2 | 5 „ 6 | | Ellis Price, Esq. (24) | 11 „ |
| 1552— 3 | 6 „ 7 | | Edward Stanley, Esq. | |

## MARY, AND PHILIP AND MARY.

| | | | | |
|---|---|---|---|---|
| 1553 | 1 | | Edward Stanley, Esq. | 6 July. |
| 1553— 4 | 1 & 1 & 2 | } | Richard Mitton, Esq. | |
| 1554— 5 | 1 „ 2 | { Rice Vaughan, Esq. } (25) | | |
| 1555 | 2 „ 3 | { Lewis Owen, Esq. | | |
| 1555— 6 | 2 „ 3 | } Dr. Ellis Price | 14 Nov. |
| | 3 „ 4 | | | |
| 1556— 7 | 3 „ 4 | } Rice Vaughan of Corsygedol, Esq. | |
| | 4 „ 5 | | | |
| 1557— 8 | 4 „ 5 | } John David Lloid, Esq. (26) | 16 „ |
| | 5 „ 6 | | | |

## ELIZABETH.

| | | | | |
|---|---|---|---|---|
| ?1558— 9 | 1 | | John Salisbury, Esq. (27) | |
| 1559—60 | 1 „ 2 | | Edward Stanley, Esq. | 9 „ |
| 1560— 1 | 2 „ 3 | | Hugh Puleston, Esq. | |
| 1561— 2 | 3 „ 4 | | John David Lloid, Esq. | 8 „ |
| 1562— 3 | 4 „ 5 | | Griffith Glynne, of Pwllheli, Esq. (28) | |
| 1563— 4 | 5 „ 6 | | Ellis Price, Esq. | 8 „ |
| 1564— 5 | 6 „ 7 | | Ellis ap William Lloid, of Rhiwaedog, Esq. | |
| 1565— 6 | 7 „ 8 | | John Lewis Owen, Esq. (29) | |
| 1566— 7 | 8 „ 9 | | Griffith Glynne, Esq. | |
| 1567— 8 | 9 „ 10 | | Ellis Price, Esq. | |
| 1568— 9 | 10 „ 11 | | Peter Salisbury, Esq. | |
| 1569—70 | 11 „ 12 | | Owen Wynne, Esq. | |

(23) *John ap Hugh ap Jevan, of Mathavarn, co. Montgomery. He is party, as Sheriff, to an original receipt for money paid to the King's use, upon 10 May, 5 Edw. VI. W.

(24) *Of Plas Iolin, co. Denbigh; afterwards an agent or *tool* of the famous Robert Dudley, Earl of Leicester. W.

(25) *Rees Vaughan; but in October, Lewis Owen was certainly Sheriff, in which year and month he was murdered. W.

(26) *Of Ceiswyn, ? son-in-law of Lewis Owen, and who defended him when attacked by banditti at the time of his murder. There is a deed at Peniarth, of John David Lloyd as Sheriff. W.

(27) *Of Rûg. W.

(28) The Griffiths of Bodegroes were his representatives.

(29) *Of Llwyn, near Dolgelly, eldest son of Lewis Owen, Esq., the Sheriff murdered in 1555. W.

| Anno Dom. | Regnal Year. | Name | Appointed. |
|---|---|---|---|
| 1570— 1 | 12 & 13 | John Yerworth, of Trefrysg, Esq. (30) | |
| 1571— 2 | 13 „ 14 | John Gwynne ap Ellis, Esq. | |
| 1572— 3 | 14 „ 15 | John Lewis Owen, Esq. | |
| 1573— 4 | 15 „ 16 | Dr. Ellis Price | |
| 1574— 5 | 16 „ 17 | Roland ap Hugh, Esq. (31) | |
| 1575— 6 | 17 „ 18 | Evan Lloyd David ap John, of Nantmynach, near Mallwyd, Esq. | |
| 1576— 7 | 18 „ 19 | John Winne ap Cadwallader, of Rhiwlas, Esq. | |
| 1577— 8 | 19 „ 20 | John Salisbury of Rug, Esq. | |
| 1578— 9 | 20 „ 1 | Ellis Price, Esq. | |
| 1579—80 | 21 „ 2 | John Price, of Gogerddan, Esq. | |
| 1580— 1 | 22 „ 3 | Jevan Lloyde, of Yale, Esq. | 30 Nov. |
| 1581— 2 | 23 „ 4 | Rece Hughes, Esq. (32) | 21 „ |
| 1582— 3 | 24 „ 5 | Richard ap Hugh ap Evan, Esq. | |
| 1583— 4 | 25 „ 6 | Peter Salisbury, of Denbigh, Esq. | |
| 1584— 5 | 26 „ 7 | Dr. Ellis Price (33) | 9 Dec. |
| 1585— 6 | 27 „ 8 | John Wynne ap Cadwallader, Esq. (34) | 22 Nov. |
| 1586— 7 | 28 „ 9 | Hugh Nanney, Esq. | 14 „ |
| 1587— 8 | 30 „ 1 | Griffith Vaughan, of Corsygedol, Esq. (35) | 4 „ |
| 1588— 9 | 31 „ 2 | John Wynne, of Gwydir, Esq. | |
| 1589—90 | 32 „ 3 | John Lewys Owen, of Llwyn, Esq. | 11 „ |
| 1590— 1 | 33 „ 4 | William Morrice ap Ellis of Cleneny, Esq. (36) | 24 Nov. |
| 1591— 2 | 34 „ 5 | Griffith Wynne, Esq. | |
| 1592— 3 | 35 „ 6 | Cadwalader Price, Esq. (37) | 4 Dec. |
| 1593— 4 | 36 „ 7 | John Vaughan, Esq. (38) | 26 Nov. |

(30) *Now called Prysg, in the parish of Llanuwchllyn. This place passed by marriage to the Vaughans of Caergai. W.

(31) *Roland Pughe, the elder, of Mathavarn?, Esq. W.

(32) *Of Maesypandy. W.

(33) In the Land Revenue Minister's Account, Dr. Ellis Price is mentioned as Sheriff in the 25th and 26th Eliz., and Peter Salisbury for the 26th and 27th Eliz., which must be an error, for Dr. Price made the Parliamentary Return, dated 10 Nov., 27 Elizabeth.

(34) *Of Rhiwlas. See 1576-7. W.               (35) See Note 22.

(36) *Afterwards Sir William Maurice, Knight. He died 10th Aug. 1622, having been Member for the County of Caernarvon, and for Beaumaris. He was a personal friend of King James I., and at Sir William Maurice's suggestion that king assumed the title of *King of Great Britain.* Orig. Letter at Porkington, from his sister, Mrs. Anne Wynn Brinker. See also Cals. State Papers, Dom. 1603-10, p. 338, published by authority of the Master of the Rolls. The tomb of this Sheriff is extant in Penmorfa Churchyard, in good preservation. W.

(37) *Eldest son and successor of the Sheriff for 1576-7 and 1585-6. W.

(38) *Of Caethley. This ancient family became extinct upon the death of the late John Vaughan, Esq., of Penmaen Dovey, some few years since. W.

| Anno Dom. | Regnal Year. | Name. | Appointed. |
|---|---|---|---|
| 1594— 5 | 37 & 38 | Morrice Lewis, of Festiniog, Esq. | 18 Nov. |
| 1595— 6 | 38 „ 9 | Robert Lloyd, of Rhiwgoch, Esq. | 27 „ |
| 1596— 7 | 39 „ 40 | John Conway, Esq. | 22 „ |
| 1597— 8 | 40 „ 1 | Lewis Owen, of Llwyn Dolgelly, Esq. | 25 „ |
| 1598— 9 | 41 „ 2 | Mathew Herbert, Esq. (39) | 28 „ |
| 1599—1600 | 42 „ 3 | Pierce Salesbury, Esq. | 2 Dec. |
| 1600— 1 | 43 „ 4 | John Wynne, of Gwydir, Esq. (40) | 24 Nov. |
| 1601— 2 | 44 „ 5 | Robert Lloyd, of Rhiwgoch, Esq. | 2 Dec. |
| 1602— 3 | 45 | Griffith Vaughan, of Gorsygedol, Esq. | 7 „ |

## JAMES I.

| | | | |
|---|---|---|---|
| 1603 | 1 | Griffith Vaughan, of Gorsygedol, Esq. | |
| 1603— 4 | 1 & 2 | Thomas Vaughan, of Pantyglas, Esq. | 1 Dec. |
| 1604— 5 | 2 „ 3 | Thomas Needham, Esq. | 5 Nov. |
| 1605— 6 | 3 „ 4 | Sir William Morrice (or Maurice), Knt. | |
| 1606— 7 | 4 „ 5 | James Price, of Ynnysmaengwyn, Esq. (afterwards Sir James) (41) | 17 „ |
| 1607— 8 | 5 „ 6 | Edeneved [or Ednyfed] Griffith, of Gwydgwian, Esq. | |
| 1608— 9 | 6 „ 7 | John Price, of Rhiwlas, Esq. (42). | 10 „ |
| 1609—10 | 7 „ 8 | Mathew Herbert, Esq. (43) | |
| 1610—11 | 8 „ 9 | William Lewis Anwil, of Park, Esq. | |
| 1611—12 | 9 „ 10 | John Wynn, of Llanvrothen, Esq. [Sir J. Wynn, of Gwydir] | 12 „ |
| 1612—13 | 10 „ 11 | John Lloyde, of Vaynol, Flintshire, Esq. (44) | 16 „ |
| 1613—14 | 11 „ 12 | John Vaughan, of Caergai, Esq. | |
| 1614—15 | 12 „ 13 | Robert Lloyde, Esq. | |
| 1615—16 | 13 „ 14 | John Lloyde, of Rhiwaedog, Esq. | |
| 1616—17 | 14 „ 15 | Lewis Gwynne, Esq. (45) | |
| 1617—18 | 15 „ 16 | John Lewes, of Festiniog, Esq. | |

(39) *Of Dolgeog, co. Montgomery.  W.

(40) *Afterwards Sir John Wynn, of Gwydir, Bart., the Historian of the Gwydir family.  He was created a Baronet in 1611, and died in 1626-7.  W.

(41) *He obtained the Ynysmaengwyn estate by his marriage with the eldest daughter and heiress of Humphrey Wynne, Esq., of that place, lineally descended from Griffith ap Llewelyn ap Kenric (see Note 6), and died in 1642 or 1643.  His portrait now remains at Ynysmaengwyn.  He was a younger son of the house of Pryse, of Gogerthan, co. Cardigan.  W.

(42) *Eldest son and successor of the Sheriff for 1592-3.  W.          (43) *Of Dolgeog.  W.

(44) *Registrar of St. Asaph.  His daughter and heiress conveyed Vaynol by marriage to the Prices of Rhiwlas.  W.

(45) *Of Dolaugwyn, brother to Humphrey Wynn, of Ynysmaengwyn, Esq.  (See Note 41.)  W.

| Anno Dom. | Regnal Year. | Name. | Appointed. |
|---|---|---|---|
| 1618 | 16 | William Wynne, of Glyn, Esq. (46) | |
| 1618—19 | 16 & 17 | Humfrey Hughes, of Gwerclas, Esq. | 9 Nov. |
| 1619—20 | 17 „ 18 | Sir James Pryse, of Ynysymayngwyn, Knt. | |
| 1620— 1 | 18 „ 19 | John Vaughan, of Caergai, Esq. | |
| 1621— 2 | 19 „ 20 | John Vaughan, of Caethley, Esq. | |
| 1622— 3 | 20 „ 1 | Thomas Lloyd, of Nantfreyer, Esq. | |
| 1623— 4 | 21 „ 2 | William Lewis Anwyl, Esq. (47) | |
| 1624— 5 | 22 „ 3 | Robert Lloyd, of Rhiwgoch, Esq. | |

## CHARLES I.

| | | | |
|---|---|---|---|
| 1625 | 1 | Robert Lloyd, of Rhiwgoch, Esq. | |
| ?1625 | 1 | William Vaughan, Esq. | |
| 1625— 6 | 1 & 2 | Rowland Pughe, Esq. (48) | |
| 1626— 7 | 2 „ 3 | Hugh Nanney, Esq. (49) | |
| 1627— 8 | 3 „ 4 | Pers [Pierce] Lloyd, of Ddol, Esq. | |
| 1628— 9 | 4 „ 5 | William Oxwicke, Esq. (50) | |
| 1629—30 | 5 „ 6 | Henry Price, of Taltreuddyn, Esq. | |
| 1630— 1 | 6 „ 7 | Robert Wynne, Esq. | |
| 1631— 2 | 7 „ 8 | John Owen, of Cleneney, Esq., (afterwards Sir John) (51) | |
| 1632— 3 | 8 „ 9 | Edmund Mericke, of Ucheldre, Esq. | |
| 1633— 4 | 9 „ 10 | Lewis Nanney, of Maes-y-pandy, Esq. | |
| 1634— 5 | 10 „ 11 | Evan Evans, of Tanybwlch, Esq. | |
| 1635— 6 | 11 „ 12 | Richard Vaughan, Esq. | |
| 1636 | 12 | John Lloyde, of Rhiwedog, Esq. | |
| 1636— 7 | 12 „ 13 | William Wynne, of Glynne, Esq. | |
| 1637— 8 | 13 „ 14 | Hugh Nanney, of Nanney, Esq. | |
| 1638— 9 | 14 „ 15 | Griffith Lloyd, Esq. (52) | |
| 1639—40 | 15 „ 16 | Thomas Phillips, Esq. | |
| 1640— 1 | 16 „ 17 | { Lewis Anwyl, Esq. (53) <br> { Griffith Nanney, Esq. (54) | |
| 1641— 2 | 17 „ 18 | John Lloyd, Esq. | |

(46) *William Wynne, of Glynn, Esq., eighth in lineal descent from Griffith ap Llewelyn ap Kenric. See Note 6. W.

(47) *Of Park ; died about 1642. W.　　　　(48) *Of Mathavarn, co. Montgomery. W.

(49) *Of Nanney. W.　　　　(50) *Of Cefn'rowen, parish of Dolgelley. W.

(51) *The celebrated Royalist. He was grandson of Sir William Maurice, Knt., and eventually successor to his large estates. See Note 36. W.

(52) *Of Maesyneuadd. His daughter and heiress married Maurice Wynne, second son of William Wynne, of Glynn, Esq. W.

(53) *Of Park and Cemmes, co. Montgomery. W.　　　　(54) *Of Nanney. W.

| Anno Dom. | Regnal Year. | Name. | Appointed. |
|---|---|---|---|
| 1642 | 18 | Griffith Nanney, Esq. | |
| 1642— 3 | 18 & 19 | Rowland Vaughan, Esq. (55) | |
| 1643— 4 | 19 „ 20 | John Morgan, Esq. (56) | |
| 1644— 5 | 20 „ 1 | William Owen, Esq. (57) | |
| 1645— 6 | 21 „ 2 | [No Sheriff appointed] | |
| 1646— 7 | 22 „ 3 | Lewis Owen, of Peniarth, Esq. | |
| 1647— 8 | 23 „ 4 | Owen Salisbury, Esq. (58) | |
| 1648— 9 | 24 | Morris Williams, of Hafodgarregog, Esq. | |

## COMMONWEALTH & CHARLES II.

| | | | |
|---|---|---|---|
| 1649 | | Morris Williams, of Hafodgarregog, Esq. | |
| 1650 | | Robert Anwil, of Park, Esq. | 13 Feb. |
| 1650— 1 | | Maurice Wynn, of Crogen, Esq. | |
| 1651— 2 | | John Lloyd, of Maesypandy, Esq. | |
| 1652— 3 | | Lewis Lloyd, of Rhiwedog, Esq. | |
| 1653— 4 | | Morris Lewis, Esq. (59) | |
| 1654— 5 | | William Vaughan, Esq. | |
| 1655— 6 | | John Anwyl, of Llanfendigaid, Esq. | |
| 1656— 7 | | Robert Wynne, of Sylfaen, Esq. (60) | |
| 1657— 8 | | Howel Vaughan, of Glanllyn, Esq. | |
| 1658— 9 | | Richard Anwyl, of Park, Esq. | |
| 1659—60 | | [Same Sheriff probably continued. No new appointment.] | |
| 1660— 1 | 12 & 13 | Humfrey Hughes, of Gwerclas, Esq. | |
| 1661— 2 | 13 „ 14 | William Salisbury, Esq. (61) | |
| 1662— 3 | 14 „ 15 | Roger Mostyn, of Dolycorsllwyn, Esq. | |
| 1663— 4 | 15 „ 16 | John Wynne, of Cwmmine, Esq. | |
| 1664— 5 | 16 „ 17 | Morris Williams, of Hafodgarregog, Esq. | |
| 1665— 6 | 17 „ 18 | Lewis Lloyd, Esq. (62) | 12 Nov. |
| 1666— 7 | 18 „ 19 | John Lloyd, of Maesypandy, Esq. | 7 „ |
| 1667— 8 | 19 „ 20 | Richard Winne, of Branas, Esq. | 6 „ |
| 1668— 9 | 20 „ 1 | Robert Winne, of Glyn, Esq. | 6 „ |
| 1669 | 21 | Charles Kyffin, of Caecoch, Esq. | 8 „ |
| 1669—70 | 21 „ 2 | John Vaughan, Esq. | 24 „ |

(55) *Of Caergai, a Welsh poet of some eminence.  W.

(56) *Of Gelli Iorwerth, parish of Trawsfynydd.  W.

(57) *Of Porkington, Shropshire, the gallant defender of Harlech Castle, for King Charles I., and younger brother of the loyal Sir John Owen, Knt.  W.

(58) *Of Rûg.  W.         (59) *Of Pengwern, Festiniog.  W.

(60) *Afterwards of Glyn, eldest son and successor of the Sheriff for 1618 and 1636-7.  W.

(61) *Of Rûg.  W.         (62) *Of Rhiwaedog.  W.

| Anno Dom. | Regnal Year. | Name. | Appointed. |
|---|---|---|---|
| 1670— 1 | 22 & 23 | Morris Wynne, of Moelyglo, Esq. (63)   . | 5 Nov. |
| 1671— 2 | 23 „ 4 | Howell Vaughan, of Vanner, Esq. (64)   . | 6 „ |
| 1672— 3 | 24 „ 5 | Nathaniel Jones, of Hendwr.   .   .   . | 7 „ |
| 1673— 4 | 25 „ 6 | Lewis Lewis of Penmaen, Esq.   .   . | 10 „ |
| 1674— 5 | 26 „ 7 | ⌠ Owen Wynne, of Glyn, Esq. (65) .   . ⌡ Hugh Tudyr, of Egryn, Esq.   .   . | 18 „ |
| 1675— 6 | 27 „ 8 | Sir John Winne, Knt. and Bart. (66) .   . | 11 „ |
| 1676— 7 | 28 „ 9 | Griffith Vaughan, Esq.   .   .   .   . | 9 „ |
| 1677— 8 | 29 „ 30 | John Nanney, of Llanfendigaid, Esq. | 15 „ |
| 1678— 9 | 30 „ 1 | Robert Wynne, of Maesyneuadd, Esq. (67) | — |
| 1679—80 | 31 „ 2 | Richard Nanney, of Cefn-deuddwr, Esq.(68) | 13 „ |
| 1680— 1 | 32 „ 3 | William Vaughan, of Caergai, Esq.   . | 4 „ |
| 1681 | 33 | Edmund Meyricke, Esq. (69)   .   .   . | |
| 1681— 2 | 33 „ 4 | William Vaughan, Esq.   .   .   .   . | 16 „ |
| 1682— 3 | 34 „ 5 | Vincent Corbet, of Ynysymaengwyn, Esq. | 22 „ |
| 1683 | 35 | Robert Pew (or Pugh), Esq.   .   .   . | 19 „ |
| 1683— 4 | 35 „ 6 | Anthony Thomas, of Hendre, Esq.   . | 17 Dec. |
| 1684— 5 | 36 „ 7 | Maurice Jones, of Hendwr, Esq.   .   . | 24 Nov. |

## JAMES II.

| 1685 | 1 | Lewis Lewis, of Penmaen, Esq.   .   . | |
| 1685— 6 | 1 & 2 | Richard Poole, of Cae-nest, Esq.   .   . | 26 Nov. |
| 1686— 7 | 2 „ 3 | Richard Mitton, Esq.   .   .   .   . | 25 „ |
| 1687— 8 | 3 | John Jones, of Uchlawrcoed, Esq. (70)   . | 29 Dec. |
| 1688 | 3 „ 4 | Sir Robert Owen, Knt. (71)   .   .   . | 5 Jan. |
| 1688 | 4 | Charles Hughes, of Gwerclas, Esq.   . | 15 Nov. |

## WILLIAM AND MARY.

| 1688— 9 | 1 | Charles Hughes, of Gwerclas, Esq.   . | |

(63) *Second son of the Sheriff for 1618 and 1636-7.  W.

(64) *Eldest son and successor of Robert Vaughan, of Hengwrt, Esq., the well known Merionethshire Antiquary.  W.

(65) *Eldest son and successor of the Sheriff for 1656-7, and 1668-9.  He died in Dec., 1682.  W.

(66) *Sir John Wynn, of Watstay, which name he altered to Wynnstay.  He died in 1719, aged 91.  W. See notes to the list of M.P.'s for Caernarvon.

(67) *Eldest son and successor to the Sheriff for 1670-1.  W.

(68) In the London Gazette for 1679, he is incorrectly called William Narmey.

(69) *Of Ucheldref.  W.

(70) *Eldest son and successor of Colonel John Jones, the Regicide.  W.

(71) *Of Glyn and Porkington, Shropshire.  He obtained Glynn by his marriage with Margaret, eldest daughter and heiress of Owen Wynne, of Glyn, Esq.  See note 65.  There are at Porkington two curious letters of proposal from him to the heiress of Glynn, and copies of them at Peniarth.  It appears that it might have been said of him, " the course of true love did not run smoothly."  W.

| Anno Dom. | Regnal Year. | Name. | Appointed. |
|---|---|---|---|
| 1689 | I | Griffith Nanney, Esq. | 16 March. |
| 1689 | I | Charles Hughes, of Gwerclas, Esq. | 10 April. |
| 1689 | I | Sir Roger Meredith, of Stansty, Bart. | 14 Nov. |
| 1689—90 | 1 & 2 | John Jones, of Mowddwy, Esq. | 24 „ |
| 1690— 1 | 2 „ 3 | John Grosvenor, of Cwmdady, Esq. | 27 „ |
| 1691 | 3 | Hugh Nanney, of Nannau. | — „ |
| 1691— 2 | 3 | Oliver Thomas, of Bala, Esq. | 21 Dec. |
| 1692 | 3 „ 4 | Thomas Owen, of Llyn-lloed, Montgomeryshire, Esq. (72) | 11 Feb. |
| 1692— 3 | 4 „ 5 | Owen Wynne, of Pengwern, Festiniog, Esq. | 17 Nov. |
| 1693 | 5 „ 6 | Owen Wynne, Esq. | 16 „ |
| 1694 | 6 | William Anwyl, of Dolfriog, Esq. | ——— |
| 1694 | 6 | Richard Owen, of Peniarth, Esq. (73) | ——— |

## WILLIAM III.

| | | | |
|---|---|---|---|
| 1694— 5 | 6 & 7 | Richard Owen, of Peniarth, Esq. | |
| 1695— 6 | 7 „ 8 | John Lloyd, of Aberllefeni, Esq. | 5 Dec. |
| 1696— 7 | 8 „ 9 | Howell Vaughan, of Vanner, Esq. | 3 „ |
| 1697— 8 | 9 „ 10 | Richard Vaughan, Esq. (74) | 23 „ |
| 1698 | 10 | Morris Jones, of Dol, Esq. | — „ |
| 1698— 9 | 10 „ 11 | William Lewis Anwil, of Park, Esq. | 12 „ |
| 1699—1700 | 11 „ 12 | Evan Wynne, of Cwmmein, Esq. | 20 Nov. |
| 1700— 1 | 12 „ 13 | John Nanney, Esq. (75) | 28 „ |
| 1702 | 13 „ 14 | Edward Holland, of Pentremawr, Esq. | 1 Jan. |

## ANNE.

| | | | |
|---|---|---|---|
| 1702 | I | Edward Holland, of Pentremawr, Esq. | |
| 1702— 3 | I | William Winn, Esq. | 2 Dec. |
| 1703 | 1 & 2 | David Lloyd, of Henddwr, Esq. | — Jan.? |
| 1703— 4 | 2 „ 3 | Maurice Williams, of Hafodgarregog, Esq. | 2 Dec. |
| 1704— 5 | 3 „ 4 | John Lloyd, of Rhiwaedog, Esq. | 18 „ |
| 1705— 6 | 4 „ 5 | Sir William Williams, Bart. (76) | 3 „ |
| 1706— 7 | 5 „ 6 | Sir Griffith Williams, of Marl, Bart. | 5 „ |
| 1707— 8 | 6 „ 7 | John Wynne, of Garthmeilio, Esq. | 18 „ |

(72) The property now belongs to the Marquis and Marchioness of Londonderry.

(73) *Eldest son and successor to the Sheriff for 1646-7. Died in 1714. W.

(74) *Of Corsygedol. W.

(75) *Of Maesypandy. W.

(76) *Of Llanvorda, in Shropshire, ancestor in the fourth lineal degree to the present Sir Watkin Williams Wynn, Bart. Sir William Williams was eldest son and successor of the Rt. Honble. Sir William Williams, Bart., Speaker of the House of Commons in 1679-80. The present Sheriff died in 1740. There are portraits of him at Wynnstay and Peniarth. W.

| Anno Dom. | Regnal Year. | Name. | Appointed. |
|---|---|---|---|
| 1708— 9 | 7 & 8 | John Vaughan, of Caergai, Esq.    .    . | 25 Nov. |
| 1709—10 | 8 „ 9 | Roger Price, of Rhiwlas, Esq.    .    . | 1 Dec. |
| 1710—11 | 9 „ 10 | Thomas Merrick, (or Meyrick), of Berth-lwyd, Esq.    .    .    .    .    . | 24 Nov. |
| 1711—12 | 10 „ 11 | Hugh Owen, of Caerberllan, Esq.    .    . | 13 Dec. |
| 1712—13 | 11 „ 12 | William Owen, of Glyn, Esq. (77)    .    . | 11   „ |
| 1713 | 12 | Richard Mitton, of Dinas Mowddwy, Esq. | 30 Nov. |
| 1713—14 | 12 „ 13 | William Wynne, of Maesyneuadd, Esq. (78) | 13 Dec. |

## GEORGE I.

| | | | |
|---|---|---|---|
| 1714 | 1 | William Wynne, of Maesyneuadd, Esq.  . | |
| 1714 | 1 | Richard Mitton, of Dinas Mowddwy, Esq. | 6 Dec. |
| 1714—15 | 1 & 2 | Lewis Owen, of Peniarth, Esq. (79)    . | 16 . „ |
| 1715—16 | 2 | John Lloyd, of Rhiwaedog, Esq.    .    . | 5  „ |
| 1716 | 2 „ 3 | John Evans, of Kyfdy, Esq.    .    . | 6 Feb. |
| 1716—17 | 3 „ 4 | Richard Weaver, of Corwen, Esq.    .    . | 6 Dec. |
| 1717—18 | 4 | William Salisbury, of Rûg, Esq.    .    . | 21   „ |
| 1718 | 4 „ 5 | Griffith Wynne, of Taltreuddyn, Esq.    . | 2 Feb. |
| 1718—19 | 5 | Roger Salisbury, of Rûg, Esq.    .    . | 21 Dec. |
| 1719—20 | 5 „ 6 | Ellis Jones, of Nantbudir, Esq.    .    . | 6 Jan. |
| 1720 | 6 | John Lloyd, of Cilan, Esq.    .    .    . | 7  „ |
| 1720— 1 | 6 „ 7 | Hugh Hughes, of Gwerclas, Esq.    .    . | 26  „ |
| 1721 | 7 „ 8 | Richard Mitton, of Mowddwy, Esq.    . | 14  „ |
| 1721— 2 | 8 „ 9 | Thomas Price, of Gwnadle, Esq.    .    . | 14 Dec. |
| 1722— 4 | 9 „ 10 | David Lloyd, of Kefnbodig, Esq.    .    . | 11   „ |
| 1724 | 10 „ 11 | Giwn (or Gwin) Lloyd, of Hendwr, Esq.(80) | 7 Jan. |
| 1724— 6 | 11 „ 12 | Robert Lloyd, of Dolyglessin, Esq.    . | 10 Dec. |
| 1726 | 12 „ 13 | Atheluston (Athelstan) Owen, of Ynys-maengwyn, Esq. (81)    .    .    .    . | 13 Jan. |
| 1726— 7 | 13 | William Wynne, of Taltreuddyn, Esq.    . | 29 Nov. |

## GEORGE II.

| | | | |
|---|---|---|---|
| 1727 | 1 | William Wynne, of Taltreuddyn, Esq.    . | |
| 1727— 8 | 1 & 2 | John Nanney, of Maesypandu, Esq.    : | 14 Dec. |
| 1728— 9 | 2 | Robert Vaughan, of Hengwrt, Esq. (82)    . | 18   „ |

(77) *And of Porkington, in Shropshire, eldest son and successor to the Sheriff for 1688.  W.

(78) *Eldest son and successor to the Sheriff for 1678-9.  He died in 1720.  W.

(79) *Eldest son and successor to the Sheriff for 1694-5.  W.

(80) *Giwn.  W.

(81) *Of Rhiwsaeson, in Montgomeryshire, and of Ynysmaengwyn, through his wife, Ann, daughter and heiress of Vincent Corbet, Esq., of that place.  W.

(82) *See note 64.  W.

| Anno Dom. | Regnal Year. | Name. | Appointed. |
|---|---|---|---|
| 1729 | 2 | Thomas Owen, of Cwmcadian, Esq. (83) . | 16 Jan. |
| 1729 | 2 & 3 | Griffith Roberts, of Blaenyddol, Esq. . | 1 Feb. |
| 1729—30 | 3 „ 4 | Foulk Lloyd, of Cilan, Esq. . . . | 18 Dec. |
| 1730— 1 | 4 „ 5 | William Price of Rhiwlas, Esq. . . | 14 „ |
| 1731— 2 | 5 „ 6 | Edward Lloyd, of Gwerclas, Esq. . . | 9 „ |
| 1732— 3 | 6 „ 7 | Hugh Thomas, of Hendre, Esq. . . | 14 „ |
| 1733— 4 | 7 „ 8 | Robert Wynne, of Maes-y-neuadd, Esq.(84) | 20 „ |
| 1734— 5 | 8 „ 9 | Robert Vaughan, of Hengwrt, Esq. . | 19 „ |
| 1735— 7 | 9 „ 10 | John Mytton, of Mowddwy, Esq. . . | 18 „ |
| 1737— 8 | 10 „ 11 | Robert Meyricke, of Ucheldre, Esq. . | — Jan.? |
| 1738 | 11 „ 12 | John Lloyd, of Vachddeiliog, Esq. . | 12 „ |
| 1738— 9 | 12 „ 13 | Richard Anwyl, of Dolfriog, Esq. . . | 21 Dec. |
| 1739—40 | 13 „ 14 | Thomas Price, of Rhug, Esq. (85) . . | 27 „ |
| 1740— 2 | 14 „ 15 | Robert Wynne, of Cwmmein, Esq. . | 24 „ |
| 1742— 3 | 15 „ 16 | Robert Griffith, of Plas-Tan-y-bwlch, Esq. | — Jan. |
| 1743— 4 | 16 „ 17 | Maurice Jones, of Ddôl, Esq. . . . | 19 „ |
| 1744— 5 | 17 „ 18 | William Lewis Anwyl, of Bodtalog, Esq. | 5 „ |
| 1745— 6 | 18 „ 19 | Edward Williams, of Peniarth, Esq. (86) . | 10 „ |
| 1746— 7 | 19 „ 20 | Robert Parry, of Goppa, Esq. . . | 16 „ |
| 1747— 8 | 20 „ 1 | Hugh Hughes Lloyd, of Gwerclas, Esq. . | 15 „ |
| 1748— 9 | 21 „ 2 | Owen Wynne, of Pengwern, Esq. . . | 14 „ |
| 1749—50 | 22 „ 3 | Owen Holland, of Pentre Mawr, Esq. . | 11 „ |
| 1750 | 23 „ 4 | William Wynne, of Park, Esq. (87) . . | 17 „ |
| 1750— 2 | 24 „ 5 | Maesmor Morris, of Rhagat, Esq. . . | 6 Dec. |
| 1752— 3 | 25 „ 6 | Hugh Vaughan, of Hengwrt, Esq. (88) . | 14 Jan. |
| 1753— 4 | 26 „ 7 | Robert Price, of Caecoch, Esq. . . | 7 Feb. |
| 1754— 5 | 27 „ 8 | John Mostyn, of Clegir, Esq. . . . | 31 Jan. |
| 1755— 6 | 28 „ 9 | William Humphreys, of Maerdu, Esq. . | 29 „ |
| 1756— 7 | 29 „ 30 | Richard Owen, of Caethly and Ynys-maengwyn, Esq. (89) . . . . | 27 „ |

(83) *And of Llynlloed, parish of Machynlleth. W.

(84) *Eldest son and successor to the Sheriff for 1713-4. W.

(85) *Of Gogerthan, Co. Cardigan, and of Rûg, in right of his wife, Maria Charlotte Pughe, the heiress of that place, and of Mathafarn. W.

(86) *Of Peniarth, in right of his wife, Jane, Viscountess Dowager Bulkeley, daughter and heiress, of the Sheriff for 1714-15. Edward Williams was a younger son of John Williams, of Chester, and of Bodelwyddan, co. Flint, a younger son of the Rt. Hon. Sir William Williams, Bart., Speaker of the House of Commons in 1679-80. W.

(87) *And of Wern, in Caernarvonshire, grandson of the Sheriff for 1656-7 ; son of his fourth son William, who marrying his cousin, Elizabeth, daughter and heiress of Maurice Jones, of Wern, obtained that estate. W.

(88) *Eldest son and successor of the Sheriff for 1728-9. W.

(89) *Eldest son of the Sheriff for 1726. He did not survive his mother, and never was owner of Caethly and Ynysmaengwyn. W.

| Anno Dom. | Regnal Year. | Name. | Appointed. |
|---|---|---|---|
| 1757— 8 | 30 & 31 | Peter Price, of Dolgammedd, Esq. . . | 4 Feb. |
| 1758— 9 | 31 „ 2 | William Wynne, of Maesyneuodd, Esq (90) | 27 Jan. |
| 1759 | 32 | Richard Mytton, of Mowddwy, Esq. . | 2 Feb. |
| 1759—60 | 32 „ 3 | Humphry Edwards, of Talgarth, Esq. . | 13 „ |
| 1760 | 33 „ 4 | Robert Vaughan Humphreys, of Caerynwch, Esq. (91) . . . . | 1 „ |

## GEORGE III.

| | | | |
|---|---|---|---|
| 1760— 1 | 1 | Robert Vaughan Humphreys, of Caerynwch, Esq. . . . . | |
| 1761— 2 | 1 & 2 | Lewis Owen, of Caerberllan, Esq. . . | 16 Feb. |
| 1762— 3 | 2 „ 3 | Robert Wynne, of Cwmmein, Esq. . | 15 „ |
| 1763— 4 | 3 „ 4 | John Mytton, of Mowddwy, Esq. . . | 4 „ |
| 1764— 5 | 4 „ 5 | William Lloyd, of Rhiwaedog, Esq. . | 10 „ |
| 1765— 6 | 5 „ 6 | John Pughe, of Garthmaelan, Esq. . . | 1 „ |
| 1766— 7 | 6 „ 7 | Edward Vaughan Pughe, of Tû Gwyn, Esq. | 17 „ |
| 1767— 8 | 7 „ 8 | Thomas Kyffin, of Brynrodin, Esq. . | 13 „ |
| 1768— 9 | 8 „ 9 | Robert Godolphin Owen, of Glynne, Esq.(92) | 15 Jan. |
| 1769—70 | 9 „ 10 | Rice James, of Doly-gelynan, Esq. . . | 27 „ |
| 1770— 1 | 10 „ 11 | Evan Gryffydth, of Plas-tan-y-bwlch, Esq. | 9 Feb. |
| 1771— 2 | 11 „ 12 | Richard Parry, of Plasynddol, Esq. . | 6 „ |
| 1772— 3 | 12 „ 13 | William Wynne, of Park, Esq. (93) . . | 17 „ |
| 1773— 4 | 13 „ 14 | Lewis Edwards, of Talgarth, Esq. . . | 8 „ |
| 1774— 5 | 14 „ 15 | Thomas Powel, of Bronbiban, Esq. (94) . | 7 „ |
| 1775— 6 | 15 „ 16 | Lewis Nanney, of Llwyn, Esq. . . | 6 „ |
| 1776— 7 | 16 „ 17 | William Williams, of Penniarth-uchaf, Esq. | 5 „ |
| 1777— 8 | 17 „ 18 | John Vaughan, of Dolmelynllyn, Esq. . | 31 Jan. |
| 1778— 9 | 18 „ 19 | Richard Price, of Rhiwlas, Esq. . . | 28 „ |
| 1779—80 | 19 „ 20 | Henry Arthur Corbet, of Ynys-y-maen-Gwyn, Esq. (95) . . . . | 1 Feb. |

(90) *Eldest son and successor to the Sheriff for 1733-4. Upon the death of his uncle, John Nanney, Esq., this Sheriff inherited the Maesypandy estate, and assumed the name of Nanney. W.

(91) *Father of Catherine, wife of the Rt. Hon. Sir Richard Richards, Knt. Lord Chief Baron. W.

(92) *And of Porkington, Shropshire, eldest son and successor to the Sheriff for 1712-13. W.

(93) *And of Wern, Caernarvonshire, eldest son and successor of the Sheriff for 1750. The present Sheriff married Jane, eldest daughter and heiress of Edward Williams, the Sheriff for 1745-6, by Jane, Lady Bulkeley, his wife, and died in 1796. W.

(94) *And of Nanteos, in Cardiganshire. W.

(95) *Grandson (through his daughter, the heiress of Ynysmaengwyn) of the Sheriff for 1726. Henry Arthur Corbet, whose patronymic was Maurice, was the youngest son of his parents, but the Ynysmaengwyn estate was left to him. He assumed the name of Corbet, but died without male issue. W.

| Anno Dom. | Regnal Year. | Name. | Appointed. |
|---|---|---|---|
| 1780 | 20 | Lewis de Saumaise, of Botalog, Esq. . | 2 Feb. |
| 1780— 1 | 20 & 21 | David Roberts, of Tan y Gaer, Esq. . | 23 „ |
| 1781— 2 | 21 „ 2 | Edward Lloyd, of Maesmor, Esq. . . | 5 „ |
| 1782— 3 | 22 „ 3 | William Humffreys, of Maerdû, Esq. . | 1 Jan. |
| 1783— 4 | 23 „ 4 | Robert Evans, of Bodwenni, Esq. . . | 10 Feb. |
| 1784 | 24 | David Roberts, of Blaenyddol, Esq. . | 11 „ |
| 1784— 5 | 24 „ 5 | Robert Howell Vaughan, of Havod Owen, Esq. (96) . . . . | 5 March. |
| 1785— 6 | 25 „ 6 | John Jones, of Cyffty, Esq. . . . | 7 Feb. |
| 1786— 7 | 26 „ 7 | Griffith Price, of Braich y ceûnant, Esq. . | 13 „ |
| 1787— 8 | 27 „ 8 | John Jones, of Rhyd y fen, Esq. . . | 12 „ |
| 1788— 9 | 28 „ 9 | Griffith Evans, of Cwm yr afon, Esq. . | 8 „ |
| 1789—90 | 29 „ 30 | Edward Lloyd, of Palau, Esq. . . | 29 April. |
| 1790— 1 | 30 „ 1 | John Wynne Pugh, of Garthmaelan, Esq. | 29 Jan. |
| 1791 | 31 | Bulkeley Hatchet, the younger, of Tyn-y-pwll, Esq. . . . . . | 5 Feb. |
| 1791 | 31 | John Williams, of Peniarth-uchaf, Esq. . | 23 „ |
| 1791— 2 | 31 „ 2 | Griffith Roberts, of Bodynllin, Esq. . | 9 March. |
| 1792— 3 | 32 „ 3 | Edward Corbet, of Ynys maen gwin, Esq.(97) | 3 Feb. |
| 1793— 4 | 33 „ 4 | William John Lenthal, of Ucheldref, Esq. | 6 „ |
| 1794— 5 | 34 „ 5 | Owen Ormsby, of Glynn, Esq. (98) . . | 5 „ |
| 1795— 6 | 35 „ 6 | Robert Lloyd, of Cefngoed, Esq. (99) . | 11 „ |
| 1796 | 36 | Sir Edward Price Lloyd, of Park, Bart. . | 5 „ |
| 1796— 7 | 36 „ 7 | William Lloyd, of Cumhusion or Comheisian, Esq. (100) . . . . . | 16 March. |
| 1797— 8 | 37 „ 8 | Bell Lloyd, of Crogen, Esq. (101) . . | 1 Feb. |
| 1798— 9 | 38 „ 9 | Robert Watkin Wynne, of Cwmmein, Esq. | 7 „ |
| 1799—1800 | 39 „ 40 | Sir Thomas Mostyn, of Corsygedol, Bart. | 1 „ |
| 1800— 1 | 40 „ 1 | Bulkeley Hatchet, of Carnygadall, Esq. . | 5 „ |

(96) *Afterwards (in 1792) created a Baronet, and died in 1796. W.

(97) *Eldest brother and successor to the Sheriff for 1779—80. The present Sheriff, Edward Maurice, Esq., of Lloran, Denbighshire, also assumed the name of Corbet, upon succeeding to the Ynysmaengwyn estate. He died in London in 1820, and was buried with great funeral pomp at Towyn. W.

(98) *And of Willowbrook, Co. Sligo. He married Margaret, eldest sister and co-heiress of the Sheriff for 1768-9, and died in 1804, leaving an only daughter, heiress to the great estates of Porkington, Glyn, Clenenney, and Willowbrook. She was the wife of William Gore, Esq., of the family of Gore, of Woodford, Co. Leitrim. He assumed the additional surname of Ormsby, and was for many years M.P. for North Shropshire. He died in 1860, and she, who was born in 1781, died in 1869. W.

(99) *A solicitor at Oswestry. W.

(100) *And of Plas Power, near Wrexham. W.

(101) In some instances the name is written William, but Bell is correct.
*He was brother of Edward Pryce, first Lord Mostyn. W.

| Anno Dom. | Regnal Year. | Name. | Appointed. |
|---|---|---|---|
| 1801— 2 | 41 & 42 | Jonathan Passingham, of Hendwr, Esq. . | 11 Feb. |
| 1802— 3 | 42 „ 3 | John Meredith Mostyn, of Clegir, Esq. . | 10 „ |
| 1803 | 43 | Hugh Owen Hatchet, of Carnygadell, Bart. | 3 „ |
| 1803— 4 | 43 „ 4 | John Forbes, of Cefnbodig, Esq. . . | 16 „ |
| 1804— 5 | 44 „ 5 | Sir Edward Pryce Lloyd, of Park, Bart.(102) | 1 „ |
| 1805— 6 | 45 „ 6 | John Edwards, of Penrhyn, Esq. (103) . | 6 „ |
| 1806 | 46 | Hugh Jones, senior, of Dolgelly, Esq. (104) | 1 „ |
| 1806— 7 | 46 „ 7 | Thomas Jones, of Ynysfaig, Esq. . . | 5 March. |
| 1807— 8 | 47 „ 8 | Richard Henry Kenrick, of Ucheldref, Esq. | 4 Feb. |
| 1808— 9 | 48 „ 9 | Lewis Price Edwards, of Talgarth, Esq.(105) | 3 „ |
| 1809—10 | 49 „ 50 | William Davies, of Ty-Ucha, Esq . . | 6 „ |
| 1810—11 | 50 „ 1 | John Davies, of Aberllefeni, Esq. . . | 31 Jan. |
| 1811—12 | 51 „ 2 | Hugh Reveley, of Brynygwin, Esq. . | 8 Feb. |
| 1812—13 | 52 „ 3 | William Wynne, of Peniarth, Esq. (106) . | 24 Jan. |
| 1813—14 | 53 „ 4 | Thomas Edwards, of Ty Issa, Esq. . . | 10 Feb. |
| 1814—15 | 54 „ 5 | William Gryffydd Oakeley, of Tany-bwlch, Esq. . . . . . | 4 „ |
| 1815—16 | 55 „ 6 | Lewis Vaughan, of Penmaen Dovey, Esq. | 13 „ |
| 1816 | 56 | Thomas Duckinfield Ashley, of Cwmlle-coediog, Esq. (107) . . . . | 12 „ |
| 1816—17 | 56 „ 7 | John Davies, of Fron-haulog, Esq. . . | 9 March. |
| 1817—18 | 57 „ 8 | Sir John Evans, of Hendremorfydd, Knt.(108) | 12 Feb. |
| 1818—19 | 58 „ 9 | John Edwards, of Coed y Bedw, Esq. . | 10 „ |
| 1819—20 | 59 „ 60 | Edward Owen, of Garthynghared, Esq.(109) | 10 „ |

## GEORGE IV.

| 1820 | I | Edward Owen, of Garthynghared, Esq. . | |

(102) *Afterwards first Lord Mostyn. W. (See preceding note.)

(103) *And of Machynlleth, afterwards created a Baronet; father of Mary Cornelia, his only child, now Marchioness of Londonderry. W.

(104) *Was appointed but did not serve the office. He had been butler, and afterwards an agent at Nanney, but was owner of Hengwrtucha. W.

(105) *Son and successor to the Sheriff for 1773-4. W.

(106) *Eldest son and successor to the Sheriff for 1772—3. It was in 1812 or 1813 that the last execution, up to the present time, took place in Merionethshire; one for a horrible murder, by a South Wales man, in Penrhyn Deudraeth, one of the men employed upon the embankment in formation across Traeth mawr, the other a forger. Both were convicted at the same Assizes. I remember well, seeing them in the old gaol at Dolgelley. W.

(107) *And of Duckinfield, in Cheshire. W.

(108) Knighted during his year of office.
  *He gave a most luxurious banquet to his Welsh friends at the Freemason's Tavern, upon his being knighted. It was long afterwards remembered. Before he was presented to the Prince Regent for the honour of knighthood, the ceremony was practised in private, Sir Robert Williames Vaughan, then M.P. for the County, acting the part of Prince. W.

(109) *Lineally descended from Lewis Owen, the Baron. See note 25. W.

| Anno Dom. | Regnal Year. | Name. | Appointed. |
|---|---|---|---|
| 1820— 1 | 1 & 2 | Thomas Fitz-hugh, of Cwmheision, Esq. . | 12 Feb. |
| 1821— 2 | 2 „ 3 | John Mytton, of Plas yn Dinas, Esq. . | 6 „ |
| 1822— 3 | 3 „ 4 | James Gill, of Pant Glas, Esq. . . | 4 „ |
| 1823 | 4 | John Wynne, of Cwmmein, Esq. . . | 31 Jan. |
| 1823— 4 | 4 „ 5 | John Wynne, of Meyarth, Esq. . . | 26 April. |
| 1824— 5 | 5 „ 6 | Athelstan Corbet, of Ynys-maen-gwyn, Esq. (110) . . . . . | 31 Jan. |
| 1825— 6 | 6 „ 7 | Francis Roberts, of Gerddiblûog, Esq. . | 2 Feb. |
| 1826— 7 | 7 „ 8 | William Casson, of Cynfal, Esq. . | 30 Jan. |
| 1827— 8 | 8 „ 9 | Thomas Hartley, of Llwyn, Esq. . . | 5 Feb. |
| 1828— 9 | 9 „ 10 | Thomas Casson, of Blaenyddol, Esq. . | 13 „ |
| 1829—30 | 10 „ 11 | William John Bankes, of Dolymoch, Esq.(111) | 11 „ |
| 1830 | 11 | Jones Panton, of Llwyngwern, Esq. . | 2 „ |

## WILLIAM IV.

| | | | |
|---|---|---|---|
| 1830— 1 | 1 | Jones Panton, of Llwyngwern, Esq. . | |
| 1831— 2 | 1 & 2 | Hugh Lloyd, of Cefenbodig (Chester) Esq. (112) . . . . . | 31 Jan. |
| 1832— 3 | 2 „ 3 | William Turner, of Croesor, Esq. . . | 6 Feb. |
| 1833— 4 | 3 „ 4 | George Jonathan Scott, of Peniarth-ucha, Esq. (113) . . . . . | 4 „ |
| 1834— 5 | 4 „ 5 | Charles Gray Harford, of Bryntirion, Esq. | 3 „ |
| 1835— 6 | 5 „ 6 | John Henry Lewis, of Dolgun, Esq. . | 7 „ |
| 1836— 7 | 6 „ 7 | John Ellerker Boulcott, of Hendreissa, Esq. | 3 „ |
| 1837 | 7 | Sir Robert Williames Vaughan, of Nannau, Bart. . . . . . | 28 Jan. |

## VICTORIA.

| | | | |
|---|---|---|---|
| 1837— 8 | 1 | Sir Robert Williames Vaughan, of Nannau, Bart. (114) . . . . | |
| 1838— 9 | 1 & 2 | John Manners Kerr, of Plas Issa, Esq.(115) | 1 Feb. |
| 1839—40 | 2 „ 3 | The Honble. Edward Lloyd Mostyn, of Plashen. (116) . . . . . | 4 „ |

(110) *Nephew and successor, through his mother, to the Sheriffs for 1779—80, and 1792—3. W.

(111) *And of Kingston House, Dorsetshire ; at one time M.P. for the University of Cambridge. W.

(112) *A Tradesman at Chester, but lineally descended from the ancient, and once powerful family of Lloyd, of Rhiwaedog. This gentleman amassed a fortune, as I recollect, it was said of £200,000, in trade, at Chester. and I believe was much respected. W.

(113) *And of Betton Strange, Shropshire. W.

(114) *Eldest son and successor to the Sheriff for 1784-5. Died in April 1843. He represented the County in Parliament from 1792 to 1836. W.

(115) *A General in the army. W. 

(116) *Now Lord Mostyn. W.

| Anno Dom. | Regnal Year. | Name. | Appointed. |
|---|---|---|---|
| 1840— 1 | 3 & 4 | George Price Lloyd, of Plasyndre, Esq. . . | 29 Jan. |
| 1841— 2 | 4 „ 5 | John Williams, of Bron Eryri, Esq. . | 5 Feb. |
| 1842— 3 | 5 „ 6 | The Honble. Thomas Price Lloyd, of Mochras. (117) . . . . . | 2 „ |
| 1843— 4 | 6 „ 7 | Owen Jones Ellis Nanney, of Cefn-deuddwr, Esq. . . . . | 1 „ |
| 1844— 5 | 7 „ 8 | David White Griffith, of Sygun, Esq. . | 31 Jan. |
| 1845— 6 | 8 „ 9 | Richard Watkin Price, of Rhiwlas, Esq. . | 3 Feb. |
| 1846— 7 | 9 „ 10 | Sir Robert Williames Vaughan, of Nannau, Bart. (118) . . . . . | 30 Jan. |
| 1847— 8 | 10 „ 11 | John Griffith Griffith, of Taltreuddyn-fawr, Esq. . . . . . . | 4 Feb. |
| 1848— 9 | 11 „ 12 | Hugh Jones, of Gwernddelwa (Hengwrt-ucha), Esq. | 11 „ |
| 1849—50 | 12 „ 13 | Robert Davies Jones [afterwards Pryce, of Cyffronydd], of Aberllefenny, Esq. . | 13 „ |
| 1850— 1 | 13 „ 14 | Edward Humphrey Griffith, of Gwastad-fryn, Esq. . . . . . | 5 „ |
| 1851— 2 | 14 „ 15 | Henry Richardson, of Aberhirnant, Esq. | 11 „ |
| 1852— 3 | 15 „ 16 | George Casson, of Blaenyddôl, Esq. . | 2 „ |
| 1853— 4 | 16 „ 17 | Thomas Arthur Bertie Mostyn, of Kylan, Esq. . . . . . . | 7 „ |
| 1854— 5 | 17 „ 18 | George Augustus Huddart, of Plas yn Penrhyn, Esq. . . . . | 30 Jan. |
| 1855— 6 | 18 „ 19 | Charles John Tottenham, of Berwyn House, Llangollen, Esq. . . . | 8 Feb. |
| 1856— 7 | 19 „ 20 | John Priestley, of Hafodgaregog, Esq. . | 30 Jan. |
| 1857— 8 | 20 „ 1 | John Nanney, of Maesyneuadd, Esq. . | 2 Feb. |
| 1858— 9 | 21 „ 2 | Edward Buckley, of Plasyn Dinas, Esq. . | 3 „ |
| 1859—60 | 22 „ 3 | Hugh John Reveley, of Brynygwin, Esq. (119) | 2 „ |
| 1860 | 23 | David Williams of Deudraeth Castle, Esq. (120) . . . . . | 23 Jan. |
| 1860— 1 | 23 „ 4 | Charles Frederick Thruston, of Talgarth Hall, Esq. . . . . | 22 Feb. |
| 1861— 2 | 24 „ 5 | David Williams, of Deudraeth Castle, Esq. | 4 „ |

(117) *Second and youngest son of the first Lord Mostyn. W.

(118) *Eldest son and successor of the Sheriff for 1837-8. He died without issue in April, 1859, and the Baronetcy became extinct. W.

(119) *Only son and successor to the Sheriff for 1811-12. W.

(120) Was excused after appointment for that year, but served the following year. Afterwards M.P. for the County. Brother of Sheriff for 1841-42.

| Anno Dom. | Regnal Year. | Name. | Appointed. |
|---|---|---|---|
| 1862— 3 | 25 & 6 | Samuel Holland, of Plas - yn - Penrhyn, Esq. (121) . . . . . . | 5 Feb. |
| 1863— 4 | 26 „ 7 | Howel Morgan, of Hengwrt-uchaf, Esq. . | 3 „ |
| 1864— 5 | 27 „ 8 | Lewis Williams, of Vronwnion, Esq. . | 3 „ |
| 1865— 6 | 28 „ 9 | Richard Meredyth Richards, of Caerynwch, Esq. (122) . . . . . . | 4 „ |
| 1866— 7 | 29 „ 30 | John Corbet, of Ynys-y-maen-gwyn, Esq. | 3 „ |
| 1867— 8 | 30 „ 1 | William Watkin Edward Wynne, of Peni-arth, Esq. (123) . . . . . | 2 „ |
| 1868— 9 | 31 „ 2 | Richard John Lloyd Price, of Rhiwlas, Esq. (124) . . . . . . | 30 Jan. |
| 1869—70 | 32 „ 3 | Henry Robertson, of Crogen, Esq. (125) . | 4 Feb. |
| 1870— 1 | 33 „ 4 | Clement Arthur Thruston, of Pennal Tower, Esq. . . . . . | 5 „ |
| 1871— 2 | 34 „ 5 | Charles Edwards, of Dolserau, Esq. (126) . | 8 „ |
| 1872— 3 | 35 „ 6 | Edward Foster Coulson, of Corsygedol, Esq. . . . . . | 5 „ |

(121) Now (1872) M.P. for the County.

(122) *Grandson and heir of Lord Chief Baron Richards. (See note 91). W. Chairman of Quarter Sessions.

(123) *Only surviving son and successor to the Sheriff for 1812-13. W. Was M.P. for the County, 1852-65.

(124) *Grandson and heir of the Sheriff for 1845-6. W.

[125] M.P. for Shrewsbury, 1859-65.

(126) M.P. for New Windsor, 1866-8.

# CHAPTER VI.

## MEMBERS OF PARLIAMENT.

ALTHOUGH in the preamble to the Statute of Rhuddlan it was recited that by "Divine Providence" (a term so often made a synonym for Conquest,) the territory of Wales, theretofore held as a fief of the English Crown, had then become an integral part of the kingdom, "et corone Regni predicti tanquam partem corporis ejusdem annexuit et univit," it does not appear that the first Edward extended to it the representative franchises secured by Magna Charta to the people of England. It is true that in the reign of his son and successor two writs appear to have been issued directing the return of a certain number of representatives for North and South Wales. (1) But no trace can be found of any subsequent or other writs addressed to Wales till after the 27th year of Hen. VIII. The

---

(1) "Representatives in Parliament for the County of Merioneth."

"So early as the 15th year of Edw. II., a writ was addressed to the Earl of Arundel, Justiciary of Wales, directing him to cause twenty-four discreet persons to be chosen from the north, and as many from the south of that principality, to serve in Parliament—*Rot. Parl.* vol. i. p. 406. And we find a similar writ in the 20th of the same King.—Prynne's *Register*, 4th part, p. 60 ; Hallam's *Middle Ages*, vol. ii. p. 299, note. To the latter of these writs a return is in existence, from which it appears that for the County of Merioneth four persons were chosen, namely :

> "Eignion Vachan,
> "Jevan, ap Gurgmn (Gurgeneu),
> "Llewelyn ap David Vaghan, and
> "Griffith ap Madoc.

"It would seem, however, that those upon whom this distinction was conferred, showed no great readiness to attend to the duties attached to it ; for I find from the return of Griffith ap Rees, Knt., the Sheriff, who also was ordered to attend the Parliament, 'quod erit ad parliamentum si tempus fuerit commode, et prædictus Eynon et alii aliquam manucaptionem de veniendo invenire nolebant.'—(*Parliament. Returns*, 20 Edw. II., formerly in the Tower Record Office.)

"All the Parliamentary Returns from 17 Edw. IV. to 1 Edw. VI., except an imperfect bundle of 33 Hen. VIII. (and it contains the names of the Members for Merionethshire in the Parliament for that year), are lost (Willis' *Notitia Parliamentaria*, vol. i. pages 7 and 169) ; but of the Representatives for the County of Merioneth, from the 1st Edw. VI. inclusive, to the present time, I have been enabled to compile probably a complete series, which is subjoined."—(From the *Archæologia Cambrensis* part iii., Supplement, July, 1846. This paper was communicated by W. W. E. Wynne, Esq.) W.

usurpation of Henry Bolingbroke, and the consequent rebellion of Owen Glyndwr, led to a series of savage enactments, (noticed in another Chapter—see Sheriffs) which deprived the Welsh of their most valuable civil rights for nearly a century and a half. Those rights were only restored to them by the offspring of the union of the white and red rose in the person of Henry VIII. By the Statute passed in the 27th year of his reign, c. 26, it was enacted "that for this present Parliament and all other Parliaments to be holden and kept for this Realm, one Knight shall be chosen and elected to the same Parliaments for every of the Shires of Brecknock, Radnor, Montgomery, and Denbigh, and for every other Shire within the said Country or Dominion of Wales; and for every Borough being a Shire-Town within the said Country or Dominion of Wales, except the Shire-Town of the County of Mereoneth, one Burgess; and the Election to be in like manner, form, and order, as Knights and Burgesses of the Parliament be elected and chosen in other Shires of this Realm; and that the Knights and Burgesses, and every of them, shall have like Dignity, Pre-eminence, and Privilege, and shall be allowed such fees as other Knights of the Parliament have and be allowed; and the Knights' fees to be levied and gathered of the Commons of the Shire that they be elected in; and the Burgesses fees to be levied and gathered as well of the Boroughs and Shire-Towns as they be Burgesses of, as of all other ancient Boroughs within the same Shires." By a subsequent Statute (35 Hen. VIII. c. 11. s. 1.) the Knights' fees were fixed at Four shillings a day, and the Burgesses' at Two shillings a day.

By the first of these Statutes a Commission was directed "to enquire and view all the said Shires," and to divide the same into Hundreds, and in the second the Execution of such Commission is recited and confirmed. (2) It is matter for regret that no trace can now be obtained of the Return to this Commission. In pursuance of the first recited Act, one Knight has always been returned for each of the Shires of Gwynedd, and a Burgess for the Borough of Caernarvon, in conjunction with the Boroughs of Criccieth, Pwllheli, Nevin and Conway. Bangor was made one of the Contributory Boroughs of Caernarvon by the Reform Act of 1832. In Anglesey, the town of Newborough alone returned the Burgess for the two Parliaments of 33 Hen. VIII., and 1 Edw. VI. But by an Act passed in the 2nd and 3rd years of the latter King, the Burgesses of Newborough were "discharged" from the payment of the fees, and the Borough of Beaumaris was directed thenceforth to return the Burgess to Parliament, and continued to do so. Early in the last century the question of the right of the Inhabitants of Newborough to vote at Elections of the Parlia-

---

(2) "Item, that the lymitacons of the Hundreds of late made within the said Shyres by vertue of his Grace's Commission directed out of his Heighness Court of Chauncerye and again returned into the same shall stande in full strengthe force and effecte according to the saide lymitacon, except suche of the same as sithe that tyme have been altered or [chaunged] by vertue of any Acte or Actes of Parliament alreadye made or that shalbe altered or changed by an Acte or Actes in this present Session to be made."—34 & 35 Hen. VIII. c. 26. s. 2.

mentary Representative was raised before a committee of the House of Commons which decided adversely to the claims of Newborough. (See note to Members for Anglesey.) By the Reform Act the towns of Holyhead, Llangefni and Amlwch, were made Contributory Boroughs, and share the representation with Beaumaris. Merionethshire to this day has no Borough or Town returning a Burgess to Parliament.

# MEMBERS FOR THE COUNTY OF ANGLESEY AND BOROUGHS OF NEWBOROUGH AND BEAUMARIS.

| Anno Dom. | Date of Return. | Regnal Year. | Name. | |
|---|---|---|---|---|
| 1541 | Dec. | 33 Hen. VIII. | Richard ap David ap Hugh Jevan ap Geffrey.(1) | Burgess. |
| 1547 | Sept.(?) | 1 Edw. VI. | Richard Bulkeley, Esq. | K.S. |
| ,, | (?)20 ,, | 1 ,, | John ap Robert Lloid. . | Burgess. |
| 1553 | 2 Feb. | 7 ,, | Lewis Owen ap Meyryk, of Frondeg, Esq. . | K.S. |
| ,, | (?)2 ,, | 7 ,, | Morrice Gruffyth, of Plas Newydd, Esq. (2) . | Burgess. |
| ,, | Sept.(?) | 1 Mary. | William Lewis, of Presaddfed, Esq. . . | K.S. |
| ,, | ,, | 1 ,, | Rowland Bulkeley, Esq. | Burgess. |
| 1554 | 2 April. | 1 ,, | Sir Richard Bulkeley, Knt. | K.S. |
| ,, | 2 ,, | 1 ,, | Rowland Bulkeley, Esq. | Burgess. |
| ,, | 8 Nov. | 1 & 2 Phil. & Mary. | Sir Richard Bulkeley, Knt. | K.S. |
| ,, | 5 ,, | 1 & 2 ,, | William (surname illegible), Merchant. . | Burgess. |
| 1555 | 10 Oct. | 2 & 3 ,, | William Lewis, Esq. . | K.S. |
| ,, | 10 ,, | 2 & 3 ,, | Hugh Goodman, Esq. . | Burgess. |
| 1558 | 20 Jan. | 4 & 5 ,, | Rowland Meredyth, of Bodowyr, Esq. . . | K.S. |
| ,, | 20 ,, | 4 & 5 ,, | William ap Ryce ap Howell, Esq. . . | Burgess. |
| 1559 | 26 ,, | 1 Elizabeth. | Rowland Meredyth, Esq. | K.S. |
| ,, | | 1 ,, | (3) | Burgess. |
| 1563 | 11 ,, | 5 ,, | Richard Bulkeley, Esq.. | K.S. |
| ,, | 11 ,, | 5 ,, | William Price, Esq. . | Burgess. |
| 1571 | 2 April. | 13 ,, | Richard Bulkeley, Esq. | K.S. |
| ,, | 2 ,, | 13 ,, | William Bulkeley. . | Burgess. |

(1) The Return of the Knight of the Shire cannot be deciphered, through decay.

The Burgesses of the 33rd year of Hen. VIII., and 1st of Edw. VI., were returned for Newborough.

(2) Son of Roland Gruffyth.

(3) The Return of the Burgess for this Parliament cannot be found.

| Anno Dom. | Date of Return. | Regnal Year. | Name. | |
|---|---|---|---|---|
| 1572 | 8 May. | 14 Elizabeth. | Lewis ap Owen, ap Merick, Esq. . . K.S. | } (4) |
| „ | 8 „ | 14 „ | Rowland Kenrick, Esq. Burgess. | |
| 1583—4 | | 26 „ | Owen Holand, of Berw, Esq. K.S. | } |
| „ | | 26 „ | Thomas Bulkeley. (?) . Burgess. | |
| 1586 | 29 Sept. | 28 „ | Sir Henry Bagnoll, of Plasnewydd, Knt. . K.S. | } |
| „ | 29 „ | 28 „ | Thomas Bulkeley, Junr., Esq. . . . . Burgess. | |
| 1588 | Oct. | 30 „ | Richard Bulkeley, of Langefney, Esq. (5) . K.S. | } |
| „ | 24 „ | 30 „ | Thomas Bulkeley, Junr., Esq. . . . . Burgess. | |
| 1593 | 19 Feb. | 35 „ | William Glynne, of Llan-vwrog, Esq. . . K.S. | } |
| „ | (?)19 „ | 35 „ | Thomas Bulkeley, of Lincoln's Inn, Esq. . Burgess. | |
| 1597 | (?)3 Oct. | 39 „ | Hugh Hughes, of Plas-coch, Esq. . . K.S. | } |
| „ | 13 „ | 39 „ | William Johnes (or Jones), of Castellmarch, Esq. Burgess. | |
| 1601 | 8 „ | 43 „ | Thomas Holland, Esq. K.S. | } |
| „ | 28 Sept. | 43 „ | William Maurice, of Clenenney, Esq. . Burgess. | |
| 1604 | Feb. | 1 James I. | Sir Richard Bulkeley, Knt. K.S. | } |
| „ | | 1 „ | William Jones, of Castell-march, Esq. . . Burgess. | |
| 1614 | April. | 12 „ | Sir Richard Bulkeley, Knt. K.S. | } |
| „ | „ | 12 „ | William Jones, Esq. . Burgess. | |
| 1620 | Dec. | 18 „ | Richard Williams, Esq. K.S. | } |
| „ | „ | 18 „ | Sampson Evans, Esq. (6) Burgess. | |
| 1624 | 12 Feb. | 21 „ | John Mostyn, of Tregar-nedd, Esq. . . K.S. | } |
| „ | 12 „ | 21 „ | Charles Jones, of Castell-march, Esq. . . Burgess. | |

(4) The Parliament of 14 Elizabeth was prorogued to the 18th year, when it was further prorogued to the 23rd year.    There were no alterations in the List of Members during that time.

(5) Thomas in Browne Willis.

(6) I cannot find the Return of the Burgess for this Parliament, and have therefore inserted the name contained in Browne Willis' and Rowland's Lists.

| Anno Dom. | Date of Return. | Regnal Year. | Name. | |
|---|---|---|---|---|
| 1625 | (?)17 May. | 1 Charles I. | Sir Sackville Trevor, Knt. | K.S. |
| ,, | 17 ,, | 1 ,, | Charles Jones, Esq. . | Burgess. |
| 1626 | 6 Feb. | 1 ,, | Richard Bulkeley, Esq. | K.S. |
| ,, | 6 ,, | 1 ,, | Charles Jones, Esq. . | Burgess. |
| 1628 | 21 ,, | 3 ,, | Richard Bulkeley, Esq. | K.S. |
| ,, | 21 ,, | 3 ,, | Charles Jones, Esq. . | Burgess. |
| 1640 | 15 Oct. | 16 ,, | John Bodvell, of Lany-grad, Esq. (7) . . | K.S. |
| | | | Richard Wood, Esq. . | K.S. |
| ,, | 15 ,, | 16 ,, | John Griffith, Senr., of Cefn-amwlch, Esq. . | Burgess. |
| | | | William Jones, Esq. . | Burgess. |
| 1646 | 31 Dec. | 22 ,, | Richard Wood, Esq. (8) | K.S. |
| 1647 | 22 Jan. | 22 ,, | William Jones, Esq. . | Burgess. |
| 1653 | 5 July. | | [See Note to Members for Caernarvon of this date.] | |
| 1654 | 12 ,, | | George Twisleton. . | K.S. |
| 1656 | 17 Sept. | | ,, ,, . | K.S. |
| ,, | 17 ,, | | Griffith Bodvill, Esq.(9) | Burgess. |
| 1659 | 13 Jan. | | Col. George Twisleton. | K.S. |
| ,, | 13 ,, | | Griffith Bodwrda, Esq. | Burgess. |
| 1660 | | 12 Charles II. | Rt. Hon. Robert, Vis-count Bulkeley. . | K.S. (10) |
| ,, | | 12 ,, | Griffyth Bodwrda, Esq. | Burgess. |
| 1661 | 4 April. | 13 ,, | Nicholas Bagnall, Esq. | K.S. |
| ,, | 4 ,, | 13 ,, | Sir Heneage Finch, Knt. and Bart. (11) . . | Burgess. |
| ,, | 18 July. | 13 ,, | John Robinson, Esq.(12) | Burgess. |
| 1679 | 13 Feb. | 31 ,, | Henry Bulkeley, Esq. . | K.S. |
| ,, | 17 ,, | 31 ,, | Richard Bulkeley, of Baron-hill, Esq. . | Burgess. |

(7) The Long Parliament. In the list at the Crown Office, Bodvell's name is run through, and Wood's inserted. On the cover of the list is written, " Several of the Members went to Oxford to the King and the House was filled with others in their places."

(8) " 8 Dec., 1646.—It was Resolved that the Speaker do issue his Warrant for a Writ to be made to elect a Knight of the Shire for Anglesey, in the place of John Bodwell, Esq., formerly chosen and sithence disabled by judgement of the House to serve any longer during this Parliament." Same day a similar Writ was ordered to be issued to elect a Burgess in the room of John Griffith, Esq., deceased.—Journals House of Commons, vol. v., p. 4.

(9) Browne Willis.

(10) Mona Antiqua. Browne Willis gives the name of Bodville as Burgess.

(11) Sir Heneage Finch, the Solicitor General, was elected for the Oxford University and Beaumaris; he made choice to sit for the University.

(12) Colonel William Robinson in Mona Antiqua.

| Anno Dom. | Date of Return. | Regnal Year. | Name. | |
|---|---|---|---|---|
| 1679 | 28 Aug. | 31 Charles II. | Richard Bulkeley, Esq.(13) | K.S. |
| ,, | 28 ,, | 31 ,, | Henry Bulkeley, Esq. | Burgess. |
| 1681 | 10 March. | 33 ,, | Richard Bulkeley, Esq. | K.S. |
| ,, | 10 ,, | 33 ,, | Henry Bulkeley, Esq. . | Burgess. |
| 1685 | 2 April. | 1 James II. | Robert, Viscount Bulkeley. | K.S. |
| ,, | 2 ,, | 1 ,, | Henry Bulkeley, Esq. . | Burgess. |
| 1689 | 16 Jan. | (Convention.) | Thomas Bulkeley, Esq. K.S. | |
| ,, | 15 ,, | ,, | Sir William Williams, of Gray's Inn, Knt. & Bart. Burgess. | (14) |
| 1690 | 13 March. | 2 Will. & Mary. | Richard, Lord Viscount Bulkeley, of Cashell. | K.S. |
| ,, | 13 ,, | 2 ,, | Hon. Thomas Bulkeley, of Dinas. . . | Burgess. |
| 1695 | 14 Nov. | 7 William III. | Rt. Hon. Richard, Viscount Bulkeley. . | K.S. |
| ,, | 7 ,, | 7 ,, | Sir William Williams, of Nantanog, Knt. & Bart.(15) | Burgess. |
| 1698 | 18 Aug. | 10 ,, | Rt. Hon. Richard, Viscount Bulkeley. . | K.S. |
| ,, | 8 ,, | 10 ,, | Owen Hughes, of Beaumaris, Esq. . . | Burgess. |
| 1701 | 30 Jan. | 12 ,, | Rt. Hon. Richard, Viscount Bulkeley. . | K.S. |
| ,, | 14 ,, | 12 ,, | Coningsby Williams, of Penmynyth, Esq. . | Burgess. |
| ,, | 4 Dec. | 13 ,, | Rt. Hon. Richard, Viscount Bulkeley. . | K.S. |
| ,, | 3 ,, | 13 ,, | Robert Bulkeley, of Beaumaris, Esq. . . | Burgess. |
| 1702 | 13 Aug. | 1 Anne. | Rt. Hon. Richard, Viscount Bulkeley. . | K.S. |
| ,, | 3 ,, | 1 ,, | Robert Bulkeley, of Beaumaris, Esq. . | Burgess. |
| 1703 | 29 Nov. | 2 ,, | Coningsby Williams, Esq. (16) . . . | Burgess. |

---

(13) Henry in Mona Antiqua.    (14) Charles Bulkeley, Coroner, made these Returns.

(15) Of Glasgoed, in London Gazette, and Llanvorda, in Mona Antiqua.

(16) "9 Nov., 1703.—Ordered, that the Speaker do issue his Warrant, &c., to elect a Burgess in the room of Robert Bulkeley, Esq., deceased."—Jour. House of Commons, vol. xiv., p. 212.

| Anno Dom. | Date of Return. | Regnal Year. | Name. | |
|---|---|---|---|---|
| 1704 | 30 Nov. | 3 Anne. | Richard, Lord Viscount Bulkeley. (17) . . | K.S. |
| 1705 | 29 May. | 4 ,, | Rt. Hon. Richard, Lord Viscount Bulkeley. . | K.S. |
| ,, | 21 ,, | 4 ,, | Hon. Henry Bertie. . | Burgess. |
| 1708 | 13 ,, | 7 ,, | Rt. Hon. Richard, Lord Viscount Bulkeley. . | K.S. |
| ,, | 15 ,, | 7 ,, | Hon. Henry Bertie. (18) | Burgess. |

(17) Son of previous Member. " 24 Oct., 1704.—Ordered, that the Speaker do issue his Warrant, &c., to elect a Knight of the Shire in the room of Richard, Viscount Bulkeley, deceased."—Journals of House of Commons, vol. xiv., p. 392.

(18) Brother to Lady Bulkeley, according to Rowland. " 27 Nov. 1708.—Petition, presented by Owen Meyrick, Esq., Mayor, Thomas Evans, Bailiff, and others, Burgesses of Newborough and Beaumaris, against the Return of Henry Bertie, Esq., for that William Owen, Esq., Mayor, John Evans, and Daniel Parry, Bailiffs of Beaumaris (being friends of Mr. Bertie), rejected the votes of the Petitioners on behalf of Sir Arthur Owen, who was duly elected ; and yet in the said Return no notice is taken of the Borough of Newborough.

" Ordered, that the merits of the said election and Return be heard on Saturday, 2 April, next." Journals House of Commons, vol. xvi., p. 21.

" 28 Nov. 1709.—Another Petition, similar to the above, which was referred to the consideration of the Committee of Privileges and Elections, &c."—Id., vol. xvi., p. 225.

" 18 Feb. 1709-10.—Mr. Compton reported from the Committee the matter as it appeared to them, touching the election for Beaumaris. The Counsel for the Petitioners alleged that the right of electing a Burgess for Beaumaris is in the Mayor, Bailiffs, and Burgesses in general of the Boroughs of Newborough and Beaumaris. And in the first place they referred to the Statute of 27 Hen. VIII., as also to that of the 35 year of the said King. The Counsel also further alleged that Newborough was a Shire Town till the reign of Edward VI., to prove which they produced an Act of 2 and 3 Edward VI., intituled ' An Act for the keeping of the Sessions and County days of the Isle of Anglesey, in Beaumaris, &c.' And it is also provided and enacted in the said Act, that the said village of Newborough and the inhabitants thereof shall be discharged from paying any wages to any Burgess which shall be returned to serve in Parliament for the town of Beaumaris and village of Newborough, or either of them. Which exemption, the Petitioners' Counsel inferred, was given to Newborough for the removal of the County Court and Session to Beaumaris : and they also produced a Charter bearing date 27 April, 17 Edward II., (1324), whereby it appeared Newborough was a Corporation at that time.

" To prove the customary usage of the Burgesses for Newborough voting at the election of a Burgess to serve for Beaumaris, they called John ap John Rowland, who said he had known Newborough 55 years ; and the inhabitants thereof have claimed a right, at times, to vote at Beaumaris at the election of a Burgess for 48 years. When Mr. Owen Hughes (who was then mayor of Newborough, and he thinks Recorder of Beaumaris), stood for a Burgess he sent to Newborough for the Burgesses to come and vote for him ; and about thirty went thither accordingly ; but they did not vote, for the election was agreed upon. He had surrendered his right as a Burgess since the last election.

" The Counsel for the Sitting Member insisted that the right of electing a Burgess for Beaumaris, is in the Mayor, Bailiffs, and capital Burgesses of Beaumaris only. They also alleged, that Newborough was not so much as a Corporation at present ; for though they had a Charter in the 17 year of Edward II., yet the last Charter that Borough had, was in the 15 year of Hen. VIII., which recited all the Charters that were before granted ; and the said Charter of Hen. VIII. was surrendered 29 Hen. prædict. To prove which they produced the original Record from the Rolls, wherein the said Charter of 15 Hen. VIII. appeared to be vacated, lines being struck through the same, and a surrender thereof entered in the margin, dated 20 October, 29 Henry VIII. Counsel further alleged that the Act of 2 and 3 Edward VI., recites that the Assizes and Sessions, which for 250 years before had been kept at Beaumaris, had been removed about 45 to the little village of Newborough upon a false representation of one, Mancus, then being Ambassador from the King of Spain to King Henry VIII., and, for that the said village is not fit to receive the Judges and Justices, or to hold Assizes or Sessions, the same are removed back to Beaumaris. It is also enacted by the said Act that Newborough and the inhabitants thereof should not from thenceforth

| Anno Dom. | Date of Return. | Regnal Year. | Name. | |
|---|---|---|---|---|
| 1710 | 26 Oct. | 9 Anne. | Rt. Hon. Richard, Lord Viscount Bulkeley. . | K.S. |
| „ | 28 „ | 9 „ | Hon. Henry Bertie. . | Burgess. |
| 1713 | 24 Sept. | 12 „ | Rt. Hon. Richard, Lord Viscount Bulkeley. . | K.S. |
| „ | 11 „ | 12 „ | Hon. Henry Bertie. . | Burgess. |
| 1715 | 10 Feb. | 1 George I. | Owen Meyrick, of Bodorgan, Esq. . | K.S. |
| „ | 10 „ | 1 „ | Hon. Henry Bertie. . | Burgess. |
| 1722 | 11 April. | 8 „ | Rt. Hon. Richard, Lord Viscount Bulkeley, of Cashell. (19) . . | K.S. |

be charged or chargeable to or with any of the charges or expences of any Burgess who from time to time should be returned to serve for the Town of Beaumaris and village of Newborough, or either of them. Therefore it was insisted that as the aforesaid surrender of the Charter determined the Corporation of Newborough, so this Act determined their right of voting in elections of a Member to serve in Parliament, as a Borough.

"And as to the allegations of the Counsel for the Petitioners, That the right of electing a Burgess for Beaumaris is in all the Burgesses of the said Borough : the Counsel for the Sitting Member produced the Charter of that Borough made in the 4th year of Queen Elizabeth, which recited many former Charters, whereby the right of electing a Burgess for Beaumaris is vested in the Mayor, Two Bailiffs, and Twenty-one Capital Burgesses thereof ; and a Return of the 39 year of Elizabeth was also produced, by which it appeared that the Mayor, Bailiffs, and Capital Burgesses, elected the Burgess to serve in that Parliament.

"Upon the evidence aforesaid, the Committee came to the following Resolution, viz.

"That it is in the opinion of the Committee that the right of electing a Burgess for Beaumaris, is in the Mayor, Bailiffs, and Capital Burgesses of Beaumaris only.

"That it is the opinion of the Committee that Henry Bertie, Esq., is duly elected for Beaumaris.

"The said Resolutions being severally read a second time, and the Question put, were agreed unto by the House.

"The Petition of Griffith Parry, Town Clerk, in custody of the Serjeant at Arms, was presented to the House and read ; setting forth that the Petitioner was heartily sorry for having fallen under the censure of the House for not obeying an Order of the Committee of Privileges and Elections, and humbly begged pardon : praying that he might be discharged, in regard his Family and affairs greatly suffer by his confinement. It was ordered, that the Petitioner be brought to the Bar of the House upon Monday morning next in order to his discharge."—Journals House of Commons, vol. xvi., pp. 323-4.

"20th Feb. 1709-10.—Griffith Parry was brought to the Bar, where he, upon his knees, received a reprimand from the Speaker ; and it was ordered that he be discharged out of Custody, he paying his Fees."—Id., vol. xvi., p. 325.

(19) "19 Oct., 1722.—A Petition of Owen Meyricke, of Bodorgan, was read ; shewing that at the last election of a Knight of the Shire, the Honourable Richard, Lord Bulkeley, and the Petitioner stood Candidates. That the greater part of the Freeholders polled for the Petitioner : that Lord Bulkeley despairing of having a majority, did largely increase the number of Freeholders by executing illegal Conveyances, and making collusive estates of several houses or hereditaments of about five-and-forty shillings per annum, to a great number of their Tenants, Servants, and other persons, to enable them to vote for the said Lord Bulkeley ; the said Lord and friends did use menacing words to deter several Freeholders from polling for the Petitioner; that by these and other practices the said Lord procured himself to be returned to the prejudice of the Petitioner.

"Ordered, that the said Petition be referred to the consideration of the Committee of Privileges and Elections : and that they do examine the matter thereof, and report the same with their opinion thereupon to the House." Id., vol. xx., . 30.

"20 Jan., 1724.—Another and similar Petition presented by the said Owen Meyricke."—Id., vol. xx., p. 238.

"13 Nov., 1724.—Another Petition presented from the said Owen Meyricke."—Id., vol. xx., p. 334.

| Anno Dom. | Date of Return. | Regnal Year. | Name. | |
|---|---|---|---|---|
| 1722 | 8 April. | 8 George I. | Hon. Henry Bertie. (20) . | Burgess. |
| 1725 | 10 „ | 11 „ | Hugh Williams, of Nant-hanog, Esq. (21) . | K.S. |

" 8 March, 1724-5.—It was ordered that the Report from the Committee of Privileges and Elections, touching the Election for Anglesey, be received upon Saturday next."—Jour. House of Commons, vol. xx., p. 433.

" 13 March, 1724-5.—Mr. Gybbon reported from the above named Committee the matter as it appeared to them, and the Resolutions made thereupon. And the said Report and Resolution being read a second time are as followeth ; viz. Upon the Petition of Owen Meyricke complaining of the undue election and return of Richard, late Lord Bulkeley : there were 217 votes polled for the said Lord, and 148 for the Petitioner. The Petitioner's Counsel objected to 111 of the said Lord's votes ; viz. 62 as not qualified by their Estates to vote ; and 49, as influenced by bribery or menaces. On the first head they called, William Lewis, Esq., who said he knew nearly all the Voters in the County ; and gave evidence of their declarations and confessions to him as follows ; viz. That 5 had only Leaseholds for years : that 21 had Freeholds by purchase within twelve months before the election, or by Conveyances executed within that time by Lord Bulkeley or others ; that 11 had no Freehold ; that 2 voted for lands, of which mortgagees were in possession ; another was only a mortgagee for years ; that the Freeholds of 15 were under the yearly value of forty shillings ; two were not rated : and that three others were rated under the value of forty shillings per annum : and the rates were produced.

" Richard Thomas said, two had confessed to him that they had no Freehold.

" William Lewis, Esq., said that 44 voters confessed to him that they had voted for Lord Bulkeley for the following reasons ; six for money given by his Lordship ; two for money given by his Lordship's directions ; twenty-eight for gifts or promises of rewards of timber, fuel, marle, or the like ; another for remittance of arrears of rent by his landlord, a friend of the said Lord ; five others because of threats by his Lordship ; and another because of threats by his Lordship's Agent.

" Thomas Evans gave similar evidence.

" Hugh Lewis said another was guilty of corrupt practices.

" On the other hand Counsel insisted that the testimony of Mr. Lewis alone was not sufficient to disqualify so many voters who had sworn to their Freeholds at the election ; and against what he (Lewis) said, they called William Lewis, of Tryselwyn, Esq., William Owen, Esq., and Mr. Hugh Price. And that upon the whole matter the Committee were of opinion that the Right Honble. Richard, late Lord Bulkeley, was duly elected : which said Resolution being read a second time, and the question put, was agreed to by the House."—Id., vol. xx., p. 440.

(20) " 18 Oct., 1722.—William Bodvell, a Burgess of Newburgh, presented a Petition, stating that the right of electing a Burgess for Beaumaris is in all the Burgesses of both Boroughs, and that the major part of the Burgesses at the last election gave their votes for the Petitioner. That Robert Coetmore, Esq., Mayor, Cadwallader Williams, and Lancelot Bulkeley, Bailiffs of Beaumaris, favouring Henry Bertie, Esq., rejected the votes of a great number of the voters for Newburgh ; and with force hindered others from entering the Guildhall of Beaumaris to vote for the Petitioner ; and by these and other practices the said Henry Bertie has been unduly returned. Ordered that the said Petition be referred to the consideration of the Committee of Privileges and Elections, &c."—Id., vol. xx., p. 25.

" 10 Jan., 1723-4.—Another, and similar Petition presented by the said William Bodvell.—Id , vol. xx., p. 230 ; and again on the 13 Nov., 1724."—Id., vol. xx., p. 335.

(21) " 17 March, 1724-5.—Ordered, that Mr. Speaker do issue his Warrant for a new Writ to be made out to elect a Knight of the Shire, in the place of the Rt. Hon. Richard, Lord Bulkeley, Viscount Cashells, deceased."—Id., vol. xx., p. 451.

" 22 April, 1725.—A Petition was presented by Thomas Lloyd, of Llanidan, against the Return of Hugh Williams, Esq., for that John Owen, the Sheriff, Mr. Williams, and others, intimidated several of the Freeholders who came to vote for the Petitioner ; and locked up others from voting for him ; also that the said Sheriff refused to poll several persons for the Petitioner ; and refused to administer the oath appointed to be taken by the Freeholders : and by many undue practices and Bribery the said Mr. Williams hath procured himself to be elected. It was therefore Ordered, that the Petition be referred to the consideration of the Committee of Privileges and Elections, &c., &c."—Id., vol. xx., p. 501.

| Anno Dom. | Date of Return. | Regnal Year. | Name. | |
|---|---|---|---|---|
| 1727 | 7 Sept. | 1 George II. | Hugh Williams, of Nant-hanog, Esq. (22) . . K.S. | ⎫ |
| „ | 6 Aug. | 1 „ | Watkin Williams Wynn, Esq. (23) . . . Burgess. | ⎬ ⎭ |

(22) "2 Feb. 1727-8.—A Petition was presented by Thomas Lloyd, and read, setting forth that the Petitioner and Hugh Williams, stood Candidates at the late election of a Knight of the Shire. That many were admitted to vote for Mr. Williams who had no right to vote : and several who were entitled to vote, and offered to poll for the Petitioner, were rejected, by which undue means, and the partiality of the Sheriff (Henry Morgan, Esq.), in holding a Court, and taking poll for Mr. Williams after the County Court had been discontinued, and in tearing and defacing the poll book, Mr. Williams procured himself to be returned, &c.

" On the same day a Petition of several of the Freeholders was presented, stating that on the 7th September the Sheriff held his Court, and opened the poll for the election, and continued the same until the evening of the next day, and then closed the poll as the Petitioners apprehended, the said Court not being adjourned over to any other time ; by reason of which, the Petitioners and others, then present, who intended to vote for Mr. Lloyd, were prevented, and they departed to their habitations ; but the said Sheriff being sensible that Mr. Lloyd had the majority thought fit to hold a Court the next day and re-open the Poll, and admitted divers persons to vote for Mr. Williams, by which means and illegal practices Mr. Williams was declared to be duly elected, though Mr. Lloyd was duly elected, and ought to have been returned, &c. It was therefore Ordered, that both the Petitions should be referred to the consideration of the Committee of Privileges and Elections, &c., &c."—Jour. House of Commons, vol. xxi., p. 31.

" 9th May, 1728.—Complaint being made to the House of some undue practice in the delivery of several of the Writs, particularly those for Anglesey, &c., &c. It was Ordered, that Mr. Robert Briscoe, Messenger attending the Great Seal, do attend the House to-morrow morning ; also, that the Clerk of the Crown do attend at the same time with the Returns for Anglesey, &c., &c."—Id., vol. xxi., p. 158.

" 10 May, 1728.—The Clerk of the Crown attended with the Returns, &c. The House being informed that Mr. Briscoe attended at the door, a motion was made that he be now called in. A Debate arose thereupon ; and a motion being made, and the Question being put, That the Debate be adjourned until this day fortnight, there were 150 For, and 90 Against it."— Id., vol. xxi., p. 159.

" 24 May, 1728.—It was Ordered, that Mr. Briscoe do attend the House that day seven-night, also the Clerk of the Crown."—Id., vol. xxi., p. 179.

" 22 Jan., 1728-9.—Another Petition was presented by the aforesaid Thomas Lloyd (similar to the preceding), against the Return of the aforesaid Mr. Williams."—Id., vol. xxi., p. 189.

" 4 Feb., 1728-9.—Another Petition presented by several of the Freeholders (similar to the preceding), against the Return of Mr. Williams."—Id., vol. xxi., p. 207. Both Petitions were Ordered to be referred to the consideration of the Committee of Privileges and Elections, &c.

(23) " 1 Feb., 1727-8.—A Petition of William Bodvill, Esq., was presented and read ; stating that at the last election for Beaumaris, Henry Bertie, Esq., Watkin Williams Wynne, Esq., and the Petitioner, stood Candidates ; that the Petitioner was duly elected, and ought to have been returned ; but Mr. John Rowlands, Mayor, and Maurice Evans, and John Green, Bailiffs, who were also guilty of other illegal practices, returned the said Mr. Wynn. Ordered to be referred to the consideration of the Committee, &c., &c."—Id., vol. xxi., p. 29.

" 13 Feb., 1727-8.—A Petition similar to the above was presented from the major part of the Burgesses of Beaumaris ; also another from the Burgesses of Newborough, complaining that the Mayor and Bailiffs of Beaumaris rejected their votes when tendered, &c. Both Petitions were ordered to be referred to the consideration of the Committee, &c., and also, that it be an instruction to the said Committee that they do hear the matter of the petitions at the same time as they hear the matter of the petition of William Bodvell, Esq., complaining of an undue return for Beaumaris."—Id., vol. xxi., p. 48.

" 22 Jan., 1728-9.—Another petition was presented from the said William Bodvell, Esq., on the same subject, which was ordered to be referred to the consideration of the Committee, &c."—Id., vol. xxi., p. 188 ; also on—

" 3 Feb., 1728-9.—Two similar Petitions to the above, one from the Burgesses of Beaumaris ; the other from the Burgesses of Newborough. Ordered to be referred, &c."—Id., vol. xxi., p. 202.

" 26 Jan., 1729-30.—The matter of the two preceding Petitions were ordered to be heard at the Bar of the House upon Thursday, 26 Feb."—Id., vol. xxi., p. 421.

| Anno Dom. | Date of Return. | Regnal Year. | Name. |
|---|---|---|---|
| 1730 | 25 March. | 3 George II. | Rt. Hon. Richard, Lord Viscount Bulkeley, of Cashell. (24) . . Burgess. |

" 26 Feb., 1729-30.—On the Order of the day being read, it was Ordered, That the merits of the election for Beaumaris be heard at the Bar of the House upon Tuesday morning next."—Journals House of Commons, vol. xxi., p. 466.

" 3 March, 1729-30.—The House proceeded to the hearing of the merits of the election for Beaumaris. Counsel were called in. Both Petitions were read, and Counsel were heard. And it being objected that the Petition of the Burgesses of Newborough was signed by some persons who had not signed the former Petitions, and that the names of some of the Petitioners were not written, or marks made by the parties themselves; the Counsel were ordered to withdraw. And it being ordered that the Counsel be called in, and be directed by Mr. Speaker to proceed only upon the matter of the Petition of the major part of the Burgesses of Beaumaris; they were recalled, and Mr. Speaker acquainted them therewith; and after further hearing, Counsel on both sides were ordered to withdraw, the House having to attend the King, and the further hearing was adjourned till two o'clock in the afternoon.

" The House being met, and the Counsel called in, they were further heard as to the right of election, which the Petitioners' Counsel insisted is in all the inhabitants of the Borough of Beaumaris, being Householders, not receiving Alms; and the sitting Member's Counsel insisted that the right of election is in the Mayor, Bailiffs, and Capital Burgesses of Beaumaris only.

" On the Petitioners' part the 19 and 26 sections of the Act of 27 Henry VIII.; the 3rd section of the Act of the 35th year of the said King; a copy of a private Act made in the 2 and 3 Edward VI.; and copies of several Returns to Parliament were read; and the Petitioners' Counsel examined a Witness.

" On the Sitting Member's part the 119 section of the Act of 34 & 35 Hen. VIII.; the Act of 21 James I.; the Charter of Beaumaris granted by Queen Elizabeth (bearing date the 22 June, in the 4th year of her reign), containing Inspeximuses of several Charters granted in former reigns, were read; and the resolution of the House of the 18 Feb., 1709-10, touching the right of election, was also read; and the Sitting Member's Counsel examined several Witnesses, and summed up their evidence. Petitioners' Counsel were heard by way of reply; and then the Counsel on both sides were directed to withdraw. And a motion being made, and the Question proposed, 'That the Right of Election of a Burgess for Beaumaris is in the Inhabitants of the said Borough of Beaumaris, being Householders, and not receiving Alms;' several Amendments were made to the Question; viz. That the word 'Inhabitant' stand part of the Question; it was negatived. An Amendment being proposed that the words, 'Mayor, Bailiffs, and Burgesses at large,' be inserted instead of the word 'Inhabitants;' it was proposed to amend the said Amendment by inserting therein between the word 'and,' and the word 'Burgess,' the word 'Capital,' and to leave out the words 'at large;' and the Question being put, that the said word 'Capital' be there inserted; it was resolved in the affirmative. And the Question being put, that these words 'at large' stand part of the said Amendment; it was negatived. And the Question being put, that the word 'only' be added to the said Amendment: it was resolved in the affirmative. Then the said Amendment so amended was agreed by the House to be made part of the Question. Another Amendment was proposed to be made to the Question by leaving out these words 'being Householders, and not receiving Alms.' And the Question being put that these words stand part of the Question; it was negatived. Then the Question so amended being put, It was Resolved, 'That the Right of electing a Burgess for Beaumaris, is in the Mayor, Bailiffs, and Capital Burgesses only of the said Borough of Beaumaris.' Then the Counsel were called in again, and Mr. Speaker acquainted them with the said Resolution. And the Petitioners' Counsel informed the House, that the House having so determined the Right of Election, they had nothing further to offer; then the Counsel were again directed to withdraw. Resolved, 'That Watkin Williams Wynn, Esq., is duly elected to serve for Beaumaris.' "—Id., vol. xxi., pp. 472-3.

(24) " 4 March, 1729-30.—Watkin Williams Wynn, Esq., being chosen Knight of the Shire for Denbigh, and Burgess for Beaumaris, made his election for Denbigh; thereupon it is Ordered, that Mr. Speaker do issue his Warrant, &c., to elect a Burgess in the room of the said Watkin Williams Wynn, Esq."—Id., vol. xxi., p. 474.

13

| Anno Dom. | Date of Return. | Regnal Year. | Name. | |
|---|---|---|---|---|
| 1734 | 9 May. | 7 George II. | Nicholas Bayly, of Plas Newydd, Esq. . . | K.S. |
| ,, | 8 ,, | 7 ,, | Rt. Hon. Richard, Lord Viscount Bulkeley, of Cashell. . . . | Burgess. |
| 1739 | 20 April. | 12 ,, | Rt. Hon. James, Lord Viscount Bulkeley, of Cashell. (25) . . | Burgess. |
| 1741 | 28 May. | 14 ,, | John Owen, of Presadd-fed, Esq. · . . | K.S. |
| ,, | 14 ,, | 14 ,, | Rt. Hon. James, Lord Viscount Bulkeley, of Cashell. . . . | Burgess. |
| 1746 | 16 July. | 20 ,, | Sir Nicholas Bayly, of Plas Newydd, Bart. . | K.S. |
| ,, | 7 ,, | 20 ,, | Rt. Hon. James, Lord Viscount Bulkeley, of Cashell. . . . | Burgess. |
| 1753 | 29 Jan. | 26 ,, | John Owen, of Presadd-fed, Esq. (26) . . | Burgess. |
| 1754 | 25 April. | 27 ,, | Sir Nicholas Bayly, of Plas Newydd, Bart. . | K.S. |
| ,, | 22 ,, | 27 ,, | Richard Price, of Vaenol, Esq. (27) . . . | Burgess. |
| 1761 | 16 ,, | 1 George III. | Owen Meyrick, Esq. (28) | K.S. |
| ,, | 2 ,, | 1 ,, | Richard Price, of Vaenol, Esq. . . . . | Burgess. |
| 1768 | 14 ,, | 8 ,, | Owen Meyrick, Esq. . | K.S. |
| ,, | 25 March. | 8 ,, | Sir Hugh Williams, of Baron Hill, Bart. . | Burgess. |
| 1770 | 12 April. | 10 ,, | Sir Nicholas Bayly, Bart. (29) | K.S. |

(25) "6 April, 1739.—Ordered, that Mr. Speaker do issue his Warrant, &c., to elect a Burgess in the room of the Rt. Hon. Lord Viscount Bulkeley, deceased."—Journals House of Commons, vol. xxiii., p. 319.

(26) "11 Jan., 1753.—Ordered, that Mr. Speaker do issue his Warrant, &c., to elect a Burgess in the room of the Rt. Hon. Lord Viscount Bulkeley, deceased."—Id., vol. xxvi., p. 520.

(27) *Also of Rhiwlas, Merionethshire. His father, William Price, Esq., married to his second wife, the Hon. Elizabeth Bulkeley, daughter of Richard, Viscount Bulkeley : she died 12th August, 1778, so Mr. Price's connection with Beaumaris. He was the last in the direct line of the Prices of Rhiwlas. W.

(28) *Of Bodorgan. W.

(29) "13 March, 1770.—Ordered, that Mr Speaker do issue his Warrant, &c., to elect a Knight of the Shire in the room of Owen Meyrick, Esq., deceased."—Id., vol. xxxii., p. 782.

| Anno Dom. | Date of Return. | Regnal Year. | Name. | |
|---|---|---|---|---|
| 1774 | 20 Oct. | 14 George III. | Rt. Hon. Thomas James Bulkeley, of Baron-hill, commonly called Lord Bulkeley, Viscount Cashell. (30) | K.S. |
| ,, | 22 ,, | 14 ,, | Sir Hugh Williams, of Castellmor, Bart. | Burgess. |
| 1780 | 14 Sept. | 20 ,, | Rt. Hon. Thomas James Bulkeley, of Baron-hill, commonly called Lord Bulkeley, Viscount Cashell. | K.S. |
| ,, | 16 ,, | 20 ,, | Hon. Sir George Warren, K.B. | Burgess. |
| 1784 | 22 April. | 24 ,, | Nicholas Bayly, of Plas Newydd, Esq. (31) | K.S. |
| ,, | 17 ,, | 24 ,, | Hon. Hugh Fortescue. | Burgess. |
| 1785 | 25 July. | 25 ,, | Sir Hugh Williams, Bart. (32) | Burgess. |
| 1790 | 28 June. | 30 ,, | Hon. William Paget, of Plas Newydd. | K.S. |
| ,, | 24 ,, | 30 ,, | Sir Hugh Williams, Bart. | Burgess. |
| 1794 | 22 Nov. | 35 ,, | Hon. Arthur Paget, of Plas Newydd. | K.S. (33) |
| ,, | 20 Oct. | 34 ,, | Sir Watkin Williams Wynn, Bart. (34) | Burgess. |
| 1796 | 6 Jan. | 36 ,, | Sir Watkin Williams Wynn, Bart. | Burgess. |

(30) *Thomas James, seventh Viscount Bulkeley, died 1822, "perantiquæ familiæ Bulkeleyorum eheu ultimus." W.

(31) *Sir Nicholas Bayley, Bart., and father of Henry, first Earl of Uxbridge, of that family. W.

(32) "11 July, 1785.—Ordered, that the Speaker do issue his Warrant, &c., to elect a Burgess in the room of the Hon. Hugh Fortescue, now Lord Fortescue, called to the House of Peers.—Journals House of Commons, vol. xl., p. 1135.

*He was the second husband of Emma, Viscountess Dowager Bulkeley, and father of Sir Robert Williams, Bart., M.P. for Caernarvonshire. W.

(33) "30 Dec., 1794.—The Speaker informed the House that during the recess he had issued his Warrant, &c., to elect a Knight of the Shire in the room of the Hon. William Paget, deceased; also a Burgess in the room of Sir Hugh Williams, Bart., deceased."—Journals House of Commons, vol. l., p. 3.

(34) *The fifth Baronet of his family; died 1840—for many years Lord Lieutenant for Denbigh and Merioneth, and M.P. for the former County. W.

| Anno Dom. | Date of Return. | Regnal Year. | Name. | |
|---|---|---|---|---|
| 1802 | 14 July. | 42 George III. | Hon. Arthur Paget, of Plas Newydd. . . | K.S. |
| ,, | 10 ,, | 42 ,, | Rt. Hon. Thomas, Lord Newborough. . . | Burgess. |
| 1807 | 12 May. | 47 ,, | Hon. Berkeley Paget, of Plas Newydd. . . | K.S. |
| ,, | 8 ,, | 47 ,, | Thomas, Lord Newborough. | Burgess. |
| ,, | 10 Dec. | 48 ,, | Sir Edward Pryce Lloyd, of Pengwern, Flint., Bart. (35) . . . | Burgess. |
| 1810 | 6 July. | 50 ,, | Hon. Berkeley Paget, of Plas Newydd. (36) . | K.S. |
| 1812 | 12 Oct. | 52 ,, | Hon. Berkeley Paget, of Plas Newydd. . . | K.S. |
| ,, | 10 ,, | 52 ,, | Thomas Frankland Lewis, of Harpton Court, Radnor, Esq.(37) | Burgess. |
| 1818 | 26 June. | 58 ,, | Hon. Berkeley Paget, of Plas Newydd. . . | K.S. |
| ,, | 22 ,, | 58 ,, | Thomas Frankland Lewis, of Harpton Court, Radnor, Esq. . | Burgess. |
| 1820 | 16 March. | 1 George IV. | Henry Paget, Esq., commonly called the Rt. Hon. the Earl of Uxbridge. (38) . . | K.S. |
| ,, | 10 ,, | 1 ,, | Thomas Frankland Lewis, of Harpton Court, Radnor, Esq. . | Burgess. |
| 1826 | 16 June. | 7 ,, | Henry Paget, Esq., commonly called the Rt. Hon. the Earl of Uxbridge, of Plasnewydd. | K.S. |

(35) "21 Jan. 1808.—The Speaker informed the House that during the recess he had issued his Warrant, &c., to elect a Burgess in the room of Lord Newborough, deceased."—Journals House of Commons, vol. lxiii., p. 3.
*Afterwards the first Lord Mostyn. W.

(36) "20 June, 1810.—Ordered, that the Speaker do issue his Warrant, &c., to elect a Knight of the Shire in the room of the Hon. Berkeley Paget, who since his election hath accepted the office of one of the Commissioners for executing the office of Treasurer of the Exchequer."—Id., vol. lxv., p. 504.

(37) *Afterwards the Rt. Hon. Thomas Frankland Lewis, and father of the late Sir George Cornewall Lewis, Bart. W.

(38) *Afterwards the second Marquis of Anglesey. W.

| Anno Dom. | Date of Return. | Regnal Year. | Name. | |
|---|---|---|---|---|
| 1826 | 13 June. | 7 George IV. | Sir Robert Williams, of Ffryars, Anglesey, Bart. (39) . . . | Burgess. |
| 1828 | 3 April. | 9 „ | Henry Paget, Esq., commonly called the Rt. Hon. the Earl of Uxbridge, of Plasnewydd. (40) . . . | K.S. |
| 1830 | 5 Aug. | 1 William IV. | Henry Paget, Esq., commonly called the Rt. Hon. the Earl of Uxbridge, of Plasnewydd. | K.S. |
| „ | 3 „ | 1 „ | Sir Robert Williams, of Ffryars, Anglesey, Bart. | Burgess. |
| 1831 | 8 Feb. | 1 „ | Sir Richard Bulkeley Williams Bulkeley, of Baron-hill, Bart.(41) . | Burgess. |
| 1832 | 19 Dec. | 3 „ | Sir Richard Bulkeley Williams Bulkeley, of Baron Hill, Bart. . | K.S. |
| „ | 10 „ | 3 „ | Frederick Paget, of Plasnewydd, Esq. . . | Burgess. |
| 1835 | 14 Jan. | 5 „ | Sir Richard Bulkeley Williams Bulkeley, of Baron-hill, Bart. . | K.S. |
| „ | 8 „ | 5 „ | Frederick Paget, of Plasnewydd, Esq. . . | Burgess. |
| 1837 | 23 Feb. | 7 „ | William Owen Stanley, of Penrhos, Esq. (42) . | K.S. |

(39) *Son and successor of Sir Hugh Williams, afore-named. W.

(40) "17 March, 1828.—Ordered, that the Speaker do issue his Warrant, &c., to elect a Knight of the Shire in the room of the Rt. Hon. Henry Paget, commonly called the Earl of Uxbridge, who since his election hath accepted the office of State Steward to the Lord Lieutenant of Ireland."—Journals House of Commons, vol. lxxxiii., p. 177.

(41) "3 Feb. 1831.—The Speaker informed the House that he had issued his Warrant, &c., to elect a Burgess in the room of Sir Robert Williams, Bart., deceased."—Id., vol. lxxxvi., p. 205.

*Son and successor of Sir Robert Williams, and owner, by bequest from his uncle—half blood—Thomas James, seventh and last Viscount Bulkeley, of the great estates of that ancient family in Anglesey and Caernarvonshire. W.

(42) "31 Jan. 1837.—Ordered, that the Speaker do issue his Warrant, &c., to elect a Knight of the Shire in the room of Sir Richard Bulkeley Williams Bulkeley, Bart., who since his election hath accepted the office of Steward of the Chiltern Hundreds."—Id., vol. xcii., p. 3.

| Anno Dom. | Date of Return. | Regnal Year. | Name. | |
|---|---|---|---|---|
| 1837 | 2 Aug. | 1 Victoria. | William Owen Stanley, of Penrhos, Esq. . | K.S. |
| ,, | 25 July. | 1 ,, | Frederick Paget, of Plas-newydd, Esq. . . | Burgess. |
| 1841 | 7 ,, | 5 ,, | Hon. William Owen Stanley, of Penrhos. | K.S. |
| ,, | 29 June. | 5 ,, | Frederick Paget, of Plas-newydd, Esq. . . | Burgess. |
| 1847 | 7 Aug. | 11 ,, | Sir Richard Bulkeley Williams Bulkeley, of Baron Hill, Bart. . | K.S. |
| ,, | 31 July. | 11 ,, | George Augustus Frederick Paget, commonly called Lord George Frederick Paget, of Plas Newydd. . . | Burgess. |
| 1852 | 14 ,, | 16 ,, | Sir Richard Bulkeley Williams Bulkeley, of Baron-hill, Bart. . | K.S. |
| ,, | 6 ,, | 16 ,, | George Augustus Frederick Paget, commonly called Lord George Frederick Paget, of Plas Newydd. . . | Burgess. |
| 1857 | 3 April. | 20 ,, | Sir Richard Bulkeley Williams Bulkeley, of Baron-hill, Bart. . | K.S. |
| ,, | 28 March. | 20 ,, | Hon. William Owen Stanley, of Penrhos.(43) | Burgess. |
| 1859 | 4 May. | 22 ,, | Sir Richard Bulkeley Williams Bulkeley, of Baron-hill, Bart. . | K.S. |
| ,, | 29 April. | 22 ,, | Hon. William Owen Stanley, of Penrhos. . | Burgess. |
| 1865 | 17 July. | 29 ,, | Sir Richard Bulkeley Williams Bulkeley, of Baron-hill, Bart. . | K.S. |

(43) *Second and youngest son of John Thomas, Lord Stanley, of Alderley, twin brother of the second Lord. He married Ellin, youngest daughter of Sir John Williams, of Bodelwyddan, Bart. W.

| Anno Dom. | Date of Return. | Regnal Year. | Name. | |
|---|---|---|---|---|
| 1865 | 11 July. | 29 Victoria. | Hon. William Owen Stanley, of Penrhos. . | Burgess. |
| 1868 | 20 Nov. | 32 „ | Richard Davies of Benarth, Caernarvonshire, Esq. . . | K.S. |
| „ | 19 „ | 32 „ | Hon. William Owen Stanley, of Penrhos.(44) | Burgess. |

(⁴⁴) On this occasion Mr. Stanley's seat was unsuccessfully contested by Morgan Lloyd, Esq., Barrister-at-law.

# MEMBERS FOR THE COUNTY AND BOROUGH OF CAERNARVON.

| Anno Dom. | Date of Return. | Regnal Year. | Name. | | |
|---|---|---|---|---|---|
| 1541 | 20 Dec. | 33 Hen. VIII. | Sir Richard Bulkeley, Knt. | K.S. | ⎫ |
| ,, | 20 ,, | 33 ,, | John Puleston, Esq. . . | Burgess. | ⎭ |
| 1547 | 12 Oct. | 1 Edw. VI. | Sir John Puleston, Knt. . | K.S. | ⎫ |
| ,, | 12 ,, | 1 ,, | Robert Puleston, Esq. (1) . | Burgess. | ⎭ |
| 1553 | 25 Jan. | 6 ,, | John Wynn ap Hugh, Esq. (2) | K.S. | ⎫ |
| ,, | 25 ,, | 6 ,, | Griffith or Gruffin Davies, Esq. | Burgess. | ⎭ |
| ,, | 6 Sept. | 1 Mary. | Maurice Wynn, gent. (3) . | K.S. | ⎫ |
| ,, | 6 ,, | 1 ,, | Henry Robins, gent. . . | Burgess. | ⎭ |
| 1554 | 2 April. | 1 ,, | Moricius [alias Moryce] Wynn, Esq. . . . . | K.S. | ⎫ |
| ,, | 2 ,, | 1 ,, | Henry Robins, Esq. . . | Burgess. | ⎭ |
| ,, | 1 Nov. | 1 & 2 Phil. & Mary. | David Lloid ap Thomas. . | K.S. | ⎫ |
| ,, | 1 ,, | 1 & 2 ,, | Henry Robins. . . . | Burgess. | ⎭ |
| 1555 | 21 Oct. | 2 & 3 ,, | Richard Griffith. . . | K.S. | ⎫ |
| ,, | 21 ,, | 2 & 3 ,, | Sir Rice Griffith, Knt. (4) . | Burgess. | ⎭ |
| 1558 | 19 Jan. | 4 & 5 ,, | William Wynn ap William, Esq. | K.S. | ⎫ |
| ,, | 19 ,, | 4 & 5 ,, | Robert Griffith, Esq. . . | Burgess. | ⎭ |
| 1558—9 | | 1 Elizabeth. | Maurice Wynne [Gwydir], Esq. (5) . . . . | K.S. | ⎫ |
| ,, | | 1 ,, | John Harrington, Esq. . | Burgess. | ⎭ |
| 1563 | 13 Jan. | 5 ,, | Morris Wynn, Esq. . . | K.S. | ⎫ |
| ,, | 13 ,, | 5 ,, | John Harrington, Esq. . | Burgess. | ⎭ |

(1) *A Branch of the once powerful family of Puleston, of Emral.  W.

(2) *Of Bodvel.  He was Standard Bearer to John Dudley, Earl of Warwick, afterwards Duke of Northumberland, in the battle between him and Kett and the rebels, near Norwich, in the reign of Edw. VI.  John Wynn's horse was shot under him, and he was himself hurt, yet he upheld the great Standard of England; for which service the Duke bestowed upon him the Isle of Bardsey, and the demesne house of the Abbot near Aberdaron, called the Courthwith.—Memoirs of distinguished Natives of the County of Caernarvon (it should be mentioned, however, that Hen Eglwys, stated by Sir John Wynn, at page 108, to be in Caernarvonshire, is in Anglesey), by Sir John Wynn, Bart., at the end of the 4to. Edition of the Hist. of Gwydir family, Ruthin, 1827, p. 120.  W.

(3) *He was of Gwydir, and father of the celebrated Sir John Wynn, Bart.  Maurice Wynn died 18 Aug., 1580, and was buried at Llanrwst.  W.

(4) *See Williams's Observations on the Snowdon Mountains, p. 176.  W.

(5) Willis says in his Corrigenda, " In his place add Robert ap Hugh."

| Anno Dom. | Date of Return. | Regnal Year. | Name. | |
|---|---|---|---|---|
| 1571—2 | | 13 Elizabeth. | John Gwynn . . . | K.S. |
| ,, | | 13 ,, | John Griffith of Lleyn . | Burgess. |
| 1572 | 23 April. | 14 ,, | Dr. John Gwynn [LL.D.] . | K.S. |
| ,, | 23 ,, | 14 ,, | John Griffith, Gent. . . | Burgess. |
| ,, | | 14 ,, | William Thomas, Esq. (6) | K.S. |
| 1584—5 | | 27 ,, | William Thomas, Esq. . | K.S. |
| ,, | | 27 ,, | Edward Griffith, Gent. (7) | Burgess. |
| 1586 | 13 Oct. | 28 ,, | John Wynn [of Gwydir], Esq. (8) . . . . | K.S. |
| ,, | 13 ,, | 28 ,, | William Griffith, LL.D. . | Burgess. |
| 1588 | 12 Nov. | 30 ,, | Hugh Gwyn of Bodvel, Esq. | K.S. |
| ,, | 12 ,, | 30 ,, | Robert Wynn, of Conway, Gent. | Burgess. |
| 1589 | 4 Feb. | 31 ,, | Hugh Gwyn of Bodvel, . | K.S. |
| ,, | 4 ,, | 31 ,, | Robert Wynn, of Conway. | Burgess. |
| 1592 | 19 Nov. | 35 ,, | Wm. Maurice, of Cleneney. (9) | K.S. |
| ,, | 19 ,, | 35 ,, | Robert Griffith, Gent. . | Burgess. |
| 1593 | 19 Feb. | 35 ,, | William Morrice, Esq. . | K.S. |
| ,, | 19 ,, | 35 ,, | Robert Griffith, Gent. . | Burgess. |
| 1597 | 24 Oct. | 39 ,, | William Maurice.(?) . . | K.S. |
| ,, | 24 ,, | 39 ,, | Nicholas Griffith.(?) . . | Burgess. |
| 1601 | 30 Sept. | 43 ,, | William Jones, of Castell-march, Esq. . . . | K.S. |
| ,, | 30 ,, | 43 ,, | Nicholas Griffith, Gent. . | Burgess. |
| 1604 | 18 March. | 1 James I. | Sir William Maurice, Knt. | K.S. |
| ,, | 18 ,, | 1 ,, | John Griffith, of Cefnam-wlch, Esq. . . . | Burgess. |
| 1609 | 15 Nov. | 7 ,, | Clement Edmonds, Esq. (10) | Burgess. |
| 1614 | | | (11) | K.S. |
| ,, | 5 April. | 12 ,, | Nicholas Griffith. . . | Burgess. |

(6) Thomas was elected in the room of Dr. Gwynn, deceased.

The Parliament of the 14 Elizabeth was prorogued to the 18th year of her reign, when it was further prorogued to the 23rd year.

(7) *There is a notice of him in the Memoirs by Sir John Wynn (referred to previously), p. 112. He was killed in Flanders, in 1586. W.

(8) *Afterwards the well-known Sir John Wynn, Bart., the Historian of the Gwydir family : he died in March, 1626-7. W.

(9) *Afterwards Sir William Maurice, Knt., who died in Aug., 1622. His tombstone remains in Penmorva Churchyard. W.

(10) He was elected in the room of John Griffith, deceased.

(11) I cannot find any return for the County for this Parliament.

14

| Anno Dom. | Date of Return. | Regnal Year. | Name. | |
|---|---|---|---|---|
| 1620 | 27 Dec. | 18 James I. | John Griffith, junior of Llynn, Esq. . . . . | K.S. |
| ,, | 30 | 18 ,, | Nicholas Griffith, of Caernarvon, Esq. . . . . | Burgess. |
| 1624 | 21 Jan. | 21 ,, | Thomas Glynne, of Glynllivon, Esq. . . . . | K.S. |
| ,, | | 21 ,, | Sir Peter Mutton, Knt. (12) | Burgess. |
| 1625 | 11 May? | 1 Charles I. | Thomas Glynne, of Glynllivon, Esq. . . . . | K.S. |
| ,, | 29 April. | 1 ,, | Edward Littleton, Esq. (13) | Burgess. |
| 1626 | 8 Jan. | 1 ,, | John Griffith, junior, of Llynn, Esq. . . . . | K.S. |
| ,, | 4(?),, | 1 ,, | Edward Littleton, of the Inner Temple, Esq. (14) . | Burgess. |
| ,, | 6 March. | 1 ,, | Robert Jones, Gent. . . | ,, |
| 1628 | 17 ,, | 3 ,, | John Griffith, Esq. . . | K.S. |
| ,, | | 3 ,, | Edward Littleton, Esq . | Burgess. |
| 1640 | Feb. | 15 ,, | Thomas Glynne, Esq. . | K.S. |
| ,, | 9 March. | 15 ,, | John Glynne, of Lincoln's Inn, Esq. (15) . . . | Burgess. |
| 1640 (16) | 2 Dec. | 16 Charles I. | John Griffith, junior, of Llyn, Esq. (17) . . | K.S. |

(12) He was Chief Justice of North Wales, and acquired the Estate of Llanerch, in Denbighshire, by purchase from Edward Gryffydd, Esq. He died Nov. 4th, 1637, and was buried at Henllan. (Pennant's Tours (1810), vol. ii. p. 176.) He was twice married, and his first wife was an orphan girl of only 12 years of age. (See 3rd Report of Hist. MSS. Commission, Appendix, p. 258.)

(13) *I believe he was one of the Judges of the North Wales Circuit. W.

In 1625 and 1628 it appears by the Crown Office List, that Edward Littleton was elected for the "Vill. de Car. [et] Burg. Lempster" [Leominster] : but elected to sit for Caernarvon.

(14) In the above List a pen is run through Littleton's name, and that of Robert Jones is substituted. Littleton was again returned for Leominster and Caernarvon, and on this occasion elected to sit for Leominster.

(15) *Afterwards Sergeant and Chief Justice of the Upper Bench under the Commonwealth and Protectorate ; also one of Cromwell's " House of Lords :"

> " Did not the learned Glynne and Maynard,
> To make good subjects traitors, strain hard ?"

After the Restoration he was received into Royal favour, and did Charles II. great service, and in consequence was knighted, and appointed King's Sergeant, and his son was created a Baronet. In the Baronetages he is stated to have been the eldest son of Sir William Glynne, of Glynllifon, but he was, unquestionably, a younger son of Sir William. W.

Obit. 1666. See Pepys' Diary (Chandos ed.), p. 74.

(16) This was the Long Parliament.

" 10th Nov., 1640.—The Speaker was ordered to issue his Warrant, &c., for the election of a Knight of the Shire for Caernarvon, because no County day did intervene between the receipt of the Writ and the day of the Appearance in Parliament ; so that the Writ was returned with a Tarde."—Jour. of House of Commons, vol. ii., p. 25.

(17) His father, John Griffith, of Cefn Amwlch, was returned to the same Parliament for Beaumaris.

| Anno Dom. | Date of Return. | Regnal Year. | Name. | |
|---|---|---|---|---|
| 1640 | 3 Dec. | 16 Charles I. | William Thomas, Esq. . | Burgess. |
| „ | | 16 „ | William Foxwist, Esq., of Caernarvon (18) . . | Burgess. |
| „ | | 16 „ | Richard Wynne, Esq. . | K.S. |
| 1647 (19) | 21 Jan. | 22 „ | Richard Wynne, of Glasin-vryn, Esq. . . . | K.S. |
| „ | 30 „ | 22 „ | William Foxwist, of Lincoln's Inn, Esq. . . | Burgess. |
| 1653 | 5 July—12 Dec. | | To this Parliament were returned for Wales without being assigned to any County, Bushy Mansell, James Phillips, James Williams, Hugh Courtenay, Richard Price and John Brown. No Burgesses were summoned. | |
| 1654 | 12 July. | | John Glyn, Sergeant-at-Law, and . . . Thomas Madryn, Esq. (20) . | K.S. |
| 1656 | ?15 Oct. | | Henry Lawrance, Esq., (21) Lord President of the Council . . . . | K.S. |
| „ | 15 „ | | Robert Williams (22) . . | Burgess. |
| 1658 | 5 Jan. | | William Glynne, of Glyn-llivon, Esq. . . . | K.S. |
| „ | 5 „ | | Robert Williams, of Conway, Esq. . . . | Burgess. |
| 1660 | | | | |
| „ | 28 March. (Convention.) | | William Glynne (23) . . | Burgess. |

(18) From a note on the cover of the Crown Office List, it appears that all the names of those who went to Oxford to the King were struck out and others appointed in their places by the Long Parliament; hence it is probable, Thomas went to Oxford and Foxwist took his place at Westminster.

(19) "8th Dec., 1646.—The Speaker was ordered to issue his Warrant to elect a Knight of the Shire in the room of John Griffith, junior, disabled by Judgment of the House to serve any longer for the County; and to elect a Burgess in the room of William Thomas, Esq., deceased."—Jour. of House of Commons, vol. v., p. 4.

(20) Mostyn according to Browne Willis. No Burgesses appear to have been summoned. This was a double Return.

(21) Henry Lawrance was elected in the room of John Glynne, Chief Justice of the Upper Bench. He (Glynne) was elected for Caernarvon and Flint, but made choice to sit for the latter Shire.

(22) Browne Willis represents Robert Williams as returned with Henry Lawrance as Knight of the Shire; but he sat as Burgess.

(23) Son and heir of John Glynne, Sergeant-at-Law. I cannot find the Return for the County.

14—2

| Anno Dom. | Date of Return. | Regnal Year. | Name. | |
|---|---|---|---|---|
| 1661 | 27 March. | 13 Charles II. | Sir Richard Wynn, of Gwydir | K.S. } |
| „ | 27 „ | 13 „ | William Griffith, of Llyn, Esq. | Burgess. } |
| 1673—4 | | 25 „ | Sir Richard Wynne . . | K.S. } |
| „ | | 25 „ | Thomas Mostyn, Esq. (?) . | Burgess. } |
| 1675 | 5 May | 27 „ | Robert Bulkeley, Viscount Cashell (24) . . . | K.S. |
| 1679 | 5 Feb. | 31 „ | Thomas Bulkeley, of Dinas, Esq. . . . . | K.S. } |
| „ | 19 „ | 31 „ | Thomas Mostyn, of Gloddaeth, Esq. . . . | Burgess. } |
| „ | 28 Aug. | 31 „ | Thomas Bulkeley, of Dinas, Esq. . . . . | K.S. } |
| „ | 20 „ | 31 „ | Thomas Mostyn, of Gloddaeth, Esq. . . . | Burgess. } |
| 1681 | 2 March. | 33 „ | Thomas Bulkeley, of Dinas, Esq. . . . . | K.S. } |
| „ | 2 „ | 33 „ | Thomas Mostyn, of Gloddaeth, Esq. . . . | Burgess. } |
| 1685 | 22 April. | 1 James II. | Thomas Bulkeley, of Dinas, Esq. . . . . | K.S. } |
| „ | 22 „ | 1 „ | John Griffith, of Llynne, Esq. | Burgess. } |
| 1689 | 19 Jan. | (Convention.) | Sir William Williams, of Vaynol, Bart. (25). . | K.S. } |
| „ | 19 „ | „ | Sir Robert Owen, Knt. (25) | Burgess. } |
| 1690 | 19 March. | 2 Will. & Mary. | Sir William Williams, of Vaynol, Bart. . . | K.S. } |
| „ | 19 „ | 2 „ | Sir Robert Owen, Knt. (26) | Burgess. } |
| 1695 | 23 Oct. | 7 William III. | Sir William Williams, of Vaynol, Bart. . . | K.S. } |
| „ | 23 „ | 7 „ | Sir Robert Owen, Knt. . | Burgess. } |

(24) "13th April, 1675.—The Speaker issued a Warrant to elect a Knight of the Shire in the room of Sir Richard Wynn, deceased."—Journals House of Commons, vol. ix., p. 315.

Second Viscount Bulkeley, of Cashel.

(25) This Return was made by John Vaughan, one of the Coroners for the County of Caernarvon.

(26) Of Cleneney and Porkington. "2nd April, 1690.—A complaint was made to the House that the High Sheriff of Caernarvon had not made his Return of the Members to serve in this present Parliament; it was ordered that he be summoned by the Sergeant at Arms attending the House to show cause why he had not made the said Return."—Jour. of House of Commons, vol. x., p. 363. "On the 4th April.—No Return being then made, he was ordered into custody."—Id., vol. x., p. 367. "On the 8th April.—The House was informed he had made his Return; and upon a Motion being made, That he be discharged from custody, it was agreed to, upon his first paying his fee."—Id., vol. x., p. 370. Samuel Hanson, of Bodvel, was the Sheriff.

| Anno Dom. | Date of Return. | Regnal Year. | Name. | |
|---|---|---|---|---|
| 1697 | 10 Feb. | 8 William III. | Thomas Bulkeley, of Dinas, Esq. . . . . | K.S. |
| „ | 10 „ | 8 „ | Sir Robert Owen, Knt. (27) | Burgess. |
| 1698 | 27 July. | 10 „ | Thomas Bulkeley, of Dinas, Esq. . . . . | K.S. |
| „ | 10 Aug. | 10 „ | Sir John Wynn, Knt. & Bart. (28) | Burgess. |
| 1701 | 18 Jan. | 12 „ | Honble. Thomas Bulkeley, of Dinas. . . . | K.S. |
| „ | 17 „ | 12 „ | Sir John Wynn, Knt. & Bart. | Burgess. |
| „ | 3 Dec. | 13 „ | Honble. Thomas Bulkeley, of Dinas . . . | K.S. |
| „ | 4 „ | 13 „ | Sir John Wynn, Knt. & Bart. | Burgess. |
| 1702 | 5 Aug. | 1 Anne. | Honble. Thomas Bulkeley, of Dinas. . . . | K.S. |
| „ | 31 July. | 1 „ | Sir John Wynn, Knt. & Bart. | Burgess. |
| 1705 | 6 June. | 4 „ | Sir John Wynn, Knt. & Bart. | K.S. |
| „ | 24 May. | 4 „ | Honble. Thomas Bulkeley, of Dinas. . . . | Burgess. |
| 1708 | 2 June. | 7 „ | Sir John Wynn, Knt. & Bart. | K.S. |
| „ | 17 May. | 7 „ | William Griffith, of Kefn- Amwlch, Esq. . . | Burgess. |
| 1710 | 30 Oct. | 9 „ | Sir John Wynn, Knt. & Bart. | K.S. |
| „ | 25 „ | 9 „ | William Griffith, of Llûn, Esq. | Burgess. |
| 1713 | 6 Sept. | 12 „ | William Griffith, of Llyne, Esq. (29) . . . . | K.S. |
| „ | 18 „ | 12 „ | Thomas Wynn, of Bodvean, Esq. . . . . | Burgess. |

(27) "14th May, 1697.—The Speaker was ordered to issue his Warrant, &c., to elect a Burgess in the room of Sir Robert Owen, Knt., deceased."—Jour. of House of Commons, vol. xii., p. 269. I cannot find any Return to this Warrant.

(28) *Of Watstay, the name of which he altered to Wynnstay. He died in 1719, aged 91. During the last years of his life he was blind, and was, I have heard, daily drawn down the Park at Wynnstay in his garden chair, to put his hands upon the great oak, still known as "Sir John Wynn's Oak." He was the last Baronet, in the direct line, of the great house of Gwydir. W.

(29) "5th March, 1714.—A petition of Sir Roger Mostyn, Baronet, was read; setting forth that the Candidates for the County of Caernarvon proposed, were William Griffith, Esq., and the Petitioner, who depended upon an Agreement at the General Meeting of the Gentlemen of the County, particularly signed by the said Mr. Griffith, by which the Petitioner was to succeed Sir John Wynn; and made no preparation for a poll; but, at the election asserted the said Agreement, and demanded performance of it; but was refused: The Petitioner polled four friends, in order to desire an Oath, in an Act for qualifying Members to sit in Parliament, to be tendered the other Candidate; who not appearing, the Petitioner had no opportunity of so doing; and desiring of the Sheriff to be satisfied therein, was answered, He had taken the Oath that morning: That the Petitioner doubting *Sir* (*sic*) William Griffith's qualifications, hopes to be judged duly elected, and submits to the House therein.—Ordered, That the said Petition be referred to the consideration of the Committee of Privileges and Elections, &c."—Jour. of House of Commons, vol. xvii., p. 486.

| Anno Dom. | Date of Return. | Regnal Year. | Name. | |
|---|---|---|---|---|
| 1715 | 14 Feb. | 1 George I. | William Griffith, of Kefn-Amwlch, Esq. . . | K.S. } |
| ,, | 8 ,, | 1 ,, | Thomas Wynn, Esq. . | Burgess. } |
| ,, | 27 April. | 1 ,, | John Griffith, of Llûn, Esq. (30) . . . . | K.S. |
| 1722 | 18 ,, | 8 ,, | John Griffith, of Cefn-Amwlch, Esq. . . | K.S. } |
| ,, | 6 ,, | 8 ,, | Thomas Wynn, of Glyn Llivon, Esq. (31) . . | Burgess. } |
| 1727 | 30 Aug. | 1 George II. | John Griffith, of Cefn-Amwlch, Esq. . . | K.S. } |
| ,, | 22 ,, | 1 ,, | Thomas Wynn, Esq. . | Burgess. } |
| 1734 (32) | 14 May. | 7 ,, | John Griffith, of Kefn-amwlch, Esq.. . . | K.S. } |
| ,, | 4 ,, | 7 ,, | Thomas Wynn, of Bodvean, Esq. . . . . | Burgess. } |
| 1740 | 2 Jan. | 13 ,, | John Wynn, of Glyn-llivon, Esq. (33) . . | K.S. |
| 1741 | 20 May. | 14 ,, | William Bodvel, of Madrin, Esq. . . . . | K.S. } |
| ,, | 11 ,, | 14 ,, | Thomas Wynn, Esq. . | Burgess. } |
| 1747 | 8 July. | 21 ,, | William Bodvel, of Madrin, Esq. . . . . | K.S. } |
| ,, | 3 ,, | 21 ,, | Sir Thomas Wynn, Bart. . | Burgess. } |

(30) "25th March, 1715.—The Speaker was ordered to issue his Warrant to elect a Knight of the Shire in the room of William Griffith, Esq., deceased."—Jour. of House of Commons, vol. xviii., p. 23.

(31) "Three petitions (dated, 24th Oct., 1722 ; 13th Jan., and 23rd Nov., 1724), were presented by William Price, Esq. (who stood Candidate with Thomas Wynn at the election held 3rd April, 1722), against the Return of the said Thomas Wynn, Esq.; which were ordered to be referred to the consideration of the Committee of Privileges and Elections, &c."—Jour. of House of Commons, vol. xx., pp. 38, 232, 347.

(32) "9th May, 1728.—A Complaint was made to the House that there had been some undue practice in the delivery of several Writs for Members to serve in this Parliament, amongst other Counties that of Caernarvon : it was,—Ordered, That Mr. Robert Briscoe, the Messenger attending the Great Seal, do attend this House to-morrow morning ; also that the Clerk of the Crown do attend with the Returns at the same time."—Journals House of Commons, vol. xxi., p. 158.

"10th May, 1728.—The Clerk of the Crown attended as ordered ; and upon a Motion being made that Mr. Briscoe be now called, a Debate arose thereupon, and the question being put, That the Debate be adjourned until this day fortnight; the House divided, when there were 150 for, and 90 against the Motion."—Id., vol. xxi., p. 159. "On the 24th May.—The Clerk of the Crown and Mr. Briscoe were ordered to attend upon that day seven-night." —Id., vol. xxi., p. 179.

(33) "15th Nov., 1739.—The Speaker was ordered to issue his Warrant to elect a Knight of the Shire in the room of John Griffith, deceased."—Id., vol. xxiii., p. 383.

| Anno Dom. | Date of Return. | Regnal Year. | Name. | |
|---|---|---|---|---|
| 1749 | 2 May. | 22 George II. | Sir William Wynne, Knt. (34) | Burgess. |
| 1754 | 29 April. | 27 „ | Sir John Wynn, of Glyn-llivon, Bart. . . . | K.S. ⎫ |
| „ | 20 „ | 27 „ | Sir William Wynne, Knt. . | Burgess. ⎬ |
| „ | 16 Dec. | 28 „ | Robert Wynne, Esq. (35) . | Burgess. |
| 1761 | 1 April. | 1 George III. | Thomas Wynn, of Glynn, Esq. . . . . | K.S. ⎫ |
| „ | 1 „ | 1 „ | Sir John Wynn, Bart. . | Burgess· ⎬ |
| 1768 | 30 March. | 8 „ | Thomas Wynn, Esq. . | K.S. ⎫ |
| „ | 28 „ | 8 „ | Glynn Wynn, Esq. . . | Burgess. ⎬ |
| 1774 | 2 Nov. | 15 „ | Thomas Assheton Smith, of Caernarvon, Esq. (36) | K.S. ⎫ |
| „ | 13 Oct. | 15 „ | Glynn Wynn, Esq. . . | Burgess. ⎬ |
| 1780 | 27 Sept. | 20 „ | John Parry, of Wernfawr, Esq. (37) . . . | K.S. ⎫ |
| „ | 12 „ | 20 „ | Glynn Wynn, Esq. . . | Burgess. ⎬ |
| 1781 | 16 July. | 21 „ | „ „ „ (38) . | Burgess. |

(34) "29th April, 1749.—The Speaker was Ordered to issue his Warrant, &c., to elect a Burgess in the room of Sir Thomas Wynn, Bart., deceased."—Jour. of House of Commons, vol. xxv., p. 842.

*Sir Thomas Wynn, of Glynllivon, the first Baronet of his family, died M.P. for Caernarvon, 13 April, 1749. He was one of the Clerks of the Board of Green Cloth, and was succeeded in the Baronetcy and estates, by his son John Wynn, Deputy Treasurer of Chelsea Hospital. W.

(35) "2nd Dec., 1754.—The Speaker was Ordered to issue his Warrant, &c., to elect a Burgess in the room of Sir William Wynne, Knt., deceased."—Jour. of House of Commons, vol. xxvii., p. 39.

(36) "9th Dec., 1774.—Sir Thomas Wynn presented a Petition against T. A. Smith, Esq., (who stood Candidate with the Petitioner), he being guilty of Bribery and Corruption; and by violence and threats deterred and prevented several Freeholders from voting for the petitioner, and that T. A. Smith, Esq., father of the said T. A. Smith, and late High Sheriff of Caernarvon, dying during his Shrievalty, having in his life time appointed Hugh Ellis, Gent., his Under Sheriff, who, from the said death, acted as Sheriff; and that the said Hugh Ellis, before the said election, not only canvassed for the said T. A. Smith, but also attended at several entertainments given by, or on behalf of the said T. A. Smith in order to procure him to be elected, and in other respects the said Hugh Ellis both before and at the election acted in a very partial and unwarrantable manner in the execution of his office: and owing to the above abuses the Petitioner was compelled to discontinue the poll, whereby the said T. A. Smith was returned, to the prejudice of the Petitioner:—Ordered, That the said Petition be taken into consideration upon Friday, the 19th May next, at 3 o'clock, p.m."—Id., vol. xxxv., p. 33.

"16th Dec., 1774.—Another petition presented by some of the Freeholders against the Return of T. A. Smith."—Id., vol. xxxv., p. 47.

"12th April, 1775.—The said Petitions were ordered to be discharged."—Id., vol. xxxv., p. 301.

(T. Assheton Smith signed the Return as Sheriff for the said election on the 2d Nov., 1774.)

(37) A Bencher of Lincoln's Inn. His Arms are in the painted window of the Hall of that Inn. He was an ancestor of the Member for 1868.

(38) "5th July, 1781.—The Speaker was ordered to issue his Warrant, &c., to elect a Burgess, in the room of Glynn Wynn, Esq., who, since his election hath accepted the office of Receiver General of His Majesty's Land Revenue within the several Counties of North Wales, and the County Palatine of Chester."—Journals House of Commons, vol. xxxviii., p. 556. He was re-elected.

| Anno Dom. | Date of Return. | Regnal Year. | Name. | |
|---|---|---|---|---|
| 1784 | 7 April. | 24 George III. | John Parry, Esq. . . | K.S. |
| ,, | 9 ,, | 24 ,, | Glynn Wynn, of Caernarvon, Esq. (39) . . . | Burgess. |
| 1790 | 25 June. | 30 ,, | Robert Williams, of Caernarvon, Esq. . . . | K.S. |
| ,, | 21 ,, | 30 ,, | Rt. Honble. Henry, Lord Paget . . . . | Burgess. |
| 1795 (40) | 4 Feb. | 35 ,, | Rt. Honble. Henry, Lord Paget (41) . . . | Burgess. |
| 1796 | 7 June. | 36 ,, | Sir Robert Williams, of Nant, Bart. . . . | K.S. |
| ,, | 4 ,, | 36 ,, | Honble. Edward Paget . | Burgess. |
| 1802 | 12 July. | 42 ,, | Sir Robert Williams, of Plas-y-Nant, Bart. . . | K.S. |
| ,, | 6 ,, | 42 ,, | Honble. Edward Paget . | Burgess. |
| 1805 | 7 Nov. | 46 ,, | Sir Robert Williams, of Plas-y-Nant, Bart. . . | K.S. |
| ,, | 31 Oct. | 46 ,, | Honble. Charles Paget. . | Burgess. |
| 1807 | 14 May. | 47 ,, | Sir Robert Williams, of Plas-y-Nant, Bart. . | K.S. |
| ,, | 5 ,, | 47 ,, | Honble. Charles Paget. . | Burgess. |
| 1812 | 14 Oct. | 52 ,, | Sir Robert Williams, of Plas-y-Nant. . . | K.S. |
| ,, | 6 ,, | 52 ,, | Honble. Charles Paget. . | Burgess. |

(39) "7th June, 1784.—A long Petition presented by some of the Burgesses of Caernarvon and its contributory Boroughs on behalf of Sir Thomas Wynne, Bart., Baron Newborough, who contested the same against Glynn Wynn, Esq., on the 9th April, 1784; wherein are Complaints of illegal and corrupt practices, more especially against the Mayor and the two Bailiffs for withholding, altering, and mutilating the Books and Records of Caernarvon; also against the Town Clerk of Pwllheli, who having custody of the Books and Records of that Borough was in the interest of the said Glynn Wynn, and refused inspection of the said Books and Records : also that the said Mayor, &c., applied to the Recorder or Town Clerk of Nefin and obtained possession of the Books, Records, &c., of that Borough, and have kept possession of them ever since, by which Acts the said Lord Newborough and his Agents could not obtain the information and satisfaction as they were by Law entitled to: The Petitioners therefore pray the House to declare the said Glynn Wynn to be unduly returned, and the said Lord Newborough to be duly elected :—It was ordered that the Petition be taken into consideration upon Tuesday, 16th Nov."—Journals House of Commons, vol. xl., p. 96.

(This Petition was not proceeded with.)  The Petitioner and Member were brothers.

*In 1784, there was a contest for the County of Caernarvon.  Two of the Candidates, I have heard, were two brothers of the Wynn of Glynllivon family—they must have been Thomas Wynn, Esq., afterwards Lord Newborough, and his brother, Colonel Glynn Wynn—and the other Candidate was William Wynne, Esq., of Wern, and afterwards of Wern and Peniarth.  There is a printed address of the latter upon this occasion, at Peniarth. W.

(40) "28th Jan., 1795.—The Speaker was ordered to issue his Warrant, &c., to elect a Burgess in the room of the Honble. Henry Paget (commonly called Lord Paget), who, since his election, hath accepted a commission of Lieutenant Colonel in His Majesty's Army."—Id., vol. l., p. 100.

(41) Afterwards Marquis of Anglesey.

| Anno Dom. | Date of Return. | Regnal Year. | Name. | | |
|---|---|---|---|---|---|
| 1818 | 24 June. | 58 George III. | Sir Robert Williams, of Nant, Bart. . . . | K.S. | } |
| ,, | 18 ,, | 58 ,, | Honble. Charles Paget. . | Burgess. | |
| 1820 | 14 Mar. | 1 George IV. | Sir Robert Williams, of Nant, Bart. . . . | K.S. | } |
| ,, | 7 ,, | 1 ,, | Honble. Sir Charles Paget, Knt. | Burgess. | |
| 1823 | 12 Jan. | 3 ,, | ,, ,, ,, ,, ,, | Burgess. | |
| 1826 | 20 June. | 7 ,, | Thomas John, Lord New-borough . . . | K.S. | } |
| ,, | 15 ,, | 7 ,, | Rt. Hon. Lord William Paget. | Burgess. | |
| 1830 | 9 Aug. | 1 William IV. | Charles Wynne Griffith Wynne, of Cefn-amwlch, Esq. . | K.S. | } |
| ,, | 2 ,, | 1 ,, | William Ormsby Gore, of Porkington, Salop, Esq.(42) | Burgess. | |
| 1831 | 6 May. | 1 ,, | Charles Wynne Griffith Wynne, of Cefn-amwlch, Esq. . | K.S. | } |
| ,, | 13 ,, | 1 ,, | Sir Charles Paget, Knt. . | Burgess. | |
| 1832 | 21 Dec. | 3 ,, | Thomas Assheton Smith, of Vaynol, Esq. . . | K.S. | } |
| ,, | 15 ,, | 3 ,, | Rear Admiral, The Honble. Sir Charles Paget. (43) . | Burgess. | |

(42) See Sheriffs of Caernarvonshire.

(43) "7th Feb., 1833.—A Petition was presented by Owen Jones Ellis Nanney, Esq., a Major in the Caernarvonshire Militia, against the return of Sir Charles Paget, elected as Burgess."—Jour. House of Commons, vol. lxxxviii., p. 17.

"5th March.—A Select Committee appointed to try the same."—Id., vol. lxxxviii., p. 139.

"6th March.—The Committee determined that Sir Charles Paget was not duly returned a Burgess to serve in this Parliament; and that Owen Jones Ellis Nanney ought to have been returned.—Ordered, That the Deputy Clerk of the Crown do attend the House to-morrow with the Return and amend the same by rasing out the name of Sir Charles Paget and insert that of Owen Jones Ellis Nanney instead."—Id., vol. lxxxviii., p. 143.

"7th March.—Ordered, That all persons who will question the election of Owen Jones Ellis Nanney, to do so within the next Fourteen days."—Id., vol. lxxxviii., p. 146.

"11th March.—A Petition presented from some of the Burgesses against Owen Jones Ellis Nanney on account of Bribery; and praying the House to declare Sir Charles Paget to be duly elected: which Petition was ordered to be taken into consideration on Thursday, 16th May, next."—Id., vol. lxxxviii., p. 155.

"18th March.—A similar petition presented."—Id., vol. lxxxviii., p. 179.

"26th March.—No Recognizances being entered into in respect of the petition of the 11th March, it was ordered to be discharged."—Id., vol. lxxxviii., p. 216.

"16th May.—The names of the Members were drawn to try the Petition complaining of an undue election."—Id., vol. lxxxviii., p. 397.

"22nd May.—Certain Statements were put in by Counsel on both sides (given). The Committee determined that Owen Jones Ellis Nanney is not duly elected, and that Sir Charles Paget is :—the Deputy Clerk of the Crown is therefore ordered to attend the House to-morrow with the last return and amend the same by rasing out the name of Owen Jones Ellis Nanney, and inserting that of the Honble. Sir Charles Paget instead. The Committee also informed the House that they had altered the Poll taken at the last election by adding to such Poll 53 names and striking off 113 (names given)."—Id., vol. lxxxviii., p. 423.

| Anno Dom. | Date of Return. | Regnal Year. | Name. | |
|---|---|---|---|---|
| 1835 | 13 Jan. | 5 William IV. | Thomas Assheton Smith, of Vaenol, Esq. . . | K.S. |
| „ | 12 „ | 5 „ | Love Parry Jones Parry, of Llanbedrog, Esq. (44) . | Burgess. |
| 1837 | 1 Aug. | 1 Victoria. | John Ralph Ormsby Gore, of Porkington, Salop, Esq. (45) . . . | K.S. |
| „ | 27 July. | 1 „ | William Bulkeley Hughes, of Plascôch, Anglesey, Esq. (46) . . . | Burgess. |
| „ | 17 Oct. | 1 „ | John Ralph Ormsby Gore, Esq. . . . . | K.S. |
| „ | 17 „ | 1 „ | William Bulkeley Hughes, Esq. . . . . | Burgess. |
| 1841 | 14 July. | 5 „ | Hon. Edward Gordon Douglas Pennant, of Penrhyn Castle. (47) . . . | K.S. |
| „ | 14 „ | 5 „ | William Bulkeley Hughes, Esq. (48) . . . . | Burgess. |

"12th June.—A petition was presented against the determination of the Committee of the 22nd May, as to the Right of Election for the Borough of Caernarvon."—Jour. House of Commons, vol. lxxxviii., p. 479.

(44) Afterwards Major-General Sir Love P. J. Parry, K.H., of Madryn.

"10th March, 1835.—A Petition presented praying for a new election for the Borough on account of there not being a sufficient number of polling places; and that the poll was closed before the Town Clock of Caernarvon had struck four, and at that time Owen Jones Ellis Nanney had about forty electors who were ready at a moment's notice to vote for him: and that upon the gross poll the number of votes were declared to be for Love Parry Jones Parry, Esq., 378, and for Owen Jones Ellis Nanney, 350; &c., it was then ordered to be taken into consideration upon Thursday, 4th June."—Jour. House of Commons, vol. xc., p. 95. "And again upon Thursday, 18 June."—Id., vol. xc., p. 237. "Upon which latter date no one appearing on behalf of the Petitioners the said Petition was discharged."—Id., vol. xc., p. 352.

(45) *Eldest son of the Member for the Caernarvon Boroughs in 1830. He succeeded his father as one of the representatives for North Shropshire, and now (1872) holds that honourable post. In Sept., 1869, he succeeded his mother as heir to the great estates of Porkington, Clenenney, Glynn, &c., &c., in the Counties of Salop, Caernarvon, and Merioneth. W.

(46) *Eldest son and successor of the late Sir William Bulkeley Hughes, Knt., of Plascoch, the representative of an old family in Anglesey. W.

(47) *In him the title of Penrhyn has been restored, as "Baron Penrhyn, of Llandegai," and it may be said that well does he represent the ancient house of Penrhyn. "Si monumentum quæris, circumspice." W.

(48) "7th Sept., 1841.—A petition presented by George Augustus Frederick Paget, commonly called Lord George Paget, against William Bulkeley Hughes, Esq., for Bribery, &c."—Jour. House of Commons, vol. xcvi., p. 560.

"22nd Sept.—The Speaker acquainted the House that he had received a report from the Examiner of Recognizances, stating that the Surety to the Petition of Lord George Paget was objectionable on the ground that a person named in the Recognizance had not acknowledged the same."—Id., vol. xcvi., p. 584.

"1st Oct.—Another Petition from Lord George Paget relative to the objections against his Recognizance."—Id., vol. xcvi., p. 596.

| Anno Dom. | Date of Return. | Regnal Year. | Name. | |
|---|---|---|---|---|
| 1847 | 9 Sept. | 11 Victoria. | Hon. Edward Gordon Douglas Pennant. . . . | K.S. |
| ,, | 9 ,, | 11 ,, | William Bulkeley Hughes, Esq. . . . . | Burgess· |
| 1852 | 17 July. | 16 ,, | Hon. Edward Gordon Douglas Pennant. . . . | K.S. |
| ,, | 17 ,, | 16 ,, | William Bulkeley Hughes, Esq. (49). . . . | Burgess. |
| 1857 | 2 April. | 20 ,, | Hon. Edward Gordon Douglas Pennant. . . | K.S. |
| ,, | 29 ,, | 20 ,, | William Bulkeley Hughes, Esq. . . . . | Burgess. |
| 1859 | 6 May. | 22 ,, | Hon. Edward Gordon Douglas Pennant. . . | K.S. |
| ,, | 28 ,, | 22 ,, | Charles Wynne, of Cefn Amwlch, Esq. (50) . . | Burgess. |
| 1865 | 4 Aug. | 28 ,, | Hon. Edward Gordon Douglas Pennant. . . | K.S. |
| | 4 ,, | 28 ,, | William Bulkeley Hughes, Esq. . . . . | Burgess. |
| 1866 | 17 ,, | 30 ,, | Hon. George Sholto Douglas Pennant. (51) . . | K.S. |
| 1868 | 27 Nov. | 32 ,, | Thomas Love Duncombe Jones Parry, of Madryn, Esq. (52) . . . | K.S. |
| ,, | 19 ,, | 32 ,, | William Bulkeley Hughes, Esq. (53) . . . | Burgess. |

"6th Oct.—A Motion was made that Lord George Paget be allowed to present another petition complaining of the last election and return for the Borough: which Motion was afterwards withdrawn."—Jour. House of Commons, vol. xcvi., p. 605.

(49) Mr. Bulkeley Hughes at this time sat in the Conservative interest, and Mr. Richard Davies (afterwards Member for Anglesey) contested the seat with him on behalf of the Liberals—but Mr. Hughes was returned by a majority of 93, the numbers being—Hughes, 369 ; Davies, 276.

(50) Mr. Bulkeley Hughes, the previous Member, contested the Seat with him in the Liberal interest, but Mr. Wynne (afterwards Wynne Finch) was returned by a majority of 52, the numbers being—Wynne, 380; Hughes, 328.

(51) "6th Aug., 1866.—The Speaker was ordered to issue his Warrant, &c., &c., to elect a Knight of the Shire in the room of the Honble. Edward Gordon Douglas Pennant, created Lord Penrhyn."—Journ. House of Commons, vol. cxxi., p. 524.

His eldest son was returned, unopposed, in his place.

(52) Eldest son of Major Genl. Sir Love Parry, who represented the Caernarvon Boroughs in 1835-37. The Hon. G. S. Douglas Pennant, the previous Member, contested the seat with him in the Conservative interest, but Mr. Jones Parry was returned by a majority of 148, the numbers being—Parry, 1963 ; Pennant, 1815.

(53) The Hon. Thos. John Wynn, of Glynllifon, contested the seat in the Conservative interest, but Mr. B. Hughes was returned by a majority of 546, the numbers being—Hughes, 1581 ; Wynn, 1035.

# KNIGHTS OF THE SHIRE FOR MERIONETH.

| Anno Dom. | Date of Return. | Regnal Year. | Name. (See Note 1, p. 86.) |
|---|---|---|---|
| 1542 | 3 Jan. | 33 Hen. VIII. | Edward Stanley, of Harlech, Gent. |
| 1547 | 4 Oct. | 1 Edw. VI. | Lewis Owen, of Dolgelley, Esq. (1) |
| 1553 | 14 Feb. | 7 ,, | Lewis Owen, Esq. |
| ,, | 26 Sept. | 1 Mary. | John Salesbury, of Rhug. |
| 1554 | 2 April. | 1 ,, | Lewis Owen, Esq. |
| 1555 | Oct. | 2 & 3 Phil. & Mary. | Elizeus (or Ellis) Price, Esq. |
| 1558 | 11 Jan. | 4 & 5 ,, | Ellis Price, of Plas Iolyn, Esq., LL.D. |
| 1559 | 10 ,, | 1 Elizabeth. | John Wyn ap Cadwalader, of Rhiwlas, Esq. |
| 1563 | 5 ,, | 5 ,, | Ellis Price, of Plasiolyn, Esq. |
| 1572 | 8 May. | 14 (2) ,, | John Lewis Owen, of Dolgelley, afterwards of Llwyn, Esq. (3) |
| 1585 | 10 Nov. | 27 ,, | Cadwalader Price, of Rhiwlas, Esq. |
| 1586 | 13 Oct. | 28 ,, | Robert Lloyd, of Rhiwgoch, Esq. (4) |
| 1588 | 12 Nov. | 30 ,, | Robert Salesbury, of Rhug, Esq. |
| 1593 | 19 Feb. | 35 ,, | Griffith Nanney, of Nanney, Esq. |
| 1597 | 3 Sept. | 39 ,, | Thomas Myddelton, Esq. (5) |
| 1601 | 27 ,, | 43 ,, | Robert Lloyd, of Rhiwgoch, Esq. |
| 1604 | 6 March. | 1 James I. | Sir Edward Herbert, of Berthddu, Knt. (6) |
| 1614 | 5 April. | 12 ,, | Robert Lloyd, of Rhiwgoch, Esq. |
| 1620 | 19 Dec. | 18 ,, | Griffith Vaughan, Esq. (7) |
| 1624 | 12 Feb. | 21 ,, | Harry Wynne, of Rhiwgoch. (8) |
| 1625 | 17 May. | 1 Charles I. | Henry Wynne, Esq. (9) |
| 1626 | 17 Feb. | 1 ,, | Edward Vaughan, Esq. |

(1) Commonly known as "The Baron," from his being Baron of the Exchequer of North Wales.

*Was murdered near Dugoed, in the Parish of Mallwyd, in October, 1555. See Pennant's "Tour in Wales." W.

(2) This Parliament was prorogued to the 18th year, when it was further prorogued to the 23rd year of Elizabeth.

(3) Son of Lewis Owen, "The Baron."

(4) *I think he was Escheator for the County then, or at some other time. W.

(5) *Afterwards Sir Thomas Myddelton, of Chirk Castle, Knt. W.

(6) *Afterwards the celebrated Lord Herbert, of Cherbury. W.

(7) *Of Corsygedol. W.

(8) *There is a monument to his memory in the North Wynnstay Chapel, in Rhuabon Church. W.

(9) *The same person as the preceding. W.

| Anno Dom. | Date of Return. | Regnal Year. | Name. |
|---|---|---|---|
| 1628 | 17 March. | 3 Charles I. | Richard Vaughan, of Corsygedol, Esq. (10) |
| 1640 | Feb. 15 | ,, | Henry Wynne, Esq. |
| ,, | 27 Oct. 16 | ,, | William Price, of Rhiwlas, Esq. (11) |
| 1646(?) | (?)22 | ,, | Col. John Jones. |
| 1647 | 26 April. 23 | ,, | Roger Pope, Esq. (12) |
| ,, | Sept. 23 | ,, | Col. John Jones. (13) |
| 1653 | 5 July. (14) | | |
| 1654 | 3 Sept. | | John Vaughan, of Cefnbodig, Esq. |
| 1656 | (?)26 Nov. | | (15) |
| 1658 | 18 Jan. | | Lewis Owen, of Peniarth, Esq. (16) |
| 1660 | 25 April. | (Convention.) | Edmund Meyricke, of Ucheldre, Esq. |

(10) *" Richard Vychan (Vaughan), the second of that name, of Corsygedol, and Plas-hên, represented the County of Meirionedd, in Parliament, and was so very fat and unwieldy that the folding-doors of the House of Commons were opened to let him in, which is never done but when the Black Rod brings a message from the King, who being then in the House of Lords, the folding-doors opened, when the rumour in the House was 'The Black Rod or the Welsh Knight is coming.' His fat, at length, grew so troublesome to him, that he brought Surgeons from London to his house at Corsygedol, to cut out the fat, and the operation was successfully performed, but by some accident soon after, some of the larger blood vessels burst open, and could not be stayed again, so he died in about the 30th year of his age " (in July, 1636).—MS. Hist. of the House of Corsygedol, at Mostyn, by Wm. Vaughan, Esq., Lieut. and M.P. for Merionethshire, and Peniarth MS., No. 71. W.

(11) This was the Long Parliament. Price having adhered to the King, and gone with him to Oxford, was disabled by this Parliament, and John Jones (afterwards Colonel in the Parliamentary Army, and one of the King's Judges was appointed by Parliament to fill the seat.

" 8th Dec., 1646.—Resolved, &c., that a Warrant be issued, under the Speaker's hand, directed to the Clerk of the Crown in Chancery, for a Writ to be issued for the Election of a Knight to serve for the County of Merioneth, in the place of Mr. Price, formerly chosen to serve for the said County, and sithence disabled."—Journ. House of Commons, vol. v., p. 5.

(12) " 26 Aug., 1647.—The Speaker was Ordered to issue his Warrant to elect a Knight of the Shire in the place of Roger Pope, deceased."—Journ. House of Commons, vol. v., p. 284.

(13) *Colonel John Jones, of Maesygarnedd, the Regicide, married a sister of Oliver Cromwell, " The Protector." W.

In Evelyn's Diary occurs the following entry :—" 17 Oct., 1660.—Scott, Scrope, Cook, and Jones, suffered for reward of their iniquities at Charing Crosse, in sight of the place where they put to death their natural Prince, and in the presence of the King, his sonn, whom they also sought to kill. I saw not their execution, but met their quarters mangl'd, and cutt, and reeking, as they were brought from the gallows in baskets on the hurdle. Oh, the miraculous providence of God !"—Vol. i., p. 326.

(14) This Parliament was convened after the dismissal by Cromwell, on the 20th April, 1653, of the " Rump," and was called the " Little " or the " Barebones " Parliament. Only 122 Members were summoned for England ; 6 for Scotland ; 5 for Ireland ; and 7 for Wales. No Member was summoned specifically for Merioneth.—(See Members for Caernarvon, 1653.)

(15) Colonel John Jones was elected for Merioneth and Denbigh, but made choice to sit for the latter County. (Browne Willis omitted to notice this.)

" 1648, 3rd April.—Order for a Thousand pounds to be bestowed on Col. John Jones as the Parliament's favor, for his great services, and to acquaint him with what Provisions and Supplies were made for the forces in Ireland (where he then was)."—Whitelock's Memorial, p. 298.

" 1648, 12th Dec.—Mr. Vaughan, one of the Members " secluded " by Col. Pride—set at liberty on the 20th." —Id., pp. 356-7.

(16) *Lewis Owen was fourth in descent, through his mother, Margaret Owen, heiress of Peniarth, from Lewis Owen, the " Baron," (see note 1). The present Member was born about the year 1622, and died in Jan., 169½. W.

| Anno Dom. | Date of Return. | Regnal Year. | Name. |
|---|---|---|---|
| 1661 | 7 May. | 13 Charles II. | Henry Wynne, of Rhiwgoch, Esq. (17) |
| 1673 | 25 March. | 25 ,, | William Price, of Rhiwlas, Esq. (18) |
| 1679 | 18 Feb. | 31 ,, | Sir John Wynn, of Rhiwgoch, Knt. & Bart. (19) |
| ,, | 2 Sept. | 31 ,, | Sir John Wynn, of Rhiwgoch, Knt. & Bart. |
| 1681 | 15 Feb. | 33 ,, | Sir Robert Owen, of Glynn, Knt. (20) |
| 1685 | 7 April. | 1 James II. | Sir John Wynn, of Rhiwgoch, Knt. & Bart. |
| 1689 | 15 Jan. | (Convention) (21) | ,, ,, ,, ,, ,, ,, |
| 1690 | 4 March. | 2 Will. & Mary. | ,, ,, ,, ,, ,, ,, |
| 1695 | 19 Nov. | 7 William III. | Hugh Nanney, of Nanney, Esq. |
| 1698 | 26 July. | 10 ,, | ,, ,, ,, ,, |
| 1701 | 4 Feb. | 12 ,, | ,, ,, ,, ,, |
| ,, | 29 April. | 13 ,, | Richard Vaughan, of Corsygedol, Esq. (22) |
| ,, | 9 Dec. | 13 ,, | ,, ,, ,, ,, |
| 1702 | 18 Aug. | 1 Anne. | ,, ,, ,, ,, |
| 1705 | 22 May. | 4 ,, | ,, ,, ,, ,, |
| 1708 | 1 June. | 7 ,, | ,, ,, ,, ,, |
| 1710 | 1 Oct. | 9 ,, | ,, ,, ,, ,, |
| 1713 | 29 Sept. | 12 ,, | ,, ,, ,, ,, |
| 1715 | 15 Feb. | 1 George I. | ,, ,, ,, ,, |
| 1722 | 24 April. | 8 ,, | ,, ,, ,, ,, |
| 1727 | 5 Sept. | 1 George II. | ,, ,, ,, ,, |
| 1734 | 7 May. | 7 ,, | William Vaughan, of Corsy-Gedol, Esq. |
| 1741 | 26 ,, | 14 ,, | ,, ,, ,, ,, |
| 1747 | 2 July. | 21 ,, | ,, ,, ,, ,, (23) |

(17) "6 Feb., 1673.—The Speaker was Ordered to issue his Warrant to elect a Knight of the Shire in the room of Henry Winne, deceased."—Journ. House of Commons, vol. ix., p. 249.

(18) Elected in the room of Henry Wynne, deceased.     (19) Son of Henry Wynne.

(20) *Of Glyn, in right of his wife, Margaret, daughter and heiress of Owen Wynne, Esq.; and paternally owner of Clenenney, in Caernarvonshire, and Porkington, in Shropshire. He died in 1698. W.

(21) This Return was made by Morris Davies and Evan Williams, Coroners for the County of Merioneth.

(22) "26 Mar., 1701.—The Speaker was Ordered to issue his Warrant to elect a Knight of the Shire in the room of Hugh Nanney, deceased."— Jour. House of Commons, vol. xiii., p. 433.

*An amusing anecdote is told as to Richard Vaughan, who was so long member for Merionethshire. There was a call of the House which he did not attend to. The Sergeant at Arms was sent to bring him to London. At Dolgelley he announced his errand, but the good people there, in league with their member, told the Sergeant that it was impossible to reach Corsygedol, at that time of year, as the mountains were impassable. "But," said he, "I see you are near an estuary, why cannot I go by boat?" "Because," was the reply, "between the sea and Corsygedol, there are impassable bogs." The Sergeant returned to London, and the Honourable Member did not attend the House that Session. W.

(23) The following is a copy of Mr. Vaughan's Address to the Electors :—

"At Foneddigion Eglwyswyr ac Uchelwyr Sir Feirionydd.

"Fy Nghydwladwŷr,

"Y disymwth a'r diddisgwyl ymddatodiad y Senedd a byrdra yr amser ir Etholiad Cyffredinol nesaf, sydd, yn ei gwneuthur yn ammhosibl i mi ymweled a chwi yn bersonol i ddiolch i chwi am yr anrhydedd a wnaeth-

| Anno Dom. | Date of Return. | Regnal Year. | Name. |
|---|---|---|---|
| 1754 | 9 May. | 27 George II. | William Vaughan, of Corsy-Gedol, Esq. |
| 1761 | 9 April. | 1 George III. | „ „ „ „ |
| 1768 | 24 March. | 8 „ | John Pughe Pryse, of Rhug and Gogerddan, Esq. |
| 1774 | 24 Feb. | 14 „ | Evan Lloyd Vaughan, of Corsygedol, Esq. |
| „ | 9 Nov. | 15 „ | „ „ „ „ „ |
| 1780 | 12 Oct. | 20 „ | „ „ „ „ „ |
| 1784 | 7 May. | 24 „ | „ „ „ „ (24) |
| 1790 | 8 July. | 30 „ | „ „ „ „ „ |
| 1792 | 25 Jan. | 32 „ | Robert Williames Vaughan, Esq. (25) |
| 1796 | 10 June. | 36 „ | Sir Robert Williames Vaughan, of Nanney, Bart. |
| 1802 | 16 July. | 42 „ | „ „ „ „ „ |
| 1805 | 12 Nov. | 46 „ | „ „ „ „ „ |
| 1807 | 19 May. | 47 „ | „ „ „ „ „ |
| 1812 | 14 Oct. | 52 „ | „ „ „ „ „ |
| 1818 | 24 June. | 58 „ | „ „ „ „ „ |
| 1820 | 14 March. | 1 George IV. | „ „ „ „ „ |
| 1826 | 15 June. | 7 „ | „ „ „ „ „ |
| 1830 | 5 Aug. | 1 William IV. | „ „ „ „ „ |
| 1831 | 10 May. | 1 „ | „ „ „ „ „ |
| 1832 | 15 Dec. | 3 „ | „ „ „ „ „ |
| 1835 | 12 Jan. | 5 „ | „ „ „ „ „ (26) |
| 1836 | 27 June. | 7 „ | Richard Richards, of Caerynwch, and Bedford Square, Middlesex, Esq. (27) |
| 1837 | 1 Aug. | 1 Victoria. | „ „ „ „ |

och i mi wrth fy newis ir ddau Barliament diwaethaf ac i gynyg fy ngwasanaeth i fod yn gynnyrcholwr i chwi yn y nesaf. Gan hyny yr wyf yn gobeithio y bydd y modd hwn o'ch Cyfarch am barhad eich ffafr, yr hyn yr wyf yr awrhon yn ei ddeisyf, yn gymeradwy gennoch oddiwrth,

" Foneddigion,

" Eich Anrhydeddwr, ach Rhwymedicaf Wasanethwr,

" WILIAM FYCHAN."

Nanney, Mehefin 20, 1747.

(From the Vaughan Correspondence, Mostyn Collection.)

(24) " 24 May, 1784.—The Speaker informed the House that the Sheriff of Merioneth had made no Return of the Member for the said County."—Jour. of House of Commons, vol. xl., p. 8.

(25) " 31 Jan., 1792.—The Speaker reported that he had issued his Warrant, &c., during the recess to elect a member in the room of Evan Lloyd Vaughan, Esq., deceased.—Jour. House of Commons, vol. xlvii. p. 3.

(26) " 9 June, 1836.—The Speaker was ordered to issue his Warrant to elect a Knight of the Shire in the room of Sir Robert Williames Vaughan who had accepted the office of Steward and Bailiff of the Chiltern Hundreds."—Jour. House of Commons, vol. xci., p. 445.

(27) The seat was contested by Sir William Wynn, Knt., of Maesyneuadd in the Liberal interest. He was defeated by a majority of 400. On the 11th July, 1836, two petitions were presented against the Return of Mr. Richard Richards, for that he held the offices of Accountant General of the Court of Exchequer, and was also one of the Masters of the said Court, and therefore incapable to serve in Parliament for the County of Merioneth ; and

| Anno Dom. | Date of Return. | Regnal Year. | Name. |
|---|---|---|---|
| 1841 | 14 July. | 5 Victoria | Richard Richards, of Caerynwch, and Bedford Square, Middlesex, Esq. |
| 1847 | 9 Aug. | 11  „ | „          „          „          „ |
| 1852 | 22 July. | 16 Victoria. | William Watkin Edward Wynne, of Peniarth, Esq. |
| 1857 | 2 April. | 20  „ | „          „          „          „    (28) |
| 1859 | 4 May | 22  „ | William Watkin Edward Wynne, Esq. (29) |
| 1865 | 31 July. | 29  „ | William Robert Maurice Wynne, of Peniarth, Esq. (30) |
| 1868 | 19 Nov. | 32  „ | David Williams, of Castle Deudraeth, Esq. (31) |
| 1870 | 22 Jan. | 33  „ | Samuel Holland, of Lasynys, Esq. (32) |

that due notice was given and delivered thereof at the opening of the Court on the 24th June (being the first day of polling) before a single vote was recorded : The Petitioners therefore prayed the House to declare the Return of Mr. Richards null and void, and that Sir William Wynn may be declared duly elected, &c."—Jour. House of Commons, vol. xci., p. 644.

"These Petitions were ordered to be taken into consideration upon Tuesday, 26th July, on which day no parties appearing on behalf of the Petitioners, the petitions were ordered to be discharged."—Id., vol. xci., p. 695.

(28) *Elected without a contest.  W.

(29) The Seat was contested by Mr. David Williams (afterwards Member) in the Liberal interest, but Mr. Wynne was returned by a majority of 38.  "On the 21st June, 1859, a Petition complaining of an undue Return and Election was presented, and it was Ordered to be referred to the General Committee of Elections."—Jour. of House of Commons, vol. cxiv., p. 224.

"On the 4th July, the Speaker reported the recognizance to be unobjectionable."—Id., vol. cxiv., p. 237.

"And on the 1st August, the Speaker informed the House that it was not intended to proceed with the Petition : it was therefore ordered to be discharged."—Id., vol. cxiv., p. 325.

(30) Eldest son of the late Member.  The Seat was again contested by Mr. D. Williams, but Mr. Wynne was returned by a majority of 31.

(31) The late Member, Mr. W. R. M. Wynne, again came forward, but after a canvass he retired from the contest, and Mr. D. Williams was returned unopposed.  Mr. Williams died 15th Dec., 1869.

(32) Lieut.-Col. C. J. Tottenham, of Plas Berwyn, contested the Seat in the Conservative interest, but Mr. Holland was returned by a majority of 647, in the room of Mr. D. Williams, deceased.

# CONSTABLES OF BEAUMARIS CASTLE.

| Anno Dom. | Appointed. | Regnal Year. | Name. |
|---|---|---|---|
| 1294 or 5 | | 23 Edward I. | William de Felton. |
| 1298—9 | | 27 ,, | John de Havering. (1) |
| 1304 or 5 | | 33 ,, | Sir John de Neubourgh, Knt. |
| 1305 or 6 | | 34 ,, | John de Medfeld. |
| 1308 or 9 | | 2 Edward II. | Simon de Monte Acuto. |
| 1311 or 12 | | 5 ,, | Sir Richard de Baskervile, Knt. |
| ,, ,, | | 5 ,, | Hugh Godard. |
| ,, ,, | | 5 ,, | Walter de Mortuo Mari. |
| 1312 | 4 March. | 5 ,, | John de Sapy. (3) |
| 1321 | 12 Oct. | 15 ,, | Giles de Bello Campo. (4) |
| 1327 | 25 March. | 1 Edward III. | ,, ,, ,, |
| ,, | 26(?) Oct. | 1 ,, | Hugh de Mortuo Mari. |
| 1328 | 29 April. | 2 ,, | Gilbert de Ellesfeld, (5) (for life). |
| 1330 | 17 Dec. | 4 ,, | Robert de Walkefare. (6) |
| 1333 | 18 Nov. | 7 ,, | William Trussell. (7) |
| 1334 | 1 Oct. | 8 ,, | ,, ,, |
| 1351 or 2 | | (?)25 ,, | Robert Pollard. |
| 1355 or 6 | | (?)29 ,, | Sir John de St. Peter, Knt. |
| 1379 or 80 | | 3 Richard II. | William Rosamond. |
| ,, ,, | | 3 ,, | Sir David Caradoc, Knt. |

(Brace (2) groups the three 1311 or 12 entries; brace (8) groups Robert Pollard and Sir John de St. Peter; brace (9) groups William Rosamond and Sir David Caradoc.)

---

(1) Havering was appointed Custos, during pleasure. He only retained the keeping for a year, for the King conferred upon him the more important offices of Justice of North Wales, and Constable and Custos of all the Castles in North Wales, except Beaumaris. Felton continued as Constable until Sir John de Neubourgh was appointed.

(2) All these names are mentioned in the Chamberlain's Accounts for the 5 & 6 years of Edw. II. ; probably some of them were Custodes or Sub-Constables.

(3) His name is mentioned in the Chamberlain's Accounts to the 15 year of Edw. II. Urrici de la Haye and John de Creswell were his Sub-Constables.

(4) Henry de Hambur, Sub-Constable.  (5) Edward de Ellesfeld, Sub-Constable.

(6) Gilbert de Walkefare, Sub-Constable.  (7) Thomas de Warrewyk, Sub-Constable.

(8) Pollard's name is mentioned in the Accounts of the 25 & 26 years of Edw. III. ; and St. Peter in those of the 29 & 30 of the same reign. The dates of appointment I cannot find.

(9) Rosamond was in all probability Constable. See next note.

16

| Anno Dom. | Appointed. | Regnal Year. | Name. |
|---|---|---|---|
| 1382 | 18 March. | 5 Richard II. | Gronw ap Tudor. (10) |
| ,, | 25 ,, | 5 ,, | Baldwin Radyngton. |
| 1385 | 31 ,, | 8 ,, | Gilbert Trussell, (for life). |
|  |  | Temp. ,, | William Lescrop. (11) |
| 1399 | 12 Oct. | 1 Henry IV. | Henry Percy. (12) |
|  |  | Temp. ,, | Thomas Bolde. |
| 1416 | 5 Nov. | 4 Henry V. | Edward Sprencheux, chevalier. (13) |
| 1418 | 20 Jan. | 5 ,, | Richard Walstede, (for life). |
| Circa 1440 |  | 18 or 19 Henry VI. | William Bulkeley, of Cheadle, Esq. (14) |
| 1446 | 10 June. | 24 ,, | Sir William Beauchampe, Knt., (for life). |
| 1459 or 60 |  | 38 ,, | Sir John Butler, Knt. (15) |
| 1461 | 4 March. | 1 Edward IV. | Sir William Hastinges, Knt. (16) |
| 1483 | 16 May. | 1 Edward V. | Henry, Duke of Buckingham. |
| ,, | 15 July. | 1 Richard III. | ,,          ,,          ,, |
| ,, | 28 Nov. | 1 ,, | Sir Richard Hudelston (or Hudelston) Knt., (for life). |
| 1485 | 10 Feb. | 2 ,, | { Robert Chamberlain. } (17) { Ralph Chamberlain. } |
| ,, | (?)20 Sept. | 1 Henry VII. | { Sir William Stanley, Knt. } (18) { William Stanley, Esq. } |
| 1495 | April. | 10 ,, | Sir Richard Crofte, Knt. |
| 1502 | 4 July. | 17 ,, | Rowland Bulkeley, Esq., (during pleasure). |
| 1502 or 3 |  | 18 ,, | Richard Pole. |
| 1509 | 3 July. | 1 Henry VIII. | Sir Rowland Vielleville, otherwise Brittayne, Knt. |
| 1535 | 13 Dec. | 27 ,, | Henry Norres, Esq., (for life). |

(10) Grant was made to Tudor of the Custody of the Castle for life, with the fee of £40, lately held by Sir David Cradock [Caradoc], Knt.   Radyngton was Constable.

(11) John Scalby, Sub-Constable.

(12) Grant was made to Henry Percy (the famous Hotspur), son of the Earl of Northumberland, of the County and Lordship of Anglesey, with Beaumaris Castle, for life.   Pat. Roll, 1 Hen. IV., part 4, no. 7.

(13) Died 4 Sept., 5 Hen. V. (A.D. 1417).

(14) See Lodge's Peerage of Ireland (Bulkeley Family Lineage), ed. 1789, vol. v., p. 18 ; and Williams's Snowdon, p. 172.

(15) He is mentioned as Constable in the Chamberlain's Account for this year (38 Hen. VI.).

(16) Chamberlain to Edw. IV.

(17) Afterwards Knighted.   Father and son ; they were appointed Constable of the Castle, and Captain of the Town, during their lives.

(18) Chamberlain to Hen. VII.   Father and son ; they were appointed Constable of the Castle, and Captain of the Town, during their lives.

| Anno Dom. | Appointed. | Regnal Year. | Name. |
|---|---|---|---|
| 1536 | 14 June. | 28 ,, | { Henry Knyvett, Esq. } (19)<br>{ Sir Richard Bulkeley, Knt. } |
|  |  |  | John, Duke of Northumberland.(20) |
| 1553 | 7 Sept. | 1 Mary. | John, Earl of Bath, (for life). |
| ,, | 19 ,, | 1 ,, | Sir Richard Bulkeley, Knt., (for life). (21) |
| 1561 | 28 May. | 3 Elizabeth. | Richard Bulkeley, Esq. (22) |
| 1617 | 11 March. | 14 James I. | Arthur Mainwaring, Esq. (23) |
| 1621 | 31 Aug. | 19 ,, | Sir Edward Lewis, Knt. (24) |
| 1631 | 14 Jan. | 6 Charles I. | Edward, Earl of Dorset. |
|  |  |  | Thomas, Viscount Bulkeley. (25) |
| 1649 | 29 May. |  | Major General Thomas Mitton, (during pleasure). (26) |
| 1652(?) | 21 Sept. |  | Robert, Viscount Bulkeley. |
| 1660 | 7 ,, | 12 Charles II. | ,,     ,,     ,,     (27) |
| 1688 | 10 Nov. | 4 James II. | Richard, Lord Bulkeley, Viscount Cashell. (28) |
| 1689 | 27 June.(29) | 1 Will. & Mary. | Richard, Lord Bulkeley, Viscount Cashell. |
| 1702 | 19 ,, | 1 Anne. | Richard Bulkeley, Esq. |
| 1716 | 10 Dec. | 3 George I. | William Bodville, Esq. |
| Circa 1725 |  | (?)12 ,, | Richard, Viscount Bulkeley. (30) |

---

(19) Afterwards Knighted. They were appointed Constable of the Castle, and Captain of the Town, during their lives.

(20) This name is mentioned in the Patent appointing John, Earl of Bath, who received the appointment upon the attainder of the said Duke. No entry can be found of the date of his appointment.

(21) This date is taken from a document at the Land Revenue Record Office, wherein it is stated he was appointed Constable for life.

(22) Afterwards Knighted.

(23) Granted in reversion after Sir Richard Bulkeley. Cal. State Papers, 1611-18, p. 443.

(24) A Gentleman of the Privy Chamber.

(25) He is mentioned as having been Constable, in the Patent appointing Robert, Viscount Bulkeley (1660). No entry can be found of the date of his appointment.

(26) Appointed owing to the delinquency of the Earl of Dorset, (vide MS. at the Land Revenue Record Office), therefore the name of Thomas, Viscount Bulkeley, ought to precede that of the Earl of Dorset, but on the Patent, appointing Robert, Viscount Butkeley (1660), the name of Thomas, Lord Bulkeley, follows that of the Earl of Dorset. Mitton was Constable at Mich., 1651.

(27) He petitioned in June(?), 1660, for continuance in the Constableship, long held by his ancestors, on which his father spent £3,000, but was forced to quit it during the Wars (Civil), in which he lost £10,000. Cal. State Papers, 1660-1, p. 87. The said Petition was granted on Sept. 7th, with a fee of 40 marks per annum. Id. p. 280.

(28) Was appointed Chancellor and Chamberlain of Anglesey, Caernarvon, and Merioneth, on the same day. The name should be "Richard, Viscount Bulkeley, of Cashell," but it is inserted as entered in the Patent Roll.

(29) The entry of appointment at the Land Revenue Office is dated 7th June.

(30) Lodge's Peerage of Ireland (Bulkeley Family Lineage), ed. 1789, vol. v., p. 28.

| Anno Dom. | Appointed. | Regnal Year. | Name. |
|---|---|---|---|
| Circa 1739 | | (?)12 George II. | James, Viscount Bulkeley. (31) |
| 1761 | 6 July. | 1 George III. | Sir Hugh Williams, of Baron Hill, Bart. |
| 1795 | 20 March. | 35 „ | Thomas James, Viscount Bulkeley. (32) |

(31) Lodge's Peerage of Ireland (Bulkeley Family Lineage), ed. 1789, vol. v., p. 28.

(32) On 25th Feb., 1783, Beaumaris Castle, &c., was granted to Thomas James, Viscount Bulkeley, for 31 years, he paying for the same £1 8s., half yearly.   On 31 March, 1807, contract was made between the Surveyor-General of the Land Revenue, and the said Thomas James Warren, Lord Bulkeley, Baron of Beaumaris, and Viscount Cashell (sic), for the sale to the said Lord Bulkeley, of the ancient Building or Castle of Beaumaris (the same being in ruins), the said Lord Bulkeley paying therefor the sum of £735.

# CONSTABLES OF CAERNARVON CASTLE.

| Anno Dom. | Appointed. | Regnal Year. | Name. |
|---|---|---|---|
| 1284 | 18 Oct. | 12 Edward I. | Thomas de Maydenhacche. (1) |
| ,, | 22 ,, | 12 ,, | John de Havering. (2) |
| 1290 | 8 May. | 18 ,, | Ada de Wetenhale. (3) |
| 1291-2 | | 20 ,, | Otto de Grandison. (4) |
| 1300 | 1 April. | 28 ,, | John de Havering. (5) |
| ,, | 8 May. | 28 ,, | Henry de Dynynton. |
| ,, | | 28 ,, | Thomas de Coston. |
| 1302-3 | | 32 ,, | Sir William Sutton, Knt. (6) |
| 1306 | 19 April. | 34 ,, | Hugh de Audele, senior. (7) |
| ,, | 2 May. | 34 ,, | Sir Hugh de Audele, Knt. (8) |
| 1306-7 | | 35 ,, | Peter de Hinkele. (9) |
| | | Temp. Edward I. | John Upton, otherwise Sir John de Hanmer. (10) |
| 1308 | 15 Jan. | 1 Edward II. | Roger de Mortuo Mari, of Chirk. (11) |
| 1311 or 12 | | 5 (?) ,, | Sir Hugh Godard, Knt. (12) |
| 1315 | 19 Feb. | 8 ,, | John de Grey. (13) |

(1) " Nuper Constab. Castri nostri de Kaernarvon, 18 Oct., 1284."—Ayloffe, p. 82.

(2) "Custos with 200 marks for its Custody."—Ayloffe, p. 92.  Afterwards Constable.

(3) Ayloffe, p. 98.

* Ada [Adam] de Wetenhall is now represented by Sir Henry Mainwaring, Bart., whose father Sir Henry Mainwaring Wetenhall, afterwards Sir Henry Mainwaring, Bart., assumed the name upon succeeding, by bequest, to the Peover Estates.  W.

(4) Custos.

(5) See note 1 to Constables of Beaumaris.

(6) Justice of North Wales, Constable of the Castle, and Mayor of the Town of Caernarvon.  Died 19 April, 1306.  Peter de Hinkele was sub-Constable.

(7) Held the Custody of the Castle, and Mayoralty of the Town from the 19th April to the 1st of May, 1306.

(8) Appointed Justice of North Wales, Constable of the Castle, and Mayor of the Town of Caernarvon.

(9) Hinkele's name is mentioned in the Chamberlain's Accounts as " sub-Const. et tam Const." in the 6 & 7 years of the Principality of Edward, Prince of Wales.

(10) See Pennant's Tours in Wales, 8vo. ed., vol. i., p. 296.  The Family Pedigree bears out the statement in Pennant as to the date and parentage of John Upton.  Lord Hanmer believes that Upton was the first of the family who assumed the territorial name of Hanmer.  He was the son of Sir John Macklesfield, one of Edward I.'s Officers.

(11) Custos.   (12) Custos.   (13) Justice of North Wales and Custos of the Castle.

| Anno Dom. | Appointed. | Regnal Year. | Name. |
|---|---|---|---|
| 1316 | 23 Nov. | 10 Edward II. | Roger de Mortuo Mari, of Chirk. (14) |
| 1321 or 22 | | 15    ,, | Thomas de Wynnesbury. (15) |
| 1321 or 22 | | (?)15    ,, | Edmund, Earl of Arundel. (16) |
| 1326 | 12 Dec. | 20    ,, | William de Shaldeford. |
| 1339 | 12 July. | 13 Edward III. | Richard, Earl of Arundel. (17) |
| | | Temp. ,, | Robert Foulehurst. |
| 1389 or 90 | | 13 Richard II. | William Bagot, Chevalier. (18) |
| 1397 | 21 April. | 20    ,, | { William Lescrop, Chevalier, & { William Audeley. } (19) |
| 1401 or 2 | | 3 Henry IV. | John Bolde. (20) |
| 1410 | 12 Jan. | 11    ,, | Thomas Barneby, (for life). (21) |
| 1427 | 18 May. | 5 Henry VI. | John Stanley. (22) |
| 1441 | 30 Sept. | 20    ,, | { John Stanley, Esq. { John Stanley. } (23) |
| 1461 | 22 Nov. | 1 Edward IV. | Sir Thomas Montgomery, Knt. |
| 1483 | 16 May. | 1 Edward V. | Henry, Duke of Buckingham. |
| ,, | 15 July. | 1 Richard III. | ,,     ,,     ,, |
| 1484 | 11 June. | 1    ,, | Sir William Stanley, Knt. of the Body. |
| 1486 | 1 Feb. | 1 Henry VII. | Sir William Stanley, Knt. Chamberlain. |
| 1495 | 21 April. | 10    ,, | Sir Richard Pole, Knt. |
| 1506 | 4 Jan. | 21    ,, | Thomas Heton. |
| ,, | 16 April. | 21    ,, | John Pyleston (or Puleston). |

(14) Justice of North Wales. Hugh de Engleton was sub-Constable in the 13 year of Edw. II.

(15) In the Chamberlain's Account he is called "sub-Const. et Custos."

(16) Custos of the Castle, and Justice of North Wales.

(17) He is mentioned as Custos, &c., in the Minister's Accounts of the 19 year of Edw. III.

(18) Custos.             (19) Custodes, appointed for their lives.

(20) *He had twenty Men at Arms and eighty Archers; and his annual maintenance amounted to £900 6s. 8d. (Ellis's Orig. Letters, vol. i., p. 14). W.

Pennant in his Tours in Wales (8vo. ed., 1810, vol. iii., p. 335) says, that Jevan ap Meredydd and Meredydd ap Hwlkin Llwyd in the year 1402 "were entrusted (under an English Captain) with the Castle of Caernarvon;" and he quotes the Hist. of the Gwydir Family as his authority. But he does not quote accurately, for Sir John Wynn's statement is that Jevan ap Meredydd and "Meredith ap Hwlkyn Llwyd of Glynllifon had the charge of the Town of Caernarvon, and an English Captain was over the Castle."—Hist. Gwydir Family, p. 53.

(21) Constable and Custos.

(22) *Original Deed at Peniarth from John de Stanley, Constable of Caernarvon and Mayor of the Town, and others of the Corporation, to Thomas Bowman, conveying to him a Burgage in the Town, (a facsimile of which forms the frontispiece to this work). It is dated 20 April, 8 Hen. VI. The Corporation Seal to this Deed is pretty entire. The Arms upon it are, Three Lions passant, or passant gardant, and an Eagle displayed as the Crest. John de Stanley was ancestor in a direct line to the Earls of Derby, and in an indirect one to my family. A house in Caernarvon, called Plas Bowman was sold by my father. W.

(23) Appointed for their lives, or longest liver, Constable and Custos.

| Anno Dom. | Appointed. | Regnal Year. | Name. |
|---|---|---|---|
| 1509 | 30 July. | 1 Henry VIII. | John Pyleston, Esq. <br> Charles Brandon, Esq. (afterwards Duke of Suffolk). (24) |
| 1523 | 1 Oct. | 15 „ | John Puleston, Esq. |
| 1550 | 8 July. | 4 Edward VI. | Sir George Blague. |
| 1551 | 29 June. | 5 „ | John Harrington, Gent. (25) |
| 1583 | 11 May. | 25 Elizabeth. | John Harrington, Esq., (for life).(26) |
| 1603 | 18 June. | 1 James I. | Roland White, Esq. (27) |
| 1622 | 18 July. | 20 „ | John Griffith, junior, of Llyn, Esq. |
| 1646(?) | | 22 Charles I. | Lord Byron. (28) |
| 1649 | 15 Nov. | | Thomas Mason, Esq. (29) |
| | | | John Bodville. (30) |
| 1663 | 13 June. | 15 Charles II. | Robert Robarts (Lord Robarts). (31) |
| 1681 | 6 July. | 33 „ | Charles Bodvile, Viscount Bodmin. |
| 1692 | 22 April. | 4 Will. & Mary. | Charles Bodvile, Earl of Radnor. (32) |
| 1713 | 4 Sept. | 12 Anne. | Richard, Lord Bulkeley, Viscount Cashell. |
| 1714 | 3 Dec. | 1 George I. | Charles Bodvile, Earl of Radnor. |
| 1724 | 17 June. | 10 „ | Thomas Wynn, Esq. (33) |
| 1727 | 12 Aug. | 1 George II. | John Wynn, of Glynnllivon, Esq. |

(24) *John Pylestone (Puleston) Sergeant at Arms, Deputy Constable upon 2 Aug., 14 Hen. VIII. (Deed of that date at Peniarth, to which Sir William Griffith, of Penrhyn, is a party.) W.

Charles Brandon, Duke of Suffolk's, name is not entered on the Chamberlain's Accounts after the 7th year of Hen. VIII.

(25) *Robert Griffith, Gent., sub-Constable upon 4 May, 6 Edw. VI. (Deed at Peniarth of that date witnessed by Griff-ap Robert Vychan of Talhenbont (Plashen) as a Magistrate of the County of Caernarvon.) W.

(26) Son of the preceding Constable.

(27) In the Calendar of State Papers, Addenda, 1580-1625, p. 424, there is a "note of a Grant to Roland White, in reversion after John Harrington, of the Office of Constable of Caernarvon; fee £60 a year. Endorsed on a grant by Queen Elizabeth, 11 May, 1579, to John Harrington of the like reversion, after his father, John Harrington."

(28) Lord Byron was Governor in 1646; was besieged and surrendered to General Mytton in that year. In a document at the Land Revenue Record Office, the name of Thomas Mason, Esq., is entered as Governor of Caernarvon, in the room of John Griffith, deceased.

(29) Governor of Caernarvon and Constable of the Castle (see preceding note).

(30) No entry can be found of the date of this appointment.

(31) "On the 2nd April, 1663, a Warrant was issued for a grant to Griffith Wynne, as Constable of the Castle and Mayor of the Town of Caernarvon for life, which was subsequently altered to —— Roberts."—(Cal. State Papers, 1663-4, p. 97.) "On the 1st June, following, a Warrant for a grant was made out for —— Roberts, as Constable."—(Id., p. 160): "and the grant was made on the 8th of the same month."—(Id., p. 165.)

(32) In the Calendar of Treasury Papers, 1697-1702, p. 253—21 Dec., 1698, mention is made of a "Report from Mr. Chetwynd, Auditor, on the petition of William Williams. The suggestions therein are notoriously false, for there was no such fee or salary as £50 per annum paid to any person for the Constableship of the Castle of Caernarvon," &c.

(33) Appointed by the Prince of Wales.

| Anno Dom. | Appointed. | Regnal Year. | Name. |
|---|---|---|---|
| 1761 | 21 March. | 1 George III. | Thomas Wynn, of Glynnllivon, Esq. (afterwards Lord Newborough). (34) |
| 1781 | 15 June. | 21 „ | William Myddleton, of the Temple, Esq. (35) |
| 1782 | 6 „ | 22 „ | Richard Howard, Esq. (36) |
| 1785 | 28 „ | 25 „ | Henry, Earl of Uxbridge. (37) |
| 1812 | 28 April. | 52 „ | Henry William, Earl of Uxbridge. |
| 1831 | 10 Jan. | 1 William IV. | Henry William, Marquis of Anglesey. |
| 1837 | 2 Dec. | 1 Victoria. | „ „ „ „ |
| 1854 | 8 Sept. | 18 „ | Rt. Hon. Henry Howard Molyneux Herbert, Earl of Caernarvon. |

(34) The Letters Patent of the 12 August revoked.    (35) The Letters Patent of the 21 March revoked.
(36) „ „ „ „ 15 June „    (37) „ „ „ „ 6 June „

# CONSTABLES OF CONWAY CASTLE.(1)

| Anno Dom. | Appointed. | Regnal Year. | Name. |
|---|---|---|---|
| 1284 | 23 Oct. | 12 Edward I. | William de Sikun.(2) |
| 1300 | 1 April. | 28 „ | John de Havering.(3) |
| 1302 | 7 Feb. | 30 „ | John de Clykum. |
| 1302— 3 | | 31 Edward I. | Sir William de Cycounz (or Sikun), Knt. |
| 1311 or 12 | | 5 Edward II. | William Bagot.(4) |
| 1319 or 20 | | 13 „ | Hugh Godard.(5) |
| „ „ | | 13 „ | Henry de Wysshbury.(6) |
| 1326 | 20 Oct. | 20 „ | William de Ercalewe.(7) |
| „ | 20 Nov. | 20 „ | Roger de Mortuo Mari, of Wigmore.(8) |
| 1327 | 26 Oct. | 1 Edward III. | Henry de Mortuo Mari.(9) |
| 1330 | 9 Nov. | 4 „ | John Lestraunge, of Mudle.(10) |
| 1337 | 21 Aug. | 11 „ | Edward de St. John le Neven.(11) |
| 1338 | 28 April. | 12 „ | „ „ „ „ |
| 1383 or 4 | | 7 Richard II. | John de Beauchamp, (for life). |
| 1403 or 4 | | 5 Henry IV. | John Bolde, Chevalier.(12) |
| 1405 or 6 | | 7 „ | John de Mascy.(13) |
| 1436 | 27 June. | 14 Henry VI. | Ralph Boteler, Chevalier, (for life). |

(1) " This ruin is the property of the Crown, under which it is held on lease by Owen Holland, Esq., at the nominal rent of 6s. 8d., and a dish of fish to Lord Hertford as often as he passes through the town."—Grose's Antiq., vol. vii., new ed. (1773), p. 27.

(2) With £150 for its Custody. Ayloffe, p. 92. Variously spelt Cicoun, Cicounz, and Chikun.

(3) See note 1 to Constables of Beaumaris.

(4) Ingelram de Merke, Sub-Constable.    (5) Custos.

(6) Constable and Custos.   Hugh de Engleton, Sub-Constable.    (7) Constable and Custos.

(8) Custos.    (9) John Sturing, Sub-Constable.

(10) Thomas de Wotton, and John Goodynogh, Sub-Constables.

(11) John de Burton, and Thomas de Upton, Sub-Constables. (St. John's name is mentioned in Chamberlains' Accounts of the 18 year of Edw. III., as Constable.)

(12) Afterwards Knighted.   He was Constable in the 6th year of Henry V. vide Chamberlains' Accounts.

(13) *" He had fifteen Men at Arms, and sixty Archers, for which he was allowed to maintain the fortress, thirty shillings and twopence, per day, amounting in the year to £714 15s. 10d."—(Ellis's Orig. Letters, vol. i., p. 14.) W.

| Anno Dom. | Appointed. | Regnal Year. | Name. |
|---|---|---|---|
| 1461 | 4 March. | 1 Edward IV. | Sir Henry Bolde, Knt, (for life). |
| 1468 | 7 Feb. | 7　　" | "　　"　　"　　" |
| 1483 | 16 May. | 1 Edward V. | Henry, Duke of Buckingham. |
| " | 15 July. | 1 Richard III. | "　　"　　"　　" |
| " | 30 Nov. | 1　　" | Thomas Tunstall, Esq., of the Royal Body, (for life).(14) |
| 1488 | 15 Sept. | 4 Henry VII. | Sir Richard Pole, Knt., of the Royal Body. |
| 1505 | 4 Jan. | 20　　" | Edward Salisbury,(during pleasure). |
| 1512 | 6 Oct. | 4 Henry VIII. | John Salisbury, (during pleasure). |
| 1516 | 6 March. | 7　　" | John Salisbury, (for life). |
| 1549 | 16 Nov. | 3 Edward VI. | Griffith John (or Jones), otherwise Griffith ap John ap Robert, (for life). |
| 1551 | 10 Aug. | 5　　" | Francis, Earl of Huntingdon, (for life). |
| | | | { Maurice Williams. <br> { John Vaughan. } (15) <br> { Robert Evans. |
| 1553 | 10 Oct. | 1 Mary. | John Herle, (for life).(16) |
| 1574 | 21 June. | 16 Elizabeth. | Robert Berry, of Ludlow, Esq., (for life).(17) |
| 1600 | 31 Jan. | 42　　" | Thomas Goodman. |
| 1605 | 21 May. | 3 James I. | { Sir Richard Herbert, Knt. } (for life). <br> { Edward Herbert, Gent. } |
| 1627 | 28 March. | 3 Charles I. | Edward, Lord Conway, Viscount Killultagh.(18) |

(14) *In Stanley's "Westminster Abbey," is an amusing account of Henry VI. going to the Chapel of S Edward, and there, in company of Sir Thomas Tunstall, the Lord Abbot, and others, selecting a spot for his own burial. W.

(15) The names, bracketed, are mentioned in the Patent appointing Sir Richard and Edward Herbert (1605) as having held the Office; as also the names of Robert Herle, Robert Berry, and Thomas Goodman; the above names are again recited in the Patent appointing Goodman to the Chief Forestarship of Snowdon, and I am of opinion that they held the Forestarship only. Herle and Berry were Constables of Conway, as well as Forestar of Snowdon. Goodman was appointed Chief Forestar 31 Jan., 42 Elizabeth. The appointments of William Vaughan, and Evans, are not entered on the Patent Rolls, nor at the Land Revenue Record Office.

(16) One of Queen Mary's Equerries. There is an Indenture at the Land Revenue Record Office, dated 19 July, 1570, wherein he (Herle) assigns the Constableship of Conway Castle unto William Gybons, Citizen, and Salter of London, for, and in consideration of a certain sum of money.

(17) On the 8th July, 1579, Berry appointed Sir William Herbert, of St. Julian, Co. Monmouth, to be his Deputy.

(18) "On March 24th, 1627, grant was made to Edward, Viscount Killultagh, and his heirs, of Conway Castle, rent reserved, 6s. 8d. per annum, and fine paid, £100."—Cal. State Papers, 1626-7, p. 107.

| Anno Dom. | Appointed. | Regnal Year. | Name. |
|---|---|---|---|
| 1643 | 1 August. | 19 Charles I. | Archbishop John Williams.(19) |
| 1645 | 19 March. | 20 „ | Sir John Owen.(20) |
| 1649 | 23 June. | | Colonel John Carter, (during pleasure).(21) |
| 1661 | 15 Feb. | 13 Charles II. | Edward, Lord Herbert, of Cherbury.(22) |
| 1679 | Nov. | 31 Charles II. | William, Lord Herbert, of Cherbury.(23) |
| 1769 | 8 Dec. | 10 George III. | John Parry, Esq.(24) |
| 1809 | 30 Oct. | 50 „ | Griffith ap Howel Vaughan, Esq.(25) |
| 1831 | 10 Jan. | 1 William IV. | „ „ „ „ |
| 1837 | 2 Dec. | 1 Victoria. | „ „ „ „ |
| 1848 | 28 March. | 11 „ | The Hon. Thomas Pryce Lloyd. |

"On 22nd May, Lord Herbert is requested to yield up possession of Conway Castle to Lord Killultagh, who had purchased it from the Commissioners for sale of the King's Land."—Id., p. 186.

(19) "Archbishop Williams, appointed by Charles I. A year afterwards Sir John Owen was appointed by Prince Rupert, but dispossessed by Williams (who with the Bishops of Bangor, St. Asaph, and Chester, declared for the Parliament) with the assistance of Col. Mitton."—Grose's Antiq., vol. vii., new ed., p. 26., et seq.

20) *He was Governor of the Town and Castle of Conway upon 20th July, and 4th August, 1645. (Original Letters at Porkington.) W.

See note 4 to Lords Lieut. of Merioneth.

(21) In the Land Revenue Record Office, Carter is appointed *vice* Lord Herbert. The Parliamentarians probably took no notice of the appointments of Archbp. Williams, and Sir John Owen.

(22) "In Feb.(?), 1661, Edward, Lord Herbert, Baron of Cherbury and Castle Island, petitioned the King for settlement on himself of the Offices of Chief Forestar of Snowdon, Constable of Conway Castle, and Keeper of the Courts, &c., of the Manor of Bardsey, granted by King James to his grandfather and father. Same date grant was made to the said Lord Herbert, of the above-named Offices."—Cal. State Papers, 1660-1, p. 522.

(23) No entries can be found, in the Patent Rolls or other Records, of the appointments from this date to 1769; but the Castle appears by entries in some Rentals at the Land Revenue Record Office, to have been let to certain persons at annual rents mentioned in such Records.

(24) M.P. for Caernarvonshire, 1789-90.            (25) See note 24 Const. of Harlech.

# CONSTABLES OF HARLECH CASTLE.

| Anno Dom. | Appointed. | Regnal Year. | Name. |
|---|---|---|---|
| 1284 | 21 Oct. | 12 Edward I. | Hugh de Wlonkeslowe, of Wlonkeslowe, Salop.(1) |
| 1285 | 3 ,, | 13 ,, | John de Benelare (or Benillarde).(2) |
| 1290 | 3 July. | 18 ,, | James de St. George. |
| 1293 | 28 Dec. | 22 ,, | Robert de Staundon. |
| 1300 | 1 April. | 28 ,, | John de Havering.(3) |
| 1303 | Sept. | 31 ,, | Vivian de Staundon.(4) |
| 1312 | 8 May. | 5 Edward II. | Thomas de Empton. |
| 1315 | | 9 ,, | Vivian de Staundon.(5) |
| 1321 | 21 April. | 14 ,, | Roger de Swynnerton (or Swyndon).(6) |
| 1323 | | 16 ,, | Oillardo de Welles.(7) |
| 1332 | 29 Dec. | 6 Edward III. | Walter de Manny, afterwards Lord Manny, K.G.(8) |
| 1393 | Sept. | 17 Richard II. | Richard Mascy, (for life). |
| 1399 | 18 Nov. | 1 Henry IV. | ,,          ,, |
| 1402 | | 3 ,, | Dycon le Mascy.(9) |
| 1404 | 8 Jan. | 5 ,, | William Hunte. |
| 1410 | 14 March. | 11 ,, | John Salghall, (for life). |
| 1439 | 12 ,, | 17 Henry VI. | Edmund Hampden, (for life). |

(1) " He was allowed £100 for its Custody."—Ayloffe's Cal., p. 92.   The name is now called Longslow.

(2) Ayloffe's Cal., p. 94.   He died in the 17 year of Edw. I.   Agnes, his wife, held the Custody of the Castle from the Feast of All Saints (1 Nov., 1289), to the Feast of the Virgin (15 Aug., 1290).

(3) See note 1 to Constables of Beaumaris.          (4) Thomas de Verdon Sub-Constable.

(5) He is mentioned in the Chamberlain's Accounts as being Constable in the 5 & 6 years of the Principality of Edward, Prince of Wales [1305-6]; also in the Accounts from the 3-7, and 9-15, of Edw. II.

(6) He held office until 27th April, 16 Edw. II.

(7) He is mentioned in the Chamberlain's Account as being Constable in September, 7 Edw. III.   Robert Bilkemore was Custos after the death of Welles, from the Feast of St. Martin (11 Nov., 1333), to Feast of Our Lord (25 Dec., 1333).

(8) Appointed for life, and died in 1372.   John de Housum (or Houson), was Sub-Constable from 10-14, Edw. III.

*In 1343-4, Bartholomew de Salle occurs as Constable, but he was probably deputy only.   W.

(9) *" He had ten men at arms, and thirty archers, and was allowed for his yearly maintenance £389 6s. 8d."—Ellis' Orig. Letters, vol. i., p. 14.   W.

| Anno Dom. | Appointed. | Regnal Year. | Name. |
|---|---|---|---|
| 1461 | 4 ,, | 1 Edward IV. | David ap Jevan, ap Einion.(10) |
| ,, | 11 August. | 1 ,, | Roger Kenaston, Esq., (for life). |
| 1464 | 26 Oct. | 4 ,, | William, Lord Herbert. |
| 1473 | Feb. | 12 ,, | Sir Roger Kenaston, Knt. |
| 1483 | 16 May. | 1 Edward V. | Henry, Duke of Buckingham. |
| ,, | 15 July. | 1 Richard III. | ,, ,, ,, |
| ,, | 15 Dec. | 1 ,, | Sir Roger Kenaston, Knt., (for life). |
| 1485 | Nov. | 1 Henry VII. | Piers Stanley.(11) |
| 1486 | 7 April. | 1 ,, | Richard Pole.(12) |
| 1504 | 28 Dec. | 20 ,, | Hugh Lewys, (during pleasure). |
| 1510—11 | | 2 Henry VIII. | Peter Stanley, (for life). |
| 1521 | 5 July. | 13 ,, | Francis Bryan, (for life).(13) |
| 1549 | 22 Dec. | 3 Edward VI. | Sir Anthony Strelley.(14) |
| 1551 | 26 March. | 5 ,, | Edward Stanley. |
| 1589 | 5 Feb. | 31 Elizabeth. | { Sir Henry Lee, Knt.(15) } (for life). { Owen Cooke, Gent. } |
| 1609 | 20 March. | 6 James I. | Ralph, Lord Eure.(16) |
| 1616 | 27 ,, | 14 ,, | Eligion Sutton, Esq. |
| 1629 | 28 April. | 5 Charles I. | Thomas Trafford, (for life). |
| 1638 | 17 Feb. | 13 ,, | William Owen, of Porkington, Esq.(17) |
| 1671 | 21 March. | 23 Charles II. | Cornelius Manley, of Bistocke, Esq., (for life). |
| 1685 | 3 Sept. | 1 James II. | Sir Evan Lloyd, of Bodidris, Bart., (for life). |
| 1692 | 29 Feb. | 4 Will. & Mary. | Charles Nicholas Eyre, Esq.(18) |

(10) The gallant defender of the Castle for Henry VI., during the Wars of the Roses. Eventually he was compelled (circa 1468) to surrender it to Sir R. Herbert, brother of William, Earl of Pembroke.

(11) Afterwards Knighted.  (12) Afterwards Knighted.  (13) Afterwards Knighted.

(14) He is mentioned as being Constable in 1558. (Vide Chamberlain's Accounts.)

(15) Afterwards K.G.

*"Old Sir Henry Lee is dead, God forgive him the injury he hath done to this poor Town."—One of the Maurice Letters at Brogyntyn [Porkington]. W.

(16) Lord President of Wales.

(17) *This was Col. Owen, the gallant Defender of Harlech Castle, for the King, and brother of Sir John Owen. W.

(18) In the Calendar of Treasury papers, 1557-1696, p. 194—21 Sept., 1691—there is a Report of Mr. Charles Chetwynd to the Lords of the Treasury, on the petition of Charles Nicholas Eyre, Esq., Carver to the Queen, who prayed for the grant of the office of Constable of Hardleigh Castle, certifying that the office had been usually granted by their Majesties predecessors by Patent, and that Sir Evan Lloyd had a grant of it during pleasure, with the usual salary of £50 per annum, and that it was then void, and would be a convenient thing for the Petitioner.

There are two Indentures at the Land Revenue Record Office; one dated 29 June, 1696, wherein he (Eyre) assigns the Constableship unto Charles Pratten, Citizen and Musician, of London, in consideration of re-

| Anno Dom. | Appointed. | Regnal Year. | Name. |
|---|---|---|---|
| 1702 | 21 Dec. | 1 Anne. | Charles Nicholas Eyre, Esq. |
| 1704 | 1 July. | 3 ,, | Richard Vaughan, of Corsygedol, Esq. |
| 1716 | 10 Dec. | 3 George I. | William Wynne, Esq.(19) |
| 1754 | 17 July. | 28 George II. | Evan Vaughan, Esq.(20) |
| 1761 | 6 May. | 1 George III. | ,, ,, ,, (21) |
| 1792 | 2 March. | 32 ,, | Sir Robert Howell Vaughan, Bart.(22) |
| ,, | 17 Dec. | 33 ,, | William Wynne Nanney, of Maesyneuadd, Esq. |
| 1796 | 28 April. | 36 ,, | Edward Williames Salesbury Vaughan, Esq.(23) |
| 1808 | 23 Jan. | 48 ,, | Griffith ap Howel Vaughan, Esq.(24) |
| 1831 | 10 June. | 1 William IV. | ,, ,, ,, ,, |
| 1837 | 2 Dec. | 1 Victoria. | ,, ,, ,, ,, |
| 1848 | 28 March. | 11 ,, | The Hon. Thomas Pryce Lloyd.(25) |

ceiving £100 : the other dated, 12 May, 1699, assigning to the said Pratten, the Castle Yard of Harlech, for, and in consideration of £30.

(19) *A younger son of Bodvean. Afterwards Knighted, and died in 1754. Was M.P. for Caernarvon Boroughs. W.

(20) *Otherwise Evan Lloyd Vaughan, of Corsygedol, Esq., grandson of Richard Vaughan, Constable. He died M.P. for Merioneth, 4 Dec., 1791. W.

(21) The Letters Patent of 17th July, 28 George II., were revoked.

(22) *Died 13 Oct., 1792. W.

(23) *Second son of Sir Robert Howel Vaughan, Bart., previously Constable. Died in 1807. W.

(24) *Of Rûg and Hengwrt, and better known as Colonel Vaughan. He was younger brother of Edward Williames Salesbury Vaughan, previous Constable. Also Constable of Conway Castle. W.

(25) Appointed at the same time (on the decease of Col. Vaughan) Constable of Conway.

# APPENDIX.

# APPENDIX.

SOME very interesting original Warrants of Lieutenancy for the year 1675, with the Returns of the High Constables of the several Commotes and Hundreds, are in the possession of Mr. A. Jones Williams, of Gelliwig, Caernarvonshire. By his permission I have extracted the following, relating to a part of Lleyn, as they are fair examples of the minute information afforded by these documents in regard to the owners of lands, and the value of their properties.

---

*To yᵉ Constables of yᵉ peace of yᵉ Comott of Dinllaen and to eu'ry of them.*

CARNARVON. } We yᵉ Deputie Lieftenants of this County who haue herevnto subscribed in pursuance of seũall Acts of Parliament made in yᵉ foureteenth and fifteenth yeare of his Maᵗⁱᵉˢ Reigne yᵗ now is for yᵉ Ordering yᵉ fforces of yᵉ seũall Counties of this Kingdome doe will ℓ require yʷ to be and personally appeare before vs at yᵉ howse of Lewis David of Carn'von vpon the 16ᵗʰ day of July next by ten of yᵉ Clocke of yᵉ same day being fryday and yᵗ there yʷ haue in readines fairely written a true perfect list of all yᵉ names of yᵉ respectiue ffreehoulds yᵗ haue any lands or tenements within yʳ sᵈ Comott with the true value of their respectiue lands yearly togeather with yᵉ names of all yᵉ Inhabitants within yʳ Comott yᵗ haue any personall estate to yᵉ value of six hundred pownds and vpwards ℓ wᵗ their personall estate be really worth for furth' therein to be done as by yᵉ sᵈ Acts is required, Hereof and of every part ℓ parcell hereof yʷ are duely to execute ℓ performe as yʷ ℓ every of yʷ will answere yᵉ Contrary at yʳ vtmost perills. Giuen vndʳ oʳ hands ℓ seales att Carnarvon yᵉ ffeifteenth day of June Anᵒ Regni Regis Caroli scᵈⁱ nunc Anglie &c, vicessimo septimo Annoꝗ Doⁿⁱ 1675.

BULKELEY.
TH. MOSTYN, of Gloddaith.
WILL GRIFFITH, of Lyne.

---

## XXJ° *Marcii* 1660.

At the meetinge then att Carn'van It was ordered by the Deputy Lieutenᵃnts there p̃sent that the sume of 50ˢ Sterlinge for Corslett furnished ℓ for the carrage bee ymposed vpon every one of these psons that bee charged wᵗʰ suche Armes ℓ 40ˢ bee paide by eũy pson charged with a Muskett furnished ℓ appʳtenᵃnć.

RI. HUGHES,
Cĺ. to the Deputy Lieutenᵃnts.

Nevyn ꝑish.

*A list of the names of all the ffreehoulders of the ꝑish & Liberties of Nevyn aforesayd & the yearely value of theire Lands.*

|  | lib'r | s | đ |
|---|---|---|---|
| William Griffyth of Llyn, Esqr | 6 | 00 | 00 |
| Thomas Madryn, Esqr | 40 | 00 | 00 |
| Griffyth Wynn of Bodvean, Esqr | 6 | 00 | 00 |
| John Gllyn Llivon, Esqr | 1 | 13 | 00 |
| Thomas Wynne Glasgoed, Esqr | 7 | 00 | 00 |
| John Wynne of Berth Aur, Esq | 00 | 10 | 00 |
| Richard Edwards of Nanhoron, gent. | 13 | 00 | 00 |
| John Williams of ystymkelyn, gent. | 6 | 00 | 00 |
| Owen Williams of Anglice, gent. | 7 | 00 | 00 |
| Robt. Meredyth of Carn'von, gent. | 4 | 00 | 00 |
| William Griffyth of Madryn issa, Esqr | 6 | 00 | 00 |
| ffrancis Griffyth of Brynodol, gent. | 00 | 13 | 00 |
| ffrancis Lloydd of Nangwnadle, gent. | 1 | 00 | 00 |
| Richard Lloyd & Barbra Anwill | 16 | 00 | 00 |
| Ellin Wynne, Widow of Nevyn | 20 | 00 | 00 |
| Robert Thomas | 7 | 00 | 00 |
| Richard Robts | 2 | 00 | 00 |
| Robert Arthur | 2 | 00 | 00 |
| James Owen | 2 | 00 | 00 |
| Catherine Davidd Wydowe | 6 | 00 | 00 |
| Hugh Jones & Ellizabeth Jones his Mother | 5 | 00 | 00 |
| Richard Hughes | 2 | 00 | 00 |
| Thomas Griffyth & Ellin his Mother | 5 | 00 | 00 |
| Robert ap Hugh & Lowry his Mother | 6 | 00 | 00 |
| Evan ap Robt Owen | 3 | 00 | 00 |
| Evan Griffyth ap Evan | 2 | 00 | 00 |
| Susanna Humphreys | 1 | 10 | 00 |
| John Evan | 1 | 10 | 00 |
| John Robts | 2 | 00 | 00 |
| David John Dđ | 1 | 00 | 00 |
| Davidd ap Robt Owen | 1 | 10 | 00 |
| Hugh Owen of Llanengan, gent. | 2 | 00 | 00 |
| Ellin Griffydd the inheretrix of Ceven Llanvair | 3 | 00 | 00 |
| Elizabeth Humphrey of Anglice | 1 | 00 | 00 |
| John Edward | 2 | 00 | 00 |
| Harry John ap Robt | 00 | 10 | 00 |
| Margaret Evans of Brynygwdion | 1 | 00 | 00 |
| Moris Jones of Meilleonen, geēt. | 1 | 10 | 00 |
| Richard Hughes of Bodwrda, gent. | 2 | 10 | 00 |

Gafflogion. *The names of the ffreehold^{rs} that have estates in the said Comot w^{th} the yearely value thereof:—videlic.*

|  | | | | li. | | |
|---|---|---|---|---|---|---|
| The hon^{ble} Robert Rob^{rts}, Esq^r., in Severall pishes there ... | | | | 120 | 00 | 00 |
| Llaneingan in tair tre soch. | | | | | | |
| The hon^{ble} Tho. Bulkely, Esq^r | ... | ... | ... | 060 | 00 | 00 |
| Nicholas Bagenall, Esq^r | ... | ... | ... | 010 | 00 | 00 |
| Llangian. S^r William Williams, Barr^t in all ... | ... | ... | 080 | 00 | 00 |
| Richard Edwards, gent, in severall pishes | ... | ... | 070 | 00 | 00 |
| Hugh Hughes | ... | ... | ... | 024 | 00 | 00 |
| Humphrey Jones tÿ yn y Cae | ... | ... | ... | 012 | 00 | 00 |
| Catherine Jones Widdow | ... | ... | ... | 015 | 00 | 00 |
| Mary Roberts Widdow | ... | ... | ... | 007 | 00 | 00 |
| John Thomas ab Williams | ... | ... | ... | 006 | 00 | 00 |
| Evan Saython his one lands ℮ barreth ... | ... | ... | 024 | 00 | 00 |
| Ellen Griffith, Spinster | ... | ... | ... | 015 | 00 | 00 |
| Love Parry | ... | ... | ... | 045 | 00 | 00 |
| Madame Gaynor Jones | ... | ... | ... | 060 | 00 | 00 |
| Griffith Vaughan, Esq^r | ... | ... | ... | 030 | 00 | 00 |
| Griffith Wynne, Esq^r | ... | ... | ... | 010 | 00 | 00 |
| John Williams | ... | ... | ... | 002 | 00 | 00 |
| Meillteyrne. Humphrey Thomas ... | ... | ... | 003 | 00 | 00 |
| Richard Trygarne, gent | ... | ... | ... | 040 | 00 | 00 |
| Robert John Prichard | ... | ... | ... | 006 | 00 | 00 |
| Griffith Wynne, Esq^r | ... | ... | ... | 008 | 00 | 00 |
| John ap Robe^rt Lewis | ... | ... | ... | 004 | 00 | 00 |
| Evan Saython, gent | ... | ... | ... | 024 | 00 | 00 |
| Edward Williams, Esq^r | ... | ... | ... | 018 | 00 | 00 |
| David Gouch | ... | ... | ... | 004 | 00 | 00 |
| Bottwnog. James Jones, gent | ... | ... | ... | 006 | 00 | 00 |
| W^m ap Ev^n Morgan, in several pishes ... | ... | ... | 20 | 00 | 00 |
| William Thomas | ... | ... | ... | 005 | 00 | 00 |
| Owen Poole | ... | ... | ... | 010 | 00 | 00 |
| Rob^t John Owen | ... | ... | ... | 005 | 00 | 00 |
| Hugh ap Ev^n | ... | ... | ... | 006 | 00 | 00 |
| Llanbedrog. Ellen Griffith, Spinster | ... | ... | 060 | 00 | 00 |
| Griffith Wynne, gent | ... | ... | ... | 060 | 00 | 00 |
| Elizabeth Hughes Widd | ... | ... | ... | 048 | 00 | 00 |
| Lewis Owen | ... | ... | ... | 004 | 00 | 00 |

*A true and ꝑfect List of the names of all the freehoulders and inhabitants within the Com̄ott of Kemitmaen with a true value of there reall estates as well in the Com̄ott as elce where in the County for hereby wee charge none that Liue out of the Com̄ott though they haue Land in the Com̄ott, Least they should be charged of there whole estates particulary in the Com̄otts, where they Liue as by this List wee haue don, the ꝑticulars thereof are as followeth.—*

|  |  |  |  |  |  | li. |
|---|---|---|---|---|---|---|
| Mrs Katherine Bodwrda<br>Hugh Bodwrda, Esqure<br>Griffith Bodwrda, Esqure | ... | ... | ... | ... | ... | 300 |
| Edward Williams of Mell, Esqr | ... | ... | ... | ... | 300 |
| John Wynne, Esquire, and his<br>mother Mrs Kath. Wynne<br>Griff ab Will. morris ...<br>Evan ap Richard ... | ... | ... | ... | ... | ... | 150 |
| Mr Griffith Carreg<br>Mrs Jane Carreg, widđ:<br>Mrs Catherin Carreg, widđ:<br>Owen ap Willm Prichard<br>Richard John ap Richard<br>John ap Richard | ... | ... | ... | ... | 100 |
| Mrs William Carreg gentł<br>John ap Humphrey<br>Evan Lewis<br>Margered Griffith<br>Harry ap Richard<br>Marry John Griffith<br>Robert Wynne<br>thomas ap Robert<br>Edward Hughes | ... | ... | ... | ... | 050 |
| Rees John Dđ ap Rees<br>John Evans<br>Rowland thomas<br>Griffith ap Prichard<br>Griffith ap Evan<br>Dauid Jon Dauid<br>Hugh Griffith an his mother<br>and sister in Lawe Ellin<br>Johnes | ... | ... | ... | ... | 050 :— |

li.

Harry ap William Prichard
Jane Richard widđ :
John ap William et mater
John Jones
thomas Johns                    ...     ...     ...     ...     050 :—
Richard Parry
Evan ap William John
Hughe Jones and
Gwen Jones widđ :

William John ap William
Arthur morrice
Evan John Griffith
William Pugh Parry
ffrancis Humphrey
Evan John ap Evan               ...     ...     ...     ...     050 :—
William John ap William et
Evan Arthure
John ap John
John Sexton

M^r Morris Griffith, gentle
Evan thomas
John ap William Davidd          ...     ...     ...     ...     100 :—
William John ap Richard
Griffith Lewis

M^r John Roberts, gente
John Griffith Eevelan
Griffith John Griffith
Thomas Williams and
Margared Griffith               ...     ...     ...     ...     100 :—
Lewis ap Humphrey
Ellin verch Evan, widđ :
Grace verch Edward, widđ.

M^r John Salisbury, Esq^r,
fox Llangwnadle and             ...     ...     ...     ...     050 :—
tydweyliog : impropria-
tion

M^r thomas Dauidd Lewis
Roger Wynne                      ...     ...     ...     ...     050 :—
William Hughes

Hugh ap Arthure
M^r John Gwnnys
William Parry                   ...     ...     ...     ...     050 :—
Robert Owen
Richard Davidd

li.

| | | | | | li. |
|---|---|---|---|---|---|
| Parry trygarne<br>John White gentł.<br>Dauid Rice, Junio<sup>r</sup><br>and Robert Evans | } | ... | ... | ... | ... | 100. |
| M<sup>r</sup> ffredericke Wynne<br>Thomas ap Richard | } | ... | ... | ... | ... | 050. |
| Hugh ap Evan James<br>Hugh ap Owen<br>Thomas Griffith<br>Elisabeth Jones, widđ. | } | ... | ... | ... | ... | 050. |
| James Jones<br>Harry Hughes<br>William Williams | } | ... | ... | ... | ... | 050. |

# ADDENDA.

---

## SHERIFFS.

---

### ANGLESEY.

| Anno Dom. | Regnal Year. | Name. | Appointed. |
|---|---|---|---|
| 1873—4 | 36 & 7 Victoria. | William Humphrey Owen, of Plas yn Penrhyn, Esq. . . . . . | 5 Feb. |

### CAERNARVON.

| | | | |
|---|---|---|---|
| 1873—4 | 36 & 7 Victoria. | Thomas Turner, of Plasbrereton, Esq. . | 5 Feb. |

### MERIONETH.

| | | | |
|---|---|---|---|
| 1873—4 | 36 & 7 Victoria. | The Hon. Charles Henry Wynn, of Rhug. | 5 Feb. |

# INDEX.

The letter *n* after a name indicates that such name will be found in the notes.

EXPLICIT.

LONDON : JOHN CAMDEN HOTTEN, 74 AND 75, PICCADILLY.